WITHDRAWN

Unimaginable Atrocities

UNIMAGINABLE ATROCITIES

Justice, Politics, and Rights at the War Crimes Tribunals

William Schabas OC MRIA

OXFORD

UNIVERSITY PRESS

OXFORD

UNIVERSITY PRESS

Great Clarendon Street, Oxford OX2 6DP
United Kingdom

Oxford University Press is a department of the University of Oxford.
It furthers the University's objective of excellence in research, scholarship,
and education by publishing worldwide. Oxford is a registered trade mark of
Oxford University Press in the UK and in certain other countries

British Library Cataloguing in Publication Data

Data available

Library of Congress Cataloguing in Publication Data

Data available

ISBN 978–0–19–965307–2

Typeset by Newgen Imaging Systems (P) Ltd, Chennai, India
Printed in Great Britain on acid-free paper by
CPI Group (UK) Ltd, Croydon, CR0 4YY

To Ben Ferencz, who was there
when it all began

CONTENTS

INTRODUCTION

'I had a great evening; it was like the Nuremberg Trials.'
Mickey (Woody Allen), after a rather grim date with Hannah's sister
Holly in the film *Hannah and Her Sisters*

Human history is marked by 'turning points', associated with the emergence of new technologies, new forms of government, and new concepts. They are signposts of the progress of humanity. Centuries from now, the Nuremberg trial will be seen as one such defining moment, if it is not already. In the Middle Ages, the Bavarian city of Nuremberg was the unofficial capital of the Holy Roman Empire. Hitler chose it as the site for his hysterical rallies. He built an enormous parade ground there that still exists. It is now a monument to Nazi atrocity. Above all, the town today evokes notions of justice. This was where the International Military Tribunal, established by the Allies in the weeks following the unconditional surrender of Germany in 1945, put the surviving leaders of the Nazi regime on trial. It is enough to say 'Nuremberg' for the idea to be understood.

Nuremberg stands for several big and influential concepts. Speaking to the American Bar Association in 1946, British Prosecutor Hartley Shawcross proposed three of them: to initiate a war of aggression is an international crime; individuals who lead their countries into such a war are personally responsible; individuals therefore have international duties which transcend the national duty of obedience imposed by particular states when to obey would constitute a crime against the law of nations. To this list, one other, drawn from the human rights movement that was also emerging at the time, might be added: atrocities committed by a government against its own people are punishable as an international crime. Nuremberg also contains the suggestion that international responsibility is imposed upon states to ensure that perpetrators of international crimes are brought to justice.

For several decades, Nuremberg stood as an interesting but neverthe-less isolated occurrence. At the time of the trial, its enthusiasts dreamed of a permanent institution. But while efforts to pursue this objective continued for a number of years after the judgment, the project stumbled and then died with the dawn of the Cold War. When I studied law, in the early 1980s, the Nuremberg trial was more a curiosity than a model. The human rights movement was at the time unsure whether Nuremberg should be revered as a defining moment, or whether it was better forgotten. The tradition of Nuremberg was only properly revived by the United Nations General Assembly in late 1989, in the days that followed the fall of the Berlin Wall. This was hardly a coincidence.

Since 1989, the use of international judicial institutions to hold account-able those who are accused of perpetrating atrocities has burgeoned. The establishment of ad hoc tribunals for the former Yugoslavia and Rwanda, in the early 1990s, initially looked like an experiment. But the idea had astounding dynamism. In 1998 the Rome Diplomatic Conference concluded with the adoption of the legislative framework of a permanent body. The Rome Statute of the International Criminal Court entered into force in 2002. Within a year, judges and a prosecutor had been elected and the institution was operational.

Increasingly, international justice is viewed as an indispensable component of efforts by the United Nations and by regional organizations to bring an end to conflict and to promote lasting peace. For example, in February 2011 when Libya's brutal regime seemed likely to put an end to the 'Arab spring', the United Nations Security Council turned to the International Criminal Court as one of the central mechanisms available to it. Weeks later, it did the same for civil war in Côte d'Ivoire. The International Criminal Court and the ad hoc tribunals are quite central to this activity. But there are also a number of so-called hybrid or internationalized institutions. And at the level of national courts, there is greatly increased reliance on international criminal law offences and concepts when justice systems respond to atrocities committed by those associated with past regimes. More limited in scope, but a source of endless fascination and media attention, is prosecution of international crimes committed outside national territory by virtue of universal jurisdiction.

This modest volume attempts to speak to some of the controversies that surround modern atrocity trials. It is written by a lawyer, but one with a bent for interdisciplinarity and a poorly concealed penchant for icono-clasm. Its ambition is to set out the complexity and the inscrutability of some of the big issues in the field that is now known generally as international criminal law. Hopefully, this discussion will stimulate the reflection of policy makers, diplomats, and journalists, as well as academics and students. Experts from these cognate disciplines are frequently intimidated by the international lawyers, who make self-assured comments about the imperatives of customary international law, often couched in confident resort to mysterious Latin maxims. One function here is to demystify some of the legal arguments.

Above all, this is a book about the policy and the politics of criminal justice. These are dimensions that lawyers often shy away from, preferring to leave the matter to other disciplines. Sometimes, they simply pretend that politics is alien to the pursuit of justice, dismissing it as a vile taint to be shunned rather than one that is to be mastered and understood. At the national level, noble efforts are made to insulate the courts from politics. Indeed, independence and impartiality of judges and prosecutors are the hallmarks of fair justice. Nevertheless, legislatures and governments necessarily intervene in policy choices. This limited role is accepted, provided that it is not driven by improper motives.

At the international level, policy and politics seem to sit much closer to the centre of the justice agenda. This is what makes international justice distinct, even peculiar. The international war crimes tribunals as well as the related initiatives are an exercise of the policy of states, individually or through collective bodies like the United Nations Security Council. Their goals are often framed with policy-oriented language: the pursuit of international peace and security, the prevention of conflict, and the transition to democratic governance. The interaction of law and politics generates several of the important issues addressed in this book, such as the selection of situations for prosecution, the 'victors' justice' critique, labelling of atrocity with loaded terms such as genocide, the tension with the prerogatives of peace, and the relationship between crimes of individuals and the state itself.

There is no pretence here at exhaustiveness. Several comprehensive textbooks already exist on the modern phenomenon of international criminal justice. Rather, this book is concerned with issues. Each of the chapters addresses a distinct conundrum. In the course of the discussion, many basic notions are explored and explained. In that sense, it is my hope that this volume may provide a useful introduction to the field. But beyond that, its objective is to provoke reflection about some of the postulates that underpin the system.

After an introduction that considers the history of international prosecution and the specificity of international criminal tribunals, the first chapter explores the general concept of international crimes. The international crimes considered here are generically referred to as 'war crimes', especially in a colloquial context. But specialists make distinctions of importance between genocide, crimes against humanity, war crimes in the technical sense, and the crime of aggression. These four categories make up the subject-matter jurisdiction of the International Criminal Court. Two of them, genocide and the crime of aggression, are examined in greater detail in distinct chapters.

Genocide, sometimes labelled the 'crime of crimes', is a source of considerable mystique. Chapter 4 ('The Genocide Mystique') considers its unique importance, offering an explanation rooted in the history of the concept and of its intriguing relationship with the cognate, crimes against humanity. Chapter 8 deals with the scope of the crime of aggression, or 'crimes against peace' as it was known at Nuremberg. At Nuremberg, the International Military Tribunal declared 'crimes against peace' to be the 'supreme international crime differing only from other war crimes in that it contains within itself the accumulated evil of the whole'. The place of the crime of aggression within the core crimes of international criminal law was recently confirmed by the amendments to the Rome Statute adopted at the 2010 Kampala Review Conference.

Critics of the international tribunals have frequently focussed upon their retroactive nature. This has often been an inevitable consequence of their political dimension, and their as yet incomplete structures. The decision to prosecute is made when the crisis is already underway, and when there is already evidence that the crimes have been committed. This is normal enough. It is no different for criminal justice at the domestic level, except that the laws and institutions already exist. Although the issue of retroactivity is likely to be less and less important, given the existence of a permanent International Criminal Court with largely prospective jurisdiction, difficulties continue to arise, especially when international crimes are prosecuted at the national level. International human rights law allows prosecution even for offences that were not codified at the time in national legislation to the extent that they were recognized as international crimes. This is frequently the subject of great debate in transitional states, challenged to deal with crimes committed by previous regimes. These questions are the subject of the second chapter, entitled '*Nullum Crimen Sine Lege*', which is the Latin formulation of the prohibition on retroactive prosecution.

The third chapter brings the reader to what may well be the greatest challenge to international justice: the selection of situations for prosecution. Because of its unavoidable political dimension, international justice (including its exercise at the national level) is by necessity not a comprehensive venture. Decisions must be made concerning those who are to be brought to justice. Inevitably, comparisons of the relative gravity and importance of atrocities perpetrated in different parts of the world must be made. This is profoundly different from the situation at the domestic level, where we assume that all serious crimes against the person will be addressed by the criminal courts. The chapter takes as its title 'Victors' Justice?', a pejorative epithet that has commonly been invoked by critics of international justice. Those who defend the system tend to shrink in shame at the charge. They often attempt to show that the choices of targets for prosecution are based upon objective criteria, or at least insist that this is the intention. But it is a tortuous argument, because in fact highly subjective decisions are often at the origin of international prosecutions.

An important thesis of the author is the significance of state policy in our understanding of the nature of international crimes. This issue is further explored in Chapter 5, which is entitled '*Mens Rea*, *Actus Reus*, and the Role of the State'. The significance of state policy is also considered with respect to the definitions of crimes. It is surely most evident concerning the crime of aggression. The new definition of the crime makes explicit the notion that only leaders capable of controlling the actions of a state can actually be prosecuted for aggression. But the link is also important for other international crimes. Without a state party component, it is difficult to distinguish between genuine crimes against humanity and the acts of serial killers, motorcycle gangs, and organized criminal networks.

The sixth chapter deals with the role of international justice in the creation of narratives about conflict. This has increasingly been understood as an element of an emerging human right to the truth. In particular, it is said that victims of atrocities are entitled to learn the circumstances of their victimization. Truth is also held out as an important component in the search for reconciliation within societies emerging from conflict. This leads naturally to the seventh chapter, which speaks to the amnesty quandary. Amnesty is used in a broad sense, describing a range of political and legal initiatives by which prosecution is put aside permanently or temporarily suspended. The difficulty has been present since Japan refused to surrender, in July 1945, unless the United States promised to leave its emperor unpunished. There have been many examples in recent times. The civil war in Sierra Leone was brought to an end with a peace agreement that pledged amnesty. In 2011 Britain and France toyed with letting the Libyan leader Muammar Gaddafi avoid prosecution at the International Criminal Court if he would peacefully leave power. While impunity under such circumstances offers immense benefits in exchange, there are several more sinister examples of self-proclaimed amnesties for tyrants, especially in Latin America. This is an issue where rigid and formulaic solutions are inadequate. Wise determinations driven by policy rather than strict principles are necessary in order to ensure that a maximum of both peace and justice is delivered.

Together, the eight chapters attempt to sketch a portrait of international criminal justice that brings out the complex relationship between policy and law. It consists of a series of canvases focussed on different themes rather than a systematic attempt to demonstrate a particular thesis or comprehensively to present the subject matter. The eight chapters are related in the same sense as a series of paintings by a single artist working with the same medium.

THE BEGINNINGS

Scholars occasionally invoke medieval precedents from the time of the Holy Roman Empire in order to show the ancient origins of international criminal prosecutions. But in reality, the phenomenon that we know today, whose institutional homes are the International Criminal Court and the United Nations ad hoc tribunals, traces its beginnings to the First World War and its aftermath. For many decades, indeed centuries, there had been an international dimension to criminal law. It was focussed on the apprehension of fugitives and their extradition to the proper jurisdiction. Where there was no traditional jurisdictional link, in the form of territory or nationality, prosecution was allowed. This was an exception to the general rule that prohibited a state from punishing crimes absent a jurisdictional nexus, that is, if it was not committed on the state's territory or by its citizens. Pirates are the classic example. There were also a few anomalous trials, but hardly anything to suggest something that was anything but ephemeral.

In May 1915, upon reliable reports from diplomats and other sources that the Armenian population in the Ottoman Empire was being massacred, Britain, France, and Russia issued a warning: 'In view of these new crimes of Turkey against humanity and civilization, the allied Governments announce publicly to the Sublime Porte that they will hold personally responsible [for] these crimes all members of the Ottoman Government and those of their agents who are implicated in such massacres.'[1] The

---

[1] 'The Ambassador in France (Sharp) to the Secretary of state, Paris, 28 May 1915', in US Foreign Relations, 1915, Supplement, p. 981. For a slightly different version, although with no substantive distinctions, see: United Nations War Crimes Commission, *History of the United Nations War Crimes Commission and the Development of the Laws of War*, London: His Majesty's Stationery Office, 1948, p. 35.

American Ambassador in Istanbul communicated the message to the Grand Vizier on behalf of the three European powers. He reported that the Ottoman leader 'expressed regret at being held personally responsible and resentment at attempted interference by foreign governments with the sovereign rights of the Turkish Government over their Armenian subjects'. Meanwhile, the ambassador added that 'persecution against Armenians [is] increasing in severity'.[2]

The great themes of contemporary international criminal law are all present in this legendary diplomatic demarche. In a substantive sense, we have the first reference in international relations to crimes against humanity, a notion that had long been used by journalists and politicians but one with no previously established legal meaning. An equivalent today might be the word 'atrocity'. The message from the three governments speaks of international accountability and is addressed to individuals and not just the state as such. Previously, defeated tyrants had often been punished, but by summary execution or exile, not by a court of law. In addition to individual citizens, the message contemplates a head of state, something the Grand Vizier understood immediately. There would be—and still is—an argument whether such persons are immune from prosecution. Immunity is a concept that is firmly anchored in international law. Indeed, it was around long before international law suggested that there was an imperative of prosecution. It is closely linked to the other great objection, national sovereignty, often raised by those whose prosecution is contemplated or by their governments.

The Grand Vizier did not say so explicitly, but he implied that the threat of criminal prosecution was politically motivated. He might have added that if Britain, France, and Russia were prepared to punish him for massacres committed against subjects of the Ottoman Empire, something more even-handed ought to have been envisaged. That way, all such persecutions, whoever the perpetrator, would be dealt with by the courts. Perhaps the leaders of Britain, France, and Russia might then have felt themselves exposed to trial for crimes perpetrated against vulnerable minorities over whom they had jurisdiction. In any event, when the war ended, the threat of criminal prosecution lingered only for those who lost the battle. In the end, Britain, France, and Russia never did make good on their promise. The Treaty of Sèvres, which was negotiated in Paris in 1919, envisaged trial of those 'responsible for the massacres committed during the continuance of the state of war on territory which formed part of the Turkish Empire on

---

[2] 'The Ambassador in Turkey (Morgenthau) to the Secretary of state, Constantinople, 18 June 1915', in US Foreign Relations, 1915, Supplement, p. 982.

1 August 1914', including the possibility that this would take place before a criminal tribunal to be created by the League of Nations. But the Treaty of Sèvres was never ratified by Ataturk's new regime. Some of the perpetrators of the Armenian massacres were brought to justice before Turkey's own courts, but most went unpunished. The unhealed wound continues to haunt Ankara's international relations nearly a century later.

The other losers in the war, the Germans, were also earmarked for prosecution. According to article 227 of the Treaty of Versailles, the victors were to create a 'special tribunal' composed of five judges, to be appointed by each of the five victorious Allied and Associated Powers, that is, the United States, Britain, France, Italy, and Japan. It was to have only one defendant, the former German Emperor, and to prosecute only one crime, 'a supreme offence against international morality and the sanctity of treaties'. The provision spoke of a 'duty to fix the punishment which it considers should be imposed'—unfortunate wording to the extent that it implies that the outcome of the trial was not in doubt. The tribunal was never actually established. Kaiser Wilhelm obtained asylum in the Netherlands, and its government refused to extradite the accused on the grounds that this would constitute retroactive punishment. The tribunal was 'international' in nature because it was established with the agreement and participation of five states, and with the consent of Germany, which, although there was much lingering unhappiness, had accepted the Treaty of Versailles.

In a sense, this is an important precedent, because it was the first international criminal tribunal to be seriously proposed. But the fact that five victorious powers and Germany might agree to something is not enough to create international law applicable to other states. That the authors of the Treaty of Versailles contemplated an international criminal tribunal to try a former head of state for a vaguely defined crime does not bring us much closer to knowing whether the victorious Allied Powers had the right to do so in the absence of Germany's consent.

The Treaty of Versailles also pledged prosecution of individuals for violations of the 'laws and customs of war'. The victors had hoped to do this before their own courts, but eventually gave in to German insistence that it be conducted by the national tribunals of the vanquished power sitting in Leipzig. A list of about 1,000 suspects was whittled down to a handful, and in the end only a few perfunctory trials took place. The defendants were U-boat captains and prisoner of war camp commanders rather than the senior leaders. The few accused who were convicted received short sentences. The trials were international in the sense that they were dictated by treaty. Moreover, the judges applied the 'laws and customs of war', a body of law whose source was not national legislation. Otherwise, German courts did nothing very different from what national tribunals had been doing for centuries.

JUSTICE AT NUREMBERG

Following the First World War, the idea of international criminal prosecution, for what the Paris Peace Conference had labelled violations of the laws and customs of war and 'massacres', rapidly waned. The revival of the idea of international prosecution was to depend upon the second great global conflict. During the inter-war period, several international bodies, most of them professional or unofficial, considered the proposals for the establishment of a permanent international criminal court. These included the International Law Association and the *Association internationale de droit pénal*. Individuals such as Henri Donnedieu de Vabres and Vaspasien Pella were involved. In 1937 the League of Nations actually adopted an agreement aiming at the establishment of an international criminal court, although the treaty never entered into force.

After proclamation of the Atlantic Charter, in mid-1941, Churchill threatened to hold Nazi leaders responsible for 'the crime without a name'. In October 1943 Roosevelt, Stalin, and Churchill spoke in the Moscow Declaration of 'evidence of atrocities, massacres and cold-blooded mass executions which are being perpetrated by Hitlerite forces in many of the countries they have overrun and from which they are now being steadily expelled'. They promised that German suspects would be returned to the countries where crimes had been committed and 'judged on the spot by the peoples whom they have outraged', while those whose offences were more generalized and without any particular geographic location would be punished by joint decision of the governments of the Allies.

Roosevelt, Stalin, and Churchill all seem to have toyed with summary execution of Nazi leaders as the way to deliver justice. It is hard to know how serious these thoughts really were. Perhaps they were more in the nature of off-hand remarks following periods of enormous tension. But as late as April 1945, as preparations were underway for the London Conference, the British government circulated an *aide-mémoire* that said:

1. HMG assume that it is beyond question that Hitler and a number of arch-criminals associated with him (including Mussolini) must, so far as they fall into Allied hands, suffer the penalty of death for their conduct leading up to the war and for the wickedness which they have either themselves perpetrated or have authorized in the conduct of the war. It would be manifestly impossible to punish war criminals of a lower grade by a capital sentence pronounced by a Military Court unless the ringleaders are dealt with with equal severity. This is really involved in the concluding sentence of the Moscow Declaration on

this subject, which reserves for the arch-criminals whose offences have no special localization treatment to be determined in due course by the Allies.

2. It being conceded that these leaders must suffer death, the question arises
whether they should be tried by some form of tribunal claiming to exercise
judicial functions, or whether the decision taken by the Allies should be reached
and enforced without the machinery of a trial. HMG thoroughly appreciate the
arguments which have been advanced in favour of some form of preliminary
trial. But HMG are also deeply impressed with the dangers and difficulties of
this course, and they wish to put before their principal Allies, in a connected
form, the arguments which have led them to think that execution without trial
is the preferable course.[3]

Yet in reality, the victors of the Second World War could never turn their
backs on the precedent set at Versailles. In 1919 a tribunal had been promised. They could do no less in 1945.

The International Military Tribunal was established in 1945 by a
treaty to which only four powers—France, the United Kingdom, the
United States, and the Soviet Union—were the initial parties. Several
of their allies later acceded to the instrument, enhancing its claim to
multilateralism if not universality. Known as the London Agreement,
it provided for the first genuinely international criminal prosecution in
that it was conducted by a tribunal created by treaty between several
states, where the accused were prosecuted not for ordinary crimes but
for offences against international law. The institution is often known as
the Nuremberg Tribunal, because that is where its only trial was held.
Actually, the official seat of the court was Berlin, where its first formal
session took place. Though 'international' in name, in the final judgment
issued on 30 September and 1 October 1946 the judges said that the four
powers had done collectively what they were entitled to do individually.
Indeed, they were the occupying powers in a state that had surrendered
unconditionally, and there seemed no doubt that they were empowered to
create a tribunal to prosecute those whom they had defeated.

Most of the literature, and particularly that in the English language, suggests that the dominant role was played by the United States. This may be a
cultural bias, however. If we had access to as much scholarship and as many
memoirs in Russian, perhaps we might see the trial through a different lens.
The Tribunal's subject-matter jurisdiction was confined to three categories:
crimes against peace, war crimes, and crimes against humanity. A fourth
count, known as the conspiracy charge, made leaders, organizers, instigators,

and accomplices who participated in the formulation or execution of a common plan or conspiracy to commit any of the other crimes individually responsible, but it was always linked to one of the other three crimes.

There was debate before the Tribunal as to whether these were truly international crimes, but the defendants did not contest the fact that if the answer was affirmative, then the prosecutions were lawful and legitimate. It was the international dimension that provided an answer to the challenge that this was retroactive law because much, if not all, of what was done by the Nazis was under the cover of legislation, however perverse.

Each of the four powers named its own prosecutor as well as two judges, one of them an alternate. The alternates participated in the deliberations and in the delivery of the judgment. The defendants complained that neutrals were not named to the bench, and that all of the eight judges had been appointed by the four victorious powers. Nobody argued that the prosecution of senior officials of a sovereign state violated rules of immunity, however. Twenty-four defendants were identified by agreement of the four prosecutors. One was soon found to be unfit to stand trial, a second committed suicide before the trial began, and a third, Martin Bormann, was tried in absentia. Bormann was never apprehended; years later, genetic evidence established that he was dead before the trial had even started. Thus, twenty-one men stood in the dock when the trial began. Three were acquitted, twelve were sentenced to death, and the others received custodial terms ranging from ten years to life.

A broadly similar institution was created at Tokyo: the International Military Tribunal for the Far East. Its legislative framework was a slightly modified version of the statute used at Nuremberg. The Tokyo Tribunal was established by decree of the American occupiers. Nevertheless, the judges were drawn from several allied powers, including Canada, the Netherlands, China, Australia, New Zealand, the Philippines, and France. The Indian judge, Radhabinob Pal, voted to acquit, offended at the idea that the victorious powers were punishing those whom they had defeated for crimes that they too had themselves committed.

When the great Nuremberg trial of the 'major war criminals' was completed, the Americans took over the courtroom and held a series of thematic trials. Nazi doctors, judges, and political leaders were tried along with senior officers from various military units such as the Wehrmacht and the SS. These were American military tribunals, and in a strictly legal sense they were no different from the war crimes courts held by most of the other countries involved in the European and Asian theatres. However, they prosecuted essentially the same crimes that were listed in the Charter of the International Military Tribunal. Probably for that reason history has accorded them a special importance. They were 'internationalized' even if the tribunals were not genuinely international. This marked the start of another important phenomenon: the implementation of international criminal law by domestic courts. The case law generated at these internationalized trials, as well as that of other national military tribunals, is generally considered to be part of the substance of international criminal law.

The Nuremberg trial is probably understood today as an exercise in accountability for Nazi atrocities perpetrated against civilians and in particular the attempted extermination of the Jews of Europe. Actually, the focus was on the launching of the war of aggression itself. In his opening address to the Tribunal, the American prosecutor, Robert Jackson, said the trial 'represents the practical effort of four of the most mighty of nations, with the support of 17 more, to utilize international law to meet the greatest menace of our times—aggressive war'. The Charter of the Tribunal addressed this under the rubric of 'crimes against peace', which was explained as 'planning, preparation, initiation or waging of a war of aggression, or a war in violation of international treaties, agreements or assurances, or participation in a common plan or conspiracy for the accomplishment of any of the foregoing'. The definition echoed the words in article 227 of the Treaty of Versailles, the unimplemented provision by which the German Emperor was to have been brought to justice following the First World War. The Tribunal dismissed objections from the Nazi lawyers who charged that this was retroactive criminal prosecution. The categories that today are at the heart of international prosecutions—war crimes and crimes against humanity—actually played a somewhat secondary role in the Nuremberg trial.

After the Second World War, with the success at Nuremberg and its sister institution in Tokyo, there were attempts to codify norms and principles of international criminal law as well as to establish a permanent international tribunal. The United Nations International Law Commission prepared a draft Code of Offences Against the Peace and Security of Mankind, and also examined procedural issues relating to the operation of an international court. By the mid-1950s, the enthusiasm generated at Nuremberg had abated. It is difficult to pinpoint the moment when this ardour for international justice began to wane.

In 1952 a committee of the United States Congress investigated the famous massacre of Polish officers and political leaders at Katyń, whose responsibility was denied by the Soviet Union at the time, but which has since been admitted. The American politicians described it as 'one of the most barbarous international crimes in world history', and recommended that those responsible be tried 'before the International World Court of Justice for committing a crime at Katyń which was in violation of the general principles of law recognized by civilized nations'.[4] They also called upon the American President 'to seek the establishment of an international commission which would investigate other mass murders and crimes against humanity'.[5] The report was tinged with Cold War rhetoric, and its exaggerated language sat comfortably within the anti-communist hysteria that prevailed at the time. But if Nuremberg had left the Soviets with any lingering taste for the international criminal justice project, this was quickly dampened by initiatives like those of the United States Congress concerning Katyń. The Katyń forest massacre is discussed in more detail in Chapter 6. 'History, International Justice, and the Right to Truth'.

It would be unfair to blame the Soviets exclusively. In Western Europe the British and French empires were in their death throes. Credible reports emerged of atrocities perpetrated by colonial police and soldiers in places such as Kenya and Algeria. Political figures in the United States feared that international justice might deal with the persecution of African Americans. In 1951 Paul Robeson presented a petition to the United Nations entitled 'We Charge Genocide' that insisted upon accountability for the lynching of black Americans, an officially tolerated practice that had yet to be eradicated in the American south. A nervous United States Congress baulked at ratifying the 1948 Genocide Convention (it would not do so for forty years). Thus, what had seemed a noble idea when it was being imposed upon the vanquished Turks in 1919, and the Germans and Japanese in 1945, was fraught with danger for all of the major powers of the post-war world if the principles and institutions of international criminal justice were to be applied universally and without distinction.

The idea of international criminal tribunals lay largely dormant for the next forty-five years. International criminal justice went into its second period of hibernation (the first was in the 1920 and 1930s). Things only began to revive in the 1980s. Developments then were propelled by the growing human rights movement, which came to insist that perpetrators of atrocities be held accountable in order to vindicate the fundamental rights of their victims and to deter future violations. This represented an important shift from an almost exclusive emphasis on defendants and prisoners as victims of an essentially oppressive criminal justice system. Instructed by the General Assembly, in the early 1980s the International Law Commission resumed work on the Code of Offences Against the

---

[4] Final Report of the Select Committee to Conduct an Investigation and Study of the Facts, Evidence, and Circumstances on the Katyń Forest Massacre, Pursuant to H. Res. 390 and H. Res. 539 (82nd Congress), p. 2.   [5] Ibid., p. 13.

Peace and Security of Mankind that had been suspended in 1954. It soon told the General Assembly that there was not much point in defining international crimes if there was no institution capable of prosecuting them.

THE THIRD PHASE: AD HOC TRIBUNALS

In 1989 the General Assembly finally gave the green light to the International Law Commission to proceed with drafting the statute of a permanent court. The end of the Cold War provided a fertile environment for the renaissance of international criminal justice. Even before the Commission submitted its final report to the General Assembly, in 1994, there were impatient calls to create temporary institutions until the permanent body could be set up. That justice and accountability had taken a big place on the international agenda became increasingly apparent. In 1990 there were cautious efforts by the United States and the United Kingdom, and subsequently by the European Union, to create an international court with jurisdiction over Iraq's aggression against Kuwait in 1990. The idea was dropped, probably because the conflict ended in a military stalemate. With Iraq defeated, attention shifted to the Balkans, where the break-up of Yugoslavia was accompanied by appalling reports of war crimes, ethnic cleansing, and gender violence. In February 1993 the Security Council voted to create the International Criminal Tribunal for the former Yugoslavia.

Senior lawyers in the United Nations had their doubts about whether the Security Council was empowered by the Charter of the United Nations to create an international criminal tribunal. Any concerns were put to rest when one of the first defendants challenged the Tribunal's creation and the judges confirmed the legality of its existence. The International Criminal Tribunal for the former Yugoslavia was more unequivocally international than its predecessors at Nuremberg and Tokyo, because of the near-universal authority of its progenitor, the United Nations Security Council. At the time of the International Tribunal's establishment, there was no victor in the conflict and, in any event, the judges were selected from various parts of the world, designated by a credible and transparent procedure that involved both the Security Council and the General Assembly. The Secretary-General specified that the Tribunal would only judge crimes that were unquestionably recognized under international law, using the precedents of the 1940s as its reference point so that this would be beyond dispute.

The Yugoslavia Tribunal was barely operational when genocide ravished the Tutsi minority of Rwanda, in 1994. A second tribunal was quickly formed by the Security Council. It was joined at the hip to that for Yugoslavia by an almost identical statute, a shared prosecutor, and a combined Appeals Chamber. The crimes were defined slightly differently, and there was an acknowledgement that the Council was doing more than simply codifying offences that had been prosecuted at Nuremberg. In particular, it was expressly given jurisdiction over war crimes perpetrated in internal armed conflict, a proposition that was still controversial as a statement of existing customary international law. The two Tribunals have operated in parallel since then, with the inevitable nuances between them in terms of legal precedent and practice. To the non-specialist, they are indistinguishable.

Although the ad hoc tribunals were thriving by the late 1990s, there was also growing dissatisfaction with their cost, and a sense that this was not an ideal model. Faced with a call to establish a tribunal for Sierra Leone, the United Nations opted for a leaner institution. The Special Court for Sierra Leone had a dramatically reduced budget compared with the other two United Nations criminal tribunals, and was designed to handle only a few trials. It was created by treaty between the United Nations and the Government of Sierra Leone rather than by resolution of the Security Council. Reflecting the joint ownership of the institution, some of the judges and the deputy prosecutor were to be appointed by the Government of Sierra Leone. The prosecutor and the international judges were appointed by the Secretary-General of the United Nations, and not elected by the General Assembly, as was the case for the Yugoslavia and Rwanda tribunals. Defence lawyers argued unsuccessfully that these features of its creation meant the Special Court did not have the same powers as the tribunals established by the Security Council, nor the required independence from the government, whose own senior officials might even be suspects. Some similar issues presented themselves with respect to the Special Tribunal for Lebanon, which also had participation of the local government in the appointment of its officials.

The Sierra Leone and Lebanon tribunals also differ from the earlier institutions in terms of funding. The first two ad hoc tribunals operate out of the general budget of the United Nations, whereas the latter two are financed by voluntary contributions from states and, in the case of the Lebanon tribunal, a contribution from the government. This form of financing is unsatisfactory for a judicial institution because of the danger that the government that pays the piper may be seen to call the tune. Like judges of national courts, those at international tribunals need to be reassured that their salaries will be paid and that their future livelihood does not depend upon whether an interested state is satisfied that the tribunal is delivering the goods. It seems too easy for the United Nations to refuse to participate in such institutions until states guarantee funding for the life of the institution. The resistance of the funders to making such commitments only confirms the fact that their ongoing financial support for the tribunals is linked to 'performance'.

In late 2010 a fifth ad hoc international criminal court was created, the International Residual Mechanism for International Tribunals. In reality, it continues the work of the Yugoslavia and Rwanda Tribunals, whose doors will close when the final trials and appeals are completed. In particular, the International Residual Mechanism ensures that there will always be a judge and a prosecutor for the few indicted fugitives who remain at large at the Rwanda tribunal (all of the suspects on the Yugoslavia Tribunal's 'most wanted' list have been apprehended), as well as an avenue for reconsideration should new evidence come to light that might exonerate a convict. A residual court has also been planned for the Special Court of Sierra Leone when its trials are completed.

THE INTERNATIONAL CRIMINAL COURT

During the 1990s, as the fledgling ad hoc tribunals for the former Yugoslavia and Rwanda were navigating in largely uncharted waters, negotiations on the establishment of a permanent international criminal court made rapid progress. Indeed, the speedy pace of the work could not have been predicted. The draft statute finalized by the International Law Commission in 1994 went through three years of intense scrutiny in a series of meetings held under the auspices of the United Nations General Assembly. During this period, the vision of the Court evolved, from that of an institution essentially subservient to the Security Council to that of a more independent body, able to set its own priorities without the entrenched domination of the great powers and the remaining superpower. In 1998 some 160 countries assembled in Rome to negotiate the Statute of the International Criminal Court. Although there was broad consensus on most of the content, when the Statute was put to a vote only 120 of the participating countries concurred. Seven of them, including the United States, China, and Israel, voted against the Statute, and another twenty-one abstained.

The most significant distinction that separates the In
Criminal Court from all of the preceding international crim
institutions is the freedom given to the Prosecutor. He or she i
a nine-year term by the Court's members and has the authority ~~to select~~
'situations' for investigation and trial. The targets of each of the earlier
tribunals had been designated by the political body that established them:
the Nazi or Japanese leaders, the Yugoslavia conflict, the Rwandan genocide, the Sierra Leone civil war, and the assassinations in Lebanon. In the
International Criminal Court, a tribunal has been created with the autonomous authority to identify those crises, conflicts, and countries upon
which its attentions are to be focussed. The only remnant of the political
guidance that characterized the earlier tribunals is the possibility for the
United Nations Security Council or a member state to refer a situation to
the Prosecutor. But even then, the Prosecutor has the discretion to decline
to investigate if he or she thinks it would not be in the 'interests of justice'. There is a mild degree of judicial supervision over this extraordinary
prosecutorial power. In theory, at any rate, the entire process of selecting
situations is supposed to obey strictly judicial criteria. In practice, it still
seems profoundly subjective but in addition, by contrast with the earlier
institutions, quite opaque. At the other international criminal tribunals,
the selection of targets was unapologetically political. The challenges that
arise with the identification of situations by the Prosecutor are considered
in Chapter 3, 'Victors' Justice?'.

The Rome Statute entered into force on 1 July 2002 after obtaining its
sixtieth ratification. A year later, following election of the judges and the
Prosecutor, it became fully operational. As of September 2011, it had been
accepted by 116 states. As its tenth anniversary approached, the Court was
active in several countries, all of them located in Africa. It is hardly a secret
that in its early years the Court has struggled to find its way. The selection of appropriate situations has seemed to be easier said than done. The
first trials have faltered upon evidentiary issues. The delays at every stage
have exceeded anything at the ad hoc tribunals, despite the extraordinarily
light case load.

WHAT MAKES A CRIMINAL TRIBUNAL 'INTERNATIONAL'?

Some of the war crimes tribunals include the word 'international' in their
name: for example, the International Military Tribunal, the International
Criminal Tribunal for the former Yugoslavia, and the International

Criminal Court. Others do not: the Special Court for Sierra Leone, the Special Tribunal for Lebanon. Obviously the name given to a tribunal is not decisive. Judges at the Special Court for Sierra Leone have ruled that they were just as 'international' as the ad hoc tribunals established by the United Nations Security Council to deal with the former Yugoslavia and Rwanda. The Sierra Leone and Lebanon tribunals owe their existence to agreements between the respective governments and the United Nations, although with the imprimatur of the Security Council. The International Criminal Court owes its existence to its treaty, the Rome Statute.

The fashionable term 'hybrid tribunal' is useful to the extent that it communicates the intermingling of the national and the international in this process. There are two main dimensions to this phenomenon; one of them concerns the personnel employed by the tribunal while the other focusses on the law that is applied. On a structural level, the tribunals for Lebanon and Sierra Leone are sometimes labelled 'hybrid' (or 'mixed-model') because of a combination of national and international involvement in selecting judges and prosecutors. They are grouped in this category along with institutions such as the Extraordinary Chambers of the Court of Cambodia, where there is also a combination of national and international judges. However, the latter is an emanation of the Cambodian legal system, as its name suggests. Some of its judges are drawn from abroad and appointed by the United Nations. The presence of non-nationals does not make a tribunal international. Many national justice systems allow for the participation of foreign citizens in their judiciary. This has long been the case with Commonwealth countries. Cyprus even has a constitution that provides that the president of the Constitutional Court must be a foreign national, although the provision has fallen into desuetude. The Constitutional Court of Cyprus is a national body, not a 'hybrid' or an international institution.

But just as the structure and personnel of a tribunal do not suffice to make it international in nature, nor does the applicable law provide a means to distinguish. Even the purest of the international tribunals provide some space for the application of national law, and especially the national law of the country concerned. Admittedly, the legislative framework may vary somewhat from one international tribunal to another depending upon the territory over which it is exercising jurisdiction. For example, the Special Court for Sierra Leone has some particular common law features, right down to the judges who like to be called 'Justice'. The Special Tribunal for Lebanon, on the other hand, has a very French bouquet, particularly at the procedural level. Even the Rome Statute of the International Criminal Court recognizes the application of 'general principles of law derived by the Court from national laws of legal systems of the world including, as appropriate, the national laws of states that would normally exercise jurisdiction over the crime'. Such deviation from symmetry or universality does not make the International Criminal Court a hybrid.

The International Military Tribunals and the first two ad hoc tribunals, as well as the International Criminal Court, only exercise jurisdiction over international crimes. But there is nothing to stop a state from establishing its own national tribunal with the same specialization, and some have done so. The fact that a national judicial institution only deals with international crimes is not enough to make it an international court. Nor does there seem to be a requirement that the jurisdiction of an international criminal court be restricted to international crimes. The Special Court for Sierra Leone was enabled to prosecute crimes under the laws of Sierra Leone in addition to war crimes and crimes against humanity, although the prosecutor chose to confine the indictments to crimes under international law. The jurisdiction of the Special Tribunal for Lebanon is limited exclusively to crimes under Lebanese law.

As a result, the 'hybrid' or 'mixed' designation to define a middle ground between the genuinely international and the purely national is a source of confusion that conceals significant distinctions. Rather than confound the difference between international and national tribunals, it is better to draw a bright line that separates them. The test should be whether the tribunal can be dissolved by the law of a single country. If that is the case, as it is in Cambodia, then the tribunal is national. Cambodia has an agreement with the United Nations by which it pledges cooperation. The agreement has been endorsed by a General Assembly resolution. Nevertheless, the legal framework of the Extraordinary Chambers is profoundly national. What the Cambodian legislator can do it can also undo. By contrast, the Special Court for Sierra Leone and the Special Tribunal for Lebanon are clearly international in nature. Not only are their statutes annexed to a treaty, they have also been blessed by Security Council resolutions. The governments of Sierra Leone and Lebanon have helped set in motion a process that they cannot, acting alone, bring to an end. The only way to conclude the work of the Sierra Leone and Lebanon tribunals is by mutual agreement of the parties that created them, or by Security Council resolution. Acting unilaterally, neither government has the power to stop the work of the institutions.

Is this of any importance, other than as a useful criterion in classifying the panorama of judicial institutions involved in international justice? Are there any legal consequences to the distinction between international and national courts? Indeed there are, according to the International Court of Justice. It concerns the classic immunities recognized under customary international law to heads of state and certain other senior government officials. In a celebrated 2002 decision, the Court said that national courts were required to respect the immunity to which foreign leaders were entitled. However, such individuals were not immune from prosecution. In particular, the International Court of Justice said they could be subject to criminal proceedings before certain international criminal courts, where they have jurisdiction. Examples include the International Criminal Tribunal for the former Yugoslavia, and the International Criminal Tribunal for Rwanda, established pursuant to Security Council resolutions under Chapter VII of the United Nations Charter, and the International Criminal Court created by the 1998 Rome Convention. The latter's Statute expressly provides, in article 27, paragraph 2, that '[i]mmunities or special procedural rules which may attach to the official capacity of a person, whether under national or international law, shall not bar the Court from exercising its jurisdiction over such a person'.[6]

Thus, there is legal importance in being able to identify 'certain international criminal courts, where they have jurisdiction'. It may be that distinctions must be made even among the international criminal tribunals. Some of them may have the power to ignore immunities, as the International Court of Justice has maintained, while others may not.

The Nuremberg judges explained that in establishing the International Military Tribunal, the four 'great powers' had 'done together what any one of them might have done singly; for it is not to be doubted that any nation has the right thus to set up special courts to administer law'.[7] To the extent that international criminal tribunals are created by sovereign states, they can have no more authority or jurisdiction than the states that create them already possess. The four ad hoc tribunals derive their authority from the United Nations itself, and have a good claim to operate on behalf of the international community. They are more than the product of an agreement between a group of states that have decided to do together what any one might do singly. On the other hand, the International Criminal Court is created by a treaty that binds its own members but cannot, in principle, do any more.

The International Court of Justice seemed to lump the International Criminal Court together with the ad hoc tribunals, giving all three the label of 'certain international criminal courts'. The Court's proposition concerning immunity makes good sense for the Security Council-created

---

[6] *Arrest Warrant of 11 April 2000 (Democratic Republic of Congo v Belgium)* [2002] ICJ Reports 3, para. 61.

[7] *France et al. v Göring et al.* (1948) 22 IMT 411, at p. 461.

tribunals, because they are created by the international community acting collectively. The logic cannot be quite the same for the International
Criminal Court. If heads of state benefit from immunity before the courts
of other states, then surely those other states cannot circumvent this
immunity by banding together to create an 'international' tribunal. They
cannot give the international court more rights and authority than they
already possess.

Yet this seems to be what happened with the issuance of an arrest warrant by the International Criminal Court against President El Bashir of
Sudan in March 2009 (and again with Muammar Gaddafi of Libya in June
2011). The judges offered an inadequate and rather superficial explanation
when they ruled that El Bashir was without immunity before the Court. At
the time the arrest warrant was issued against El Bashir, the British newspaper *The Guardian* presciently observed that this also meant the heads
of state of other non-member states, like the United States, might be subject to prosecution by the Court. However enthusiastic Washington may
now be about the arrest warrants directed at El Bashir and Gaddafi, it is
doubtful that this extends to a general recognition that no head of state
benefits from immunity before the Court, including its own. The United
States undoubtedly takes the view that the International Criminal Court
cannot exercise jurisdiction over its own president. Why then should the
same rule not apply to the presidents of Sudan and Libya?

WHY IS INTERNATIONAL JUSTICE DIFFERENT?

Of course, international criminal law does not require international criminal tribunals any more than public international law in general requires
a world court. International law existed long before there was an international judicial institution. International law, including international
criminal law, is alive and well in domestic courts. For many years, human
rights activists have encouraged the exercise of universal jurisdiction,
which is one mechanism with the potential to bring international criminal
law into the sphere of national justice institutions. Implementing the legislation of the Rome Statute has also enhanced the profile of international
criminal law within the domestic legal sphere. The growing number of
judges and lawyers who work at the international level and then return to
their own justice systems is also not without its effect. They bring back the
lessons they have learned before international courts and apply them in
their old, familiar environments.

In principle, national criminal justice systems address themselves to
'outlaws', that is, individuals whose behaviour is incompatible with the

shared values of the society in which they live. Those who violate these norms expose themselves to criminal prosecution and punishment. In the case of the most serious crimes against the person, such as murder, modern societies assume that punishable acts will be investigated and the perpetrators brought to book, more or less without exception. Modern-day human rights law says this is a duty owed to the victim. Usually relatively lengthy terms of imprisonment are imposed, with varying justifications, including deterrence of the perpetrator and of others, delivering the 'just deserts' to the offender, and protecting society by isolating dangerous individuals.

International criminal justice is different from 'ordinary' prosecution at the domestic level in several respects. First and foremost, the crimes are not the same. In one sense, international crimes such as genocide resemble ordinary crimes such as murder. But they also require additional elements of context, intent, scale, or gravity. While so-called ordinary crimes are the work of social deviants, international crimes usually require some degree of involvement by the state, that is, by the very organ whose purpose it is to protect society. Serial killers may perpetrate monstrous and horrible crimes, but we do not expect this to require international intervention. Their crimes inspire awe, yet nothing compels their internationalization.

It is the involvement of the state or of a state-like body that lifts ordinary crimes into the international arena, a subject explored in detail in Chapter 5 ('Mens Rea, Actus Reus, and the Role of the State'). Often the state itself operates as a giant criminal organization. Invariably, international prosecution is selective rather than comprehensive, focussing on organizers and leaders. More often than not, it comes in the aftermath of a conflict and is meted out to those who have been defeated rather than in a balanced manner as would be the case with ordinary crimes. And what is its purpose? As with ordinary crimes, it is difficult to prove a significant deterrent effect because we can more easily identify those who continue to violate the law than those who may have been convinced that crime does not pay. It may also be retributive, delivering just deserts to offenders and providing victims with a measure of acknowledgement. International justice is also said to promote the goals of the international community, and in particular the quest for a world without war, where disputes are settled peacefully. This is a huge burden, and one that is not associated with the prosecution of ordinary crimes.

In addressing all of these dimensions of international justice, there is a tendency towards mechanistic transposition to the international level of ideas and principles that have been derived from national criminal justice.

But international justice is different. Its political dimensions are inescapable. Its objectives necessarily involve goals related to conflict prevention and conflict resolution. It is this political aspect of the process that makes international justice so unique, and so fascinating. If it can work effectively, there is the potential to contribute to addressing some of the great problems of our time.

1

'UNIMAGINABLE ATROCITIES': IDENTIFYING INTERNATIONAL CRIMES

'Mindful that during this century millions of children, women and men have been victims of unimaginable atrocities that deeply shock the conscience of humanity', declares the preamble of the Rome Statute. The Statute goes on to define four categories of 'unimaginable atrocities': genocide, crimes against humanity, war crimes, and the crime of aggression. In ordinary conversation, the idea of such atrocities that shock humanity's conscience would likely be explained as 'war crimes'. Colloquially we often use the term 'war crimes' to describe a range of international crimes. These include those susceptible of commission in time of peace as well as in wartime, such as genocide and crimes against humanity. The term 'war crimes' may even be used to refer to the crime of aggression, which really governs the origin of a war (*jus ad bellum*) rather than how it is carried out (*jus in bello*).

The Nuremberg court is frequently described as a 'war crimes tribunal', although its central focus was actually not the laws of armed conflict, in the narrow sense, but the aggressive plan of the Nazi leaders. When journalists today speak of a 'war crimes tribunal', they generally mean this broader concept, one that includes genocide, crimes against humanity, and, perhaps, aggression. For specialists, 'war crimes' are only one of the categories of international prosecution contemplated by the international tribunals. Such 'war crimes' consist of offences relating to conduct on the battlefield, the treatment of wounded combatants and prisoners of war, and the protection of civilians. Necessarily, they can only be committed in the context of an armed conflict. The definitions of war crimes are fraught with technical rules, crafted to reassure generals and colonels that law will not overly encumber their freedom to wage war.

Obviously, the label 'war crimes' brings with it imprecision and inaccuracy, notably because it is now recognized that two momentous categories of international crime may be committed in peacetime. We have important recent examples of peacetime atrocities, such as those attributable to the Khmer Rouge in Cambodia during the late 1970s, or to the Indonesian regime in 1965, or the Haitian dictatorship of Jean-Claude Duvalier. Nevertheless, it is probably true to say that most manifestations of atrocity crimes do indeed take place in the context of armed conflict. Moreover, the incorporation of the crime of aggression within the Rome Statute recalls the famous pronouncement at Nuremberg: waging of unjust war is the 'supreme international crime differing only from other war crimes in that it contains within itself the accumulated evil of the whole'.[1]

The statutes of the international criminal tribunals for the former Yugoslavia, Rwanda and Sierra Leone circumscribe their jurisdiction as consisting of 'serious violations of international humanitarian law'. This expression, proposed by the Security Council in the resolutions setting up the tribunals, is probably no more precise than 'war crimes'. Furthermore, genocide and crimes against humanity, which are part of the jurisdiction of these tribunals, might just as well be thought of as having their origins in human rights law rather than international humanitarian law, which is a more modern term for the law of armed conflict. The prohibition of genocide is simply the most extreme and radical form of protection of ethnic minorities and condemnation of racial discrimination. The broader concept of crimes against humanity covers what would be called, in another context, gross and systematic violations of human rights. Indeed, in 1991, after decades of incessant redrafting of the Code of Offences Against the Peace and Security of Mankind, the United Nations International Law Commission proposed replacing the notion of crimes against humanity with 'systematic or mass violations of human rights'.

INTERNATIONAL CRIMINAL LAW

Academic writers and publishers appear to prefer the term 'international criminal law' to describe the discipline and the crimes that it covers. The French language distinguishes between *droit international pénal* and *droit pénal international*, and there are similar formulations in other languages (*Völkerstrafrecht* and *Internationales Strafrecht*; *derecho internacional penal* and *derecho penal internacional*). The difference between the two concepts appears to reside largely in the types of crimes they address. Thus,

---

[1] *France* et al. v *Göring* et al. (1948) 22 IMT 411, at p. 427.

droit international pénal refers to a body of norms governing relationships between states in the suppression of so-called 'ordinary' crimes, such as murder and rape. In English, the term 'transnational criminal law' is often employed. When criminal activity takes on cross-border dimensions, there must be rules to determine which state may punish the crime and the extent to which a state that cannot or does not intend to punish the crime will assist another in bringing the suspect to justice. By contrast, *droit pénal international* is focussed on crimes that are deemed to be international in nature. They are crimes 'of concern to the international community', something that cannot be said, it seems, of 'ordinary' murder and rape, not to mention impaired driving and shoplifting. Piracy is the historic example of such crimes of international concern that fall within the rubric of *droit pénal international*. French is sometimes a bit better than English in capturing certain subtleties, although its taxonomy in this area still leaves much that is unsettled.

There are now several volumes from various publishers that bear the title *International Criminal Law* or some variant upon it. They concern themselves with the substance of the crimes punished at Nuremberg and Tokyo and by the modern-day international tribunals, as well as with the obligations upon states that flow from the branding of such crimes as 'international', and with the institutions involved in enforcement. A growing number of universities offer courses on this subject, generally tagged as 'international criminal law'. But this always requires an explanation, because 'international criminal law' is usually meant to cover genocide, crimes against humanity, and war crimes (and sometimes the crime of aggression), and the tribunals that exercise jurisdiction over them. These courses do not as a general rule devote attention to such 'transnational' crimes as hijacking, piracy, money laundering and drug trafficking.

The *Oxford Companion to International Criminal Justice*, edited by Antonio Cassese and published in 2009, is a kind of encyclopedia in the field. The *Companion* has only a short entry that deals with hijacking and money laundering and similar offences; it is entitled 'Treaty-based crimes'. Such crimes are usually governed by what are often called 'suppression conventions'. Clearly, this subject is quite peripheral to the 'field' covered by the *Companion*. But other writers, such as Cherif Bassiouni, opt for a larger definition of international criminal law that includes the suppression conventions. By way of explanation, Professor Bassiouni acknowledges that this makes it more difficult to present the discipline of international criminal law as a neat, cohesive area of study. An even broader approach posits the inclusion of any crime that has been defined internationally. This extends the scope of the field to acts such as paedophilia and a range of environmental issues.

The 'treaty crimes' and the suppression conventions are more suitably discussed under the heading of 'transnational' crime. Their international dimension is mainly a consequence of the cross-border issues that arise as a result of their commission and with related law-enforcement problems. To be sure, there is controversy here. Some countries have attempted to insert drug crimes and terrorism into the jurisdictional provisions of the Rome Statute of the International Criminal Court. The first major decision of the Special Tribunal for Lebanon, in February 2011, contends that terrorism has finally joined the ranks of international crimes whose existence flows from customary international law. But the repeated failure to incorporate terrorism and drug crimes in the jurisdiction of the International Criminal Court corroborates the impression that they belong to a different, albeit related, genus.

The investigation and prosecution of 'war crimes' form a body of criminal law that is profoundly informed by the modern discipline of human rights. Much of the interest in the field of individual lawyers and activists is an inexorable product of personal commitment to the promotion of human rights rather than an obsession with the social benefits of criminal justice in general. The major human rights bodies within the United Nations, and especially the High Commissioner for Human Rights, have engaged very actively with international criminal justice institutions and objectives. Two of the High Commissioners, Louise Arbour and Navenathem Pillay, were themselves veterans of the international criminal tribunals, the former as Prosecutor at the ad hoc tribunals, the latter as judge and President of the International Criminal Tribunal for Rwanda and then as a member of the Appeals Chamber of the International Criminal Court. International human rights non-governmental organizations have put impunity and justice issues at the centre of their priorities.

The discipline of international criminal law may also be circumscribed in an institutional sense, a matter addressed in more detail in the Introduction to this volume. It can be considered to be the preserve of international criminal courts and tribunals, as distinct from national justice systems. International cooperation to suppress crime, as well as the concept of international crimes, has existed in one form or another for many centuries. International courts and tribunals, on the other hand, are a phenomenon that does not really begin until the end of the First World War, and even then in a half-baked form. They only became a permanent feature of the global legal order in the 1990s.

The problem with a purely institutional approach is that it excludes the very important activities of national courts in the prosecution of international crimes, where issues such as universal jurisdiction and the non-application of statutory limitation become relevant. The definition of an act as an international crime is highly significant at the national judicial level. It has important consequences even if there are no international institutions for prosecution. Thus, a framework that focusses solely on the international institutions does not tell the entire story.

PIRACY, THE FIRST INTERNATIONAL CRIME

Piracy is usually described as the first 'international crime'. Pirates have been called *hostis humani generis*—enemies of all humankind—as a justification for the international criminalization of their activity. For some, they are the ancestors of modern-day *génocidaires*. But it is very difficult to equate the two categories of international crime. Literature and cinema romanticize the lives of pirates, and children disguise themselves with eye-patches and toy cutlasses for costume parties. Even modern-day pirates are treated by some as quasi-heroic figures, who do little more than balance the scales of social justice between rich and poor. Of course, they are bad news if you are a wealthy ship owner or an insurance company. But the poor peasants living on the sea coast of war-torn Somalia may not necessarily share the same perspective.

Piracy is not an 'unimaginable atrocity'. Piracy is treated as an 'international crime' not because of the terrible horror or shock associated with its commission, but because it requires international cooperation for its repression. Pirates operate on the high seas, where no state can exercise territorial jurisdiction. Historically, it became accepted that a pirate could be prosecuted by the country that apprehended him (or her), regardless of the pirate's nationality or where the crime was committed. This is now known as 'universal jurisdiction'. Subsequently, other crimes have been added to the list of international crimes, essentially on the basis of the same rationale. These include a range of acts with an international dimension, including trade in pornography, narcotic drugs, and elephant ivory, and the disruption of undersea telecommunications cables. A report prepared by the Secretary-General of the United Nations in 2010 shows enormous variation in national legislative provisions authorizing universal jurisdiction, ranging from piracy to the disposal of toxic waste and currency-related matters. Yet universal jurisdiction is a subject that seems to generate more heat than light. In reality, there is very little actual practice, and only a handful of offenders has ended in prison as a result of its exercise.

In the early twentieth century, international lawmakers began to contemplate a new kind of international crime. Such acts were criminal not because of their transnational dimension or because they were committed outside the normal territorial limits of sovereign states; rather, they were quintessentially national acts, generally perpetrated by individuals with the connivance or complicity of governments. Precisely for this reason, they went unpunished. These were the work not of international outlaws but of states themselves. Their condemnation emerged at the same time as states, international organizations, and civil society began insisting that human rights violations were no longer sheltered from scrutiny by the protective shield of sovereignty. They are truly 'unimaginable atrocities'.

The initial manifestations of this new development appeared at the end of the First World War. The unprecedented destruction and loss of life that resulted from the conflict compelled outcries that those responsible should be brought to justice. The Treaty of Versailles announced the prosecution of the deposed German emperor for 'a supreme offence against international morality and the sanctity of treaties'. The charge is the precursor of what the Rome Statute of the International Criminal Court labels the crime of aggression.

Even more ambitious, in terms of challenging state sovereignty over the treatment of its own citizens, were the efforts to bring Ottoman leaders to justice for what today is called the Armenian genocide. The initial threat of prosecution was contained in the joint declaration of Britain, France, and Russia, as discussed in the Introduction to this book. An early draft referred to 'these new crimes of Turkey against Christianity and civilization'. That was nothing particularly innovative, because the major European powers had long asserted their entitlement to intervene in Turkish affairs in order to protect Christian minorities. Known as the 'capitulations', the idea traces its origins as far back as the Crusades. When the authors of the declaration replaced the word 'Christianity' with 'humanity' they turned a corner. The atrocities attributed to Turkey offended the fundamental values of all human beings as well as the interests of the European states concerned with the crimes. It was more than just a matter of protecting kin groups. Like the plan to prosecute the Kaiser, however, nothing concrete really came of this.

Still, the idea had taken hold, and it led to successful trials at Nuremberg and Tokyo following the Second World War. Carl Schmitt, who spent the Second World War as professor of law at the University of Berlin and who was a member of the Nazi party, recognized this tectonic shift in the legal landscape. In an opinion written for the defendants at the Nuremberg trial, he contested the claim that crimes against peace were an international offence on much the same basis as piracy. In his essay entitled 'Das internationalrechtliche Verbrechen des Angriffskrieges und der Grundsatz *"Nullum crimine, nulla poena sine lege"'* (published in English as 'The International Crime of the War of Aggression and the Principle *"Nullum crimen, nulla poena sine lege"'*[2]), he explained that piracy was really nothing more than robbery at sea. The particular features of its commission lead to 'certain practical consequences for the responsibility of other states' but do not 'make piracy into an international crime in a special sense'. Schmitt challenged the analogy that appeared, and that continues to appear, in academic writing between the international crime of piracy and the criminalization of aggressive war, acknowledging, however, that 'equal treatment of pirate and war criminal is easily made propagandistically comprehensible to public opinion'.

Schmitt was correct to distinguish between piracy and the new, emerging concept of crimes against peace. He had cleverly identified one of the weaker aspects in the arguments of those in favour of new categories of international crime. His plea failed at Nuremberg, of course. Schmitt's understanding was purely static, typical of his exceedingly conservative world view. Nuremberg was part of a dynamic process. As the American Prosecutor, Robert Jackson, explained, 'every custom has its origin in some single act'.

In addition to crimes against peace, the post-Second World War tribunals also punished what were labelled 'violations of the laws and customs of war'. Some of these 'war crimes' had been condemned since ancient times. In the *Iliad*, for example, Achilles is rebuked for dragging the body of Hector around the walls of Troy after he has slain the Trojan hero in battle. Achilles had violated the customs of war. In ancient times there was no international criminal tribunal to hold Achilles accountable, but he was given his due punishment, by the gods. Homer's idea that there are norms that stand above the state in order to protect fundamental values, such as the inherent dignity of a dead body, returns in Sophocles's *Antigone*.

To war crimes and crimes against peace, Nuremberg and Tokyo added a third category of international crime, perhaps the most radical of all. Initially discussed under the rubric of 'atrocities, persecutions and deportations', it was subsequently labelled 'crimes against humanity'. This broad concept contemplated unimaginable atrocities committed by a state against its own population. It was developed in order to ensure that Nazi leaders would

---

[2] Carl Schmitt, *Writings on War*, Cambridge: Polity, 2011, pp. 123–97.

not go unpunished for the acts perpetrated within Germany's borders. For greater clarity, the words 'any civilian population' were included at the end of the earliest definition and they have remained there ever since.

A NEW GENERATION OF INTERNATIONAL CRIMES

There is a manifestation of this debate during a seminal period in the codification of international crimes. In late 1946, weeks after the conclusion of the Nuremberg trial, a resolution was tabled in the General Assembly of the United Nations aimed at recognition of genocide as an international crime. The preamble of the draft text said: 'Whereas the punishment of the very serious crime of genocide when committed in time of peace lies within the exclusive territorial jurisdiction of the judiciary of every state concerned, while crimes of a relatively lesser importance such as piracy, trade in women, children, drugs, obscene publications are declared as international crimes and have been made matters of international concern....'[3] This language was lost in the final version of the resolution, but not apparently because there was any controversy about the ideas that it contained. The text recognizes the notion of international crimes in a general sense. It also acknowledges the existence of a new class of international crime, one that is 'very serious' as opposed to the traditional international crimes that are of 'relatively lesser importance'. This is the shift in international law about which Carl Schmitt was so disturbed in his 1945 essay, as described above. But then, Schmitt had clients to defend, as well as his own sordid past.

In the Rome Statute of the International Criminal Court, this body of substantive law is described as 'the most serious crimes of concern to the international community as a whole'. The Rome Statute list comprises genocide, crimes against humanity, war crimes, and the crime of aggression. Piracy or trade in obscene publications, crimes mentioned as being of 'relatively lesser importance' in the draft 1946 General Assembly resolution, are nowhere to be found. Yet there can be no doubt about their status as international crimes. The divide remains between a first generation of international crimes, such as piracy, and the second: genocide, crimes against humanity, war crimes, and the crime of aggression. The former are the work of international scofflaws operating outside the framework of sovereign states, while the latter are generally attributed to leaders and policy makers within states or state-like entities, along with the generals and bureaucrats who implement such policies.

---

[3] UN Doc. A/BUR/50.

In its February 2011 decision, the Appeals Chamber of the Special Tribunal for Lebanon concluded that international terrorism had emerged as an international crime given the evolution of customary international law. The Chamber discussed how this process had taken place. It noted that it was not enough to demonstrate that a crime was universally punished for it to be deemed international, pointing to murder as an example. According to the Appeals Chamber,

> To turn into an international crime, a domestic offence needs to be regarded by the world community as an attack on universal values (such as peace or human rights) or on values held to be of paramount importance in that community; in addition, it is necessary that States and intergovernmental organizations, through their acts and pronouncements, sanction this attitude by clearly expressing the view that the world community considers the offence at issue as amounting to an international crime.[4]

Previous tribunals have baulked at trying to explain why a crime should be deemed international. They have generally contented themselves with assuming this to be the case for the crimes listed in their statutes. But the Special Tribunal for Lebanon is confined to crimes under Lebanese law and has no explicit jurisdiction over international crimes. The Appeals Chamber wanted to apply the definitions of international crimes to the interpretation of Lebanese law. Consequently, it had to determine whether international terrorism could be included within the list of international crimes. In so doing, it felt compelled to discuss how and why a hitherto ordinary crime may migrate to the international category.

The definition provided by the Appeals Chamber of the Special Tribunal for Lebanon does not distinguish between the first generation of international crimes, which the draft 1946 General Assembly resolution had described as being of 'relatively lesser importance', and the second generation, which could claim the pedigree of 'the most serious crimes of concern to the international community as a whole'. Its explanation blurs the distinction by suggesting that all international crimes respond to the same logic. However, the destruction of undersea telecommunications cables or trade in elephant ivory, although an international crime contemplated by suppression conventions, can hardly be viewed as 'an attack on universal values (such as peace or human rights) or on values held to be of paramount importance in that community'.

---

[4] *Unnamed defendant* (STL-11-01/I), Interlocutory Decision on the Applicable Law: Terrorism, Conspiracy, Homicide, Perpetration, Cumulative Charging, 16 February 2011, para. 91.

They do not belong to the genus of 'unimaginable atrocities that shock the conscience of humanity'.

Some crimes perhaps merit international status for the reason that, as the Appeals Chamber of the Special Tribunal for Lebanon said, they constitute an 'attack on universal values'. Others belong to the category for no better reason than that the international community has decided they should. This may have been the reasoning behind the Appeals Chamber's pronouncement.

Introductory courses in criminal law often begin by endeavouring to explain why certain acts are criminalized. After all, not every act that causes harm to other human beings, or to property, to animals, or the environment, will justify deprivation of liberty. Two convenient Latin expressions are employed: *malum prohibitum* and *malum in se*. A crime that is *malum prohibitum* constitutes wrongful conduct because lawmakers decide this should be the case, whereas the expression *malum in se* describes crimes that address fundamental human values, whose perpetration is viewed as naturally or inherently evil. *Mala prohibita* crimes can often be identified because their repression varies greatly from one jurisdiction to another, whereas *mala in se* crimes present themselves as being more universal in nature. In travelling from one country to another, no tourist will bother to inquire whether murder or rape is prohibited; these crimes are *mala in se*. But it is often useful to know whether one can drink alcohol in public, or at all, or whether certain forms of sexual activity are allowed, and if women must keep their heads covered, as in Iran, or uncovered, as in France.

Sometimes, however, it is not apparent whether behaviour is prohibited because it is *malum in se* or *malum prohibitum*. Traffic in certain narcotic drugs, such as marijuana, and even its consumption, is subject to serious penalties in some countries, while tolerated in others and virtually legalized in a few. International conventions proscribing the traffic of such a drug suggest its seriousness, but this is hard to square with calls from many public policy makers for outright decriminalization, and the notoriety of its widespread casual use. Adultery is another example of a rather common phenomenon in human life that some states have chosen to criminalize. Others entirely ignore the practice, and some have leaders who notoriously indulge in it. One difficulty in identifying crimes that are *mala in se* arises because of changing values. This no doubt explains why many states that once punished adultery no longer do so. It seems that adultery might have been *mala in se* a century or two ago, and that this is no longer the case. The proposition is tautological, however, because if concepts of *malum in se* criminality change over time, then how can it be said that they manifest fundamental human values regarding dignity or good and evil?

Although the analogy is not a perfect one, the *malum prohibitum/malum in se* categorization can be usefully transposed to the field of international criminal law. The Rome Statute of the International Criminal Court describes its subject-matter jurisdiction as comprising 'the most serious crimes of concern to the international community as a whole'. It suggests that such crimes constitute 'unimaginable atrocities that deeply shock the conscience of humanity', eloquent words that have been borrowed for the title of this book. In other words, they are *mala in se*. When the Rome Statute was being drafted, there were unsuccessful proposals to include drug crimes and terrorism on the list. Some states probably considered that these crimes were not serious enough for the Court. Others may not have disputed their seriousness but perhaps took the view that the issues were better addressed in the context of transnational criminal law, using mutual legal assistance and extradition to bring offenders before national courts. In the case of terrorism, there were concerns about definition, lest a crime earmarked for political outlaws actually characterize the conduct of states with large armies and fearsome weapons. By contrast, there was never any doubt about the fact that the 'crime of crimes', genocide, belonged within the subject-matter jurisdiction of the International Criminal Court. The debate about the types of crime to be included in the remit of the Court revived in preparation for the 2010 Kampala Review Conference. With insufficient support for amendments to add drug trafficking and terrorism to the Statute, the proposals were excluded from the Conference agenda, shelved for another day, as they had been at the Rome Conference more than a decade earlier.

This is not to say that the insertion of an offence within the jurisdiction of the International Criminal Court provides irrefutable proof of its status as a serious international crime. Like the national legislator who may define a particular conduct as *malum prohibitum*, so the members of the International Criminal Court may agree to include minor or insignificant matters within the institution's jurisdiction. It is for them to decide, because the norms they adopt apply to them alone. In other words, we might say that a crime is an international crime because international lawmakers so decide. It is a bit paradoxical for the Rome Statute to declare that it deals with 'the most serious crimes of concern to the international community as a whole'. Is a crime 'most serious' because it is of concern to the international community? Is the fact that a crime is of 'concern to the international community' evidence of its 'most serious' status? This is the dog chasing its tail. Perhaps the answer is that it is a bit of both, just as it is in national criminal justice. Some crimes are obviously *mala in se* and others are *mala prohibita*, and many sit somewhere in between.

INTERNATIONAL CRIMES AND CUSTOMARY LAW

There is no problem with this essentially subjective and positivist approach when we are concerned with international crimes as they are defined in treaties. That is because, in principle, the norms set out in the treaties only apply to the states that have accepted them and to acts over which those states may exercise criminal jurisdiction. Yet by agreeing in an international convention that certain behaviour constitutes an international crime, states cannot indirectly legislate for others who have not participated in the negotiations or subsequently ratified the agreement. However, this does not mean that there is no international criminality simply because states have chosen not to ratify or accede to the relevant conventions. This is where the real difficulty in identifying international crimes arises.

Genocide is a crime within the jurisdiction of the International Criminal Court, but as early as 1951 it was described by the International Court of Justice as a universal prohibition, one that exists even in the absence of a treaty. Crimes against peace, war crimes, and crimes against humanity were dealt with at Nuremberg despite the fact that at the time of their commission there was no treaty authorizing their prosecution as international offences. More recently, the Special Court for Sierra Leone convicted several individuals of recruiting child soldiers at a time when this was not a crime in any international treaty. Thus, some crimes are international crimes even if they are not recognized in a universally applicable treaty. Furthermore, some crimes listed in international treaties may not actually be international crimes in the sense of general or customary international law. Finally, treaty definitions of international crimes may not correspond to their scope under customary international law.

The inclusion of a crime in the Rome Statute offers compelling evidence of its universal prohibition and its status as an international crime, regardless of adherence to a particular treaty. International drug trafficking and terrorism have thus far been excluded from the jurisdiction of the International Criminal Court. That might suggest there is no broad consensus that they belong within the category of international crimes or, at any rate, with those 'most serious crimes of concern to the international community as a whole'. Yet it is certainly arguable that their absence from the Rome Statute does not necessarily mean they are not serious crimes of international concern. After all, they are addressed in many other specific treaties aimed at the repression of transnational crime. An excellent example of a war crime that is not adequately included in the Rome Statute is the 'employment of . . . weapons calculated to cause unnecessary suffering'. The text appears in the Statute of the International Criminal Tribunal for the former Yugoslavia, which was deemed by the United Nations Security Council to reflect customary international law. But delegates to the Rome Conference, which was held five years after the Statute of the Yugoslavia Tribunal was adopted, could not agree on a similar text, essentially out of concern from certain major powers that its universal application might extend to nuclear weapons.

There are also examples of crimes whose international dimension remains controversial even though they are included in the Rome Statute. The war crime of transferring settlers into an occupied territory was included in the Statute, but over the objections of Israel. It argued that this offence was not of a customary nature. Some replied that Israel's argument was simply wrong in law, while others said that the drafters of the Rome Statute were free to create new crimes and to innovate. The former relied on a *malum in se* type argument, while the latter took the *malum prohibitum* route.

Why does this matter? There are significant legal consequences to the classification of behaviour as an international crime. The first is to authorize states to prosecute such crimes before their own domestic courts even in the absence of a jurisdictional link. Normally, the justice system of a particular state can only address crimes committed on its territory or by its nationals. If the crime is deemed to be international, these limitations may not apply. There seems to be little question that genocide can be prosecuted by courts anywhere in the world, regardless of whether the state holding the trial has any direct association with the crime. There are recent examples of genocide trials held in such states without any objection from the country that would normally exercise jurisdiction, confirming both the international nature of the crime and the acceptability of the exercise of such universal jurisdiction, as it is known. The 2010 report of the Secretary-General of the United Nations to the General Assembly provides further confirmation. The same cannot be said of drug trafficking or terrorism, or even of the transfer of settlers into an occupied territory, where there is no noteworthy pattern of prosecutions by courts in the absence of a significant jurisdictional link.

There is also a related proposition by which states are under an obligation to prosecute international crimes, to the extent that they have custody of a suspect and even in the absence of a jurisdictional connection. This takes universal jurisdiction up one notch, from a concept that is permissive to one that is mandatory. It has a Latin formulation, *aut dedere aut judicare*, meaning 'extradite or prosecute'. Treaties dealing with torture and enforced disappearance, and with certain war crimes, impose such an obligation. In 2009 Belgium filed an application against Senegal before the International Court of Justice arguing that the latter had failed to honour its duty to prosecute the exiled leader of Chad for crimes of torture, as required by the 1984 Torture Convention.

There is little practice, however, to suggest that states consider that they are bound to prosecute international crimes if this is not dictated by a treaty. Human rights activists regularly argue for the enforcement of such an obligation, but they are often met with resistance from state officials and indifference from legislatures. When courts in the United Kingdom refused to extradite four Rwandan genocide suspects so that they could stand trial in Rwanda, the accused returned to their homes and their ordinary lives in England's green and pleasant land. The British parliament did not respond by enacting legislation to allow genocide prosecutions under universal jurisdiction. There was no sense of any obligation to ensure that, given the failure of the courts to allow extradition, the four men should be prosecuted by the domestic justice system of the United Kingdom.

A more doubtful consequence of the universal acceptance of a crime as being international in nature is the removal of immunities. Some contend that there is simply no immunity for heads of state and similar officials where international crimes are concerned. Chilean dictator Augusto Pinochet invoked immunity before the English courts in 1998 and 1999, but without real success. Judges ruled that he had no immunity to a prosecution for the international crime of torture because it could not have been part of his official functions. But three years later, the International Court of Justice took a different approach. It rejected the bold proposition that there is no immunity of heads of state for international crimes. According to the Court, the fact that an individual is being prosecuted for an international crime leaves the classic immunity from the jurisdiction of a foreign court intact. As international law currently stands, a head of state and some senior officials benefit from immunity, regardless of the crime committed, to the extent they find themselves before the courts of another state. They only lose their immunity before an international criminal tribunal, something discussed in the Introduction to this volume.

The Universal Declaration of Human Rights affirms the prohibition of retroactive criminal offences as a general proposition: 'No one shall be held guilty of any penal offence on account of any act or omission which did not constitute a penal offence, under national or international law, at the time when it was committed.' Similar provisions appear in most constitutions.

When regimes change, there may be efforts to prosecute crimes committed in the past. Because the former tyrants sheltered themselves from the law, new legislation may be required. The defendants then argue that this is retroactive prosecution. But according to the Universal Declaration of Human Rights—which was adopted in 1948 with an eye to Nuremberg—a state may enact retroactive criminal legislation provided that this is aimed at crimes already recognized under international law. A defendant before a national court cannot succeed with an argument based upon the fact that there was no such crime in the domestic criminal law at the time the act was perpetrated if the prosecution can show that there was nevertheless such a crime under international law. Here, demonstrating that conduct was prohibited as an international crime may prove decisive to the success or failure of prosecution. This issue is discussed in Chapter 2, 'Nullum Crimen Sine Lege'.

The starting point in any identification of international crimes is the principle that they are the exception, not the rule. The prosecution of crime is an attribute of state sovereignty, and it can be internationalized only by exception. Just as states are free to enact criminal prohibitions for acts that are *mala prohibita*, they may likewise agree with other states to internationalize the prosecution of such crimes. Theoretically, there is no reason why two or more states that punish adultery as a crime in their national law could not agree, by treaty or by custom, to the internationalization of such offences. They could even create an international tribunal and give it jurisdiction to punish the behaviour. But obviously this could have no effect outside the borders of the states concerned. Any attempt by them to prosecute adultery committed elsewhere would violate the sovereignty of the state where the 'crime' was committed. In other words, such states could make adultery an international crime, but only in a technical sense.

The International Criminal Tribunal for the former Yugoslavia was established by the United Nations Security Council in 1993. Judges were given jurisdiction to prosecute 'the laws or customs of war' in accordance with article 3 of their Statute. An exemplary list of such violations was provided, but it was preceded with the words 'shall include, but not be limited to'. The judges were given the authority to determine just what such violations might be. They could well have confined their inquiry to applicable treaties, on the premise that only when a state has explicitly accepted the existence of a crime can it be determined that specific crimes are punishable. They went further. In its first major ruling, the Appeals Chamber of the Tribunal held that the reference to 'laws or customs of war' was an 'umbrella' provision encompassing all serious violations of international humanitarian law entailing individual criminal responsibility, as defined in either customary law or applicable treaties.[5]

Since then, judges of the Tribunal have registered convictions for crimes that are not specifically listed in the Statute, such as 'unlawful attacks on civilians', when these have been 'launched deliberately against civilians or civilian objects in the course of an armed conflict and are not justified by military necessity'. According to the International Criminal Tribunal for the former Yugoslavia, such attacks 'must have caused deaths and/or serious bodily injuries within the civilian population or extensive damage to civilian objects'. The judges have said: 'Such attacks are in direct contravention of the prohibitions expressly recognised in international law including the relevant provisions of Protocol Additional I [of 1977 to the Geneva Conventions of 1949]'.[6] In effect, the Yugoslavia Tribunal has added offences to the list of international crimes that were not explicit in the text. By way of explanation, the Tribunal's Appeals Chamber has said that 'serious violations' must 'constitute a breach of a rule protecting important values, and the breach must involve grave consequences for the victim'.[7] Something similar appears in article 7 of the Rome Statute, which defines crimes against humanity. Alongside a quite specific list of punishable acts is the residual category of 'other inhumane acts'. These must be 'of a similar character intentionally causing great suffering, or serious injury to body or to mental or physical health'.

ORDINARY CRIMES, HUMAN RIGHTS, AND COMPLEMENTARITY

In recent decades, human rights law has added new dimensions to the debate about the definition of crime. For example, there is now much authority for the proposition that victims of certain serious crimes have a fundamental right to see the perpetrators brought to justice. It is sometimes said that a distinguishing feature of international crimes is the duty imposed upon states to ensure their prosecution. But according to human rights courts, that obligation is indeed broader. In fact, it has nothing to do with whether the crime is international or not.

In one case, the European Court of Human Rights held that there had been a violation of the European Convention on Human Rights because

---

[5] *Tadić* (IT-94-1-AR72), Decision on the Defence Motion for Interlocutory Appeal on Jurisdiction, 2 October 1995, para. 94.

[6] *Kordić* et al. (IT-95-14/2-T), Judgment, 26 February 2001, para. 328; *Kordić* et al. (IT-95-14/2-A), Judgment, 17 December 2004, para. 40.

[7] *Kunarac* et al. (IT-96-23/1-A), Judgment, 12 June 2002, para. 66; *Kvočka* et al. (IT-98-30/1-T), Judgment, 2 November 2001, para. 123.

rape was not being adequately investigated by the Bulgarian justice system.[8] This was a single, isolated rape committed by an individual, and not a systematic rape perpetrated as part of an attack on a civilian population during wartime or other conflict. Of course rape has always been a crime under Bulgarian law. But when the authorities refused to proceed because the victim of a 'date rape' offered no proof of physical resistance, the European Court held that her rights had been breached. By insisting on physical resistance in order to prove lack of consent, the legal regime of Bulgaria violated the right of the victim to have justice done. This is not exactly the *malum in se* argument, but it is close enough. The justification is not 'fundamental human values' but rather 'fundamental human rights', which is perhaps a distinction without a real difference. It is doubtful that an international human rights court would blame a country's justice system for failure adequately to investigate a case of petty theft or trespass, however, despite the protection of the right to property in the relevant treaties.

The concept of 'serious crimes' is also used as a term of art by international human rights law. Article 6(2) of the International Covenant on Civil and Political Rights affirms that in states that retain capital punishment, the death penalty may only be imposed for the 'most serious crimes'. Human rights monitoring mechanisms support the view that this concept is confined to murder. Drug trafficking and non-violent economic crimes, even on a very large scale, do not satisfy the criterion, although a few states continue to execute traffickers in drugs, fraudsters, and even adulterers. Along somewhat the same lines, the Refugee Convention allows the *refoulement* of a refugee to a country where he or she might fear persecution if the person has been convicted of a 'very serious crime'. It also withdraws refugee protection from the perpetrator of a 'serious non-political crime'. That the concept of seriousness is an international standard means, inexorably, that it should only apply to crimes that are *mala in se* or that have been universally prohibited by treaty. International law cannot leave individual states with the option of deciding what constitute 'serious crimes' for the purpose of determining their treaty obligations.

Human rights law also indicates that certain offences, deemed criminal in many national justice systems, run counter to entitlements such as the right to equality and the right to privacy. In a series of judgments, the European Court of Human Rights ruled that the prohibition of homosexual activity between consenting adults in private was a violation of the European Convention on Human Rights.[9] Similar decisions have been

---

[8] *MC* v *Bulgaria* (App. No. 39272/98), Judgment, 4 December 2003.
[9] *Dudgeon* v *United Kingdom*, Series A, No. 45, 22 October 1981; *Norris* v *Ireland*, Series A, No. 142, 26 October 1988; *Modinos* v *Cyprus*, Series A, No. 259, 22 April 1993.

issued by several national constitutional courts.[10] This is of less relevance to the discussion of international crimes.

The 11 September 2001 attacks on the World Trade Centre in New York City prompted many to claim this was a crime against humanity, thereby framing the matter as an international crime. The rationale seems to have been the sheer horror of the acts and the number of victims. There was less talk of crimes against humanity when trains were bombed at Madrid's Atocha station in 2004, and a year later when a small gang of terrorist bombers attacked buses and underground trains in London. But in July 2011 prosecutors in Norway suggested they might lay charges against a home-grown neo-Nazi terrorist for an appalling bombing followed by the mass killing of teenagers at a summer camp. Qualitatively, it is difficult to distinguish between the World Trade Centre attack, the London and Madrid bombings, and the Norwegian terrorist. This is really the problem with broadening the scope of international crimes. We must be capable of drawing lines of demarcation. The explanation for internationalizing the World Trade Centre attacks was often that such crimes 'shock the conscience'. Yet a single murder or a single rape also shocks the conscience. Sometimes we think of such crimes, especially when associated with sadism or perversion, as 'unimaginable'. Why, then, do we not establish international criminal tribunals to deal with murder? Why do states not attempt to exercise universal jurisdiction over the crime of murder? Why do we not threaten to strip the immunity from a head of state who is involved in a murder?

The relevance of a distinction between 'ordinary' murder and murder *qua* genocide or crimes against humanity presents itself when international tribunals assess the appropriateness of trial before national courts. Such issues have arisen in transfer decisions by the International Criminal Tribunal for Rwanda. As part of its completion strategy, the Security Council expected the Tribunal to transfer its less important cases to national justice systems. In the first such application, when Norway offered to try an accused, judges of the International Tribunal refused authorization. They faulted Norway because it would only proceed on charges of murder, rather than genocide, which was not yet provided for in its national legislation. Yet Norway was willing to prosecute Michel Bagaragaza for homicidal acts that were, in substance, part of the 1994 genocide. The Tribunal seemed to feel that murder alone did not adequately stigmatize the crime.[11] It held

[10] *Lawrence* v *Texas*, 539 US 558 (2003).

[11] *Bagaragaza* (ICTR-2005-86-R11bis), Decision on the Prosecution Motion for Referral to the Kingdom of Norway, 19 May 2006; *Bagaragaza* (ICTR-2005-86-AR11bis), Decision on Rule 11 *bis* Appeal, 30 August 2006.

that transfer could only be allowed if Bagaragaza was to be tried under the label of an international crime.

Similar difficulties may arise at the International Criminal Court in debates about the admissibility of cases. The statutes of the ad hoc tribunals indicate no deference for national criminal courts, but at the International Criminal Court there is a quite explicit presumption in their favour. This is known as 'complementarity'. The International Criminal Court may proceed only if the national justice system is unwilling or unable to investigate or prosecute. If the *Bagaragaza* case is any guide, the international judges may reject the validity of national prosecutions to the extent that they proceed against suspects charged only with ordinary crimes, such as murder, rather than with the international crimes as set out in the Rome Statute. There is considerable academic authority supporting this approach, although as yet there have been no judicial decisions on the point.

Whether such a rigorous approach makes sense depends upon one's view of the fundamental justification for international criminalization. Some take the position that certain crimes must be defined as international because of their heinousness. They are the 'unimaginable atrocities' that 'shock the conscience'. Perhaps this is another way of expressing the *malum in se* principle. If this view is adopted, then it is right to insist that international crimes not be treated as 'lesser' offences, such as murder and rape. This seems to be the understanding of the judges in the referral decisions, discussed above. It is also strongly advocated by many with respect to the implementing legislation of the Rome Statute. States are told that they are required to incorporate the crimes listed in the Statute in order to comply with their obligations. Nowhere does the Statute actually say this, however.

A LINK WITH THE STATE

It seems more sensible to take the view that if a state prosecutes ordinary crimes, such as murder, without characterizing them as genocide, crimes against humanity, or war crimes, it is doing an adequate job of addressing impunity. After all, the purpose of the exercise is to bring an offender to justice. Domestic prosecutors will surely prefer to proceed on charges of ordinary murder rather than the international crimes because they are not required to prove complex contextual elements and to sensitize judges to unfamiliar legal sources. As for international tribunals, they are overburdened with cases of perpetrators who escape prosecution altogether. If nothing else, it seems a waste of resources for them to step in when national systems are active, even if the charges in a particular indictment are not international in nature. Of course, where a domestic prosecution involves a crime committed elsewhere, under universal jurisdiction, there can be no choice but to use the international characterization.

Most international crimes are actually crimes under ordinary law, but with the addition of contextual elements. The crime against humanity of murder requires proof of an intentional homicide; it must also be shown that the act took place as part of a widespread or systematic attack on a civilian population. Most but not all international crimes are underpinned by ordinary crimes. For example, the Rome Statute makes it an offence to recruit children under fifteen into the armed forces. Some countries have more or less automatically added this to their national laws as part of the exercise of implementing the Rome Statute. But in the past it would have made no sense to incorporate such a crime in domestic legislation. That is because the recruitment of soldiers—be they children or adults—was a prerogative of the state, and could only take place pursuant to legislation. Why would a state legislate to prohibit behaviour that it alone could carry out? A similar example exists with the crime against humanity of persecution. It may involve the enactment of discriminatory legislation directed against racial, ethnic, or religious minorities. The Nuremberg Laws adopted by the Nazis in 1935 are often cited as an example. Here, too, since the crime itself involves legislation, it is somewhat illogical to prohibit the conduct by means of domestic criminal law.

Earlier generations of international crime, such as piracy and trafficking in obscene publications, were based not upon the degree of evil but rather on pragmatic concerns relating to enforcement of transnational crime and crime committed on the high seas. Perhaps there is a similarly pragmatic explanation for the internationalization of genocide, crimes against humanity, and war crimes. Taken from this perspective, crime is internationalized primarily because of impunity before the national jurisdiction, that is, because national justice systems fail to prosecute. The reason why they fail is, as a general rule, because the government itself is complicit. The regime that has the duty to prosecute is responsible for the violations or has made a political decision to shelter the perpetrators. In other words, such crimes go unpunished not because of the scale of the evil but rather because of the relationship between the state and the perpetrator. States will not agree that international law can address *any* crime that is left unpunished by their own courts, but they have been willing, in recent decades, to accept that this may take place exceptionally. That is why they are so careful in defining the international crimes.

The crime of torture presents an interesting example. In the Rome Statute, it is subsumed explicitly under the definitions of both crimes against humanity and war crimes. It could also be punished as an act of genocide, because it may cause 'serious bodily or mental harm'. But in all three cases there must be an additional contextual element that elevates the crime from 'ordinary' torture to torture as a form of genocide, crimes against humanity, or war crime. In other words, single and isolated acts of torture are not punishable under the Rome Statute. Yet torture is also considered to be an international crime in accordance with the 1984 Convention Against Torture and Other Cruel, Inhuman or Degrading Treatment or Punishment. The Convention sets out various obligations respecting the crime of torture, including a duty to prosecute, using universal jurisdiction if necessary. A similar scheme was established in 2006 under the International Convention for the Protection of All Persons from Enforced Disappearance.

We might question why single acts of torture (and enforced disappearance) are treated as international crimes, yet murder and rape are not. Surely they are of comparable and perhaps superior gravity? The answer is actually quite straightforward. Torture is defined in the 1984 Convention as an act involving 'the instigation of or with the consent or acquiescence of a public official or other person acting in an official capacity'. In other words, the link with the state is decisive. Absent such a connection, torture perpetrated by one individual against another is an ordinary crime with no international dimension, on the same footing as murder and rape.

The more pragmatic approach has much merit. There is the advantage of focussing our attention on the state rather than on the individual. In addition to explaining why some crimes are already defined as international, this vision provides useful guidance in determining which new crimes to add to the list. Drug crimes probably do not belong in the list, because they are not as a rule committed by states or with their complicity. National justice systems are usually more than willing to prosecute such offences and fall short only because of failings in international cooperation mechanisms. Thus, drug crimes belong with the earlier generation of international crime, whose common denominator is international cooperation to facilitate national prosecution, rather than international prosecution. The same can be said of terrorism. The threat and the use of weapons of mass destruction, on the other hand, constitute a matter largely within the remit of states. Their justice systems cannot be expected to prosecute such crimes when they are committed by the government itself. Consequently, international prosecution is necessary.

Probably no single explanation accounts completely for inclusion in or exclusion from the list of international crimes. The same is true at the national level, which is why we require both the *malum in se* and the *malum prohibitum* paradigms in order to explain the content of criminal law. While the objective gravity of the crime initially seems important, on closer scrutiny this is not such a clear-cut proposition. A single murder is not an international crime, yet it seems objectively more serious than the act of recruiting an adolescent into the armed forces, something that is included in article 8 of the Rome Statute. Inevitably, however, there is great subjectivity in these determinations. Advocates of the rights of children consider recruitment and enlistment to rank high on the list of *mala in se*. Others might question this on the grounds that it does not threaten fundamental human values, such as the right to life. Not only does the debate continue, it also evolves, influenced by the priorities of states, the core issues of human rights, and the agendas of international civil society.

2

NULLUM CRIMEN SINE LEGE

> The power of precedent, when analyzed, is the power of the beaten track.
>
> Robert Jackson speaking to the *Barreau* in Paris,
> 2 April 1946, citing Benjamin Cardozo

Only the law can define a crime and a penalty: *nullum crimen* [*nulla peona*] *sine lege*. To respect the principle of legality, the scope of the crime and the applicable punishment must be set out in clear terms *before* its commission. This is affirmed in article 11(2) of the Universal Declaration of Human Rights, as well as in virtually all human rights treaties and national constitutions: 'No one shall be held guilty of any penal offence on account of any act or omission which did not constitute a penal offence, under national or international law, at the time when it was committed.' Often called the principle of legality, it has been described as a peremptory norm (*jus cogens*) of international human rights law.[1] Retroactivity is an issue that has obsessed international criminal justice since its earliest days. At the international criminal tribunals, it has been a source of unceasing controversy.

With the adoption of the Rome Statute and the development of an international criminal justice regime whose application promises to be universal, the issue of retroactive punishment ought to be largely laid to rest. The principle of *nullum crimen* is set out in article 23 of the Rome Statute, but this hardly seems necessary because the International Criminal Court can only exercise jurisdiction over crimes defined in its own texts on a prospective basis, that is, for crimes perpetrated after the Statute has entered into force. Indeed, in the initial cases before the Court, the issue has hardly arisen, in contrast with the experience at all of the earlier international criminal tribunals.

---

[1] *Unnamed defendant* (STL-11-01/I), Interlocutory Decision on the Applicable Law: Terrorism, Conspiracy, Homicide, Perpetration, Cumulative Charging, 16 February 2011, para. 45.

But arguments about retroactive prosecution persist at both the judicial and political levels. The development of international criminal law is accompanied by constant attempts to reassess the past. Although human longevity makes prosecution for many old offences increasingly unlikely, because the perpetrators continue to die off or become unfit to stand trial, many difficulties remain. In 2008 Spanish prosecutor Baltazar Garzón launched an investigation into the crime against humanity of enforced disappearance committed in the years immediately following the Civil War, raising questions as to whether international law applicable in the early 1940s recognized that crimes against humanity could be committed in peacetime. The same point has arisen recently with respect to trials concerning post-Second World War atrocities in the Baltic states, and the acts of the Khmer Rouge in Cambodia during the 1970s. An important decision of the Grand Chamber of the European Court of Human Rights, *Kononov* v *Latvia* of 17 May 2010, ruled favourably upon the legality of a trial held in the 1990s of a pro-Soviet partisan for the summary execution of Nazi sympathizers at the height of the Second World War.

When the first international prosecutions were being conceived at the Paris Peace Conference in 1919, the Commission on Responsibilities said that 'premeditation of a war of aggression...is conduct which the public conscience reproves and which history will condemn' but that it could not be considered 'an act directly contrary to positive law'. The Commission advised against trials based upon 'the acts which brought about the war', but said that in the future 'penal sanctions should be provided for such grave outrages against the elementary principles of international law'. When the Commission considered prosecution for breaches of the 'laws and principles of humanity', the American negotiators, Robert Lansing and James Brown Scott, objected. They argued that this was a moral standard, and that such breaches were not recognized in the laws applicable at the time. They insisted that 'an act could not be a crime in the legal sense of the word, unless it were made so by law, and that the commission of an act declared to be a crime by law could not be punished unless the law prescribed the penalty to be inflicted'.[2]

The issue returned at Nuremberg and Tokyo. Even before the trial began, lawyers for the Nazi defendants filed a motion challenging the indictment because the charge of crimes against peace, which had never before been codified, was 'repugnant to a principle of jurisprudence sacred to the civilized world, the partial violation of which by Hitler's Germany

---

[2] *Violations of the Laws and Customs of War, Reports of Majority and Dissenting Reports of America and Japanese Members of the Commission on Responsibilities, Conference of Paris, 1919,* Oxford: Clarendon Press, 1919; (1920) 14 *American Journal of International Law* 95, at pp. 118, 120, 145.

has been vehemently discountenanced outside and inside the Reich'. They noted that the maxim *nullum crimen sine lege* 'is precisely not a rule of expediency but it derives from the recognition of the fact that any defendant must needs [sic] consider himself unjustly treated if he is punished under an *ex post facto* law'.[3] The defence counsel were influenced by a legal opinion from the great German jurist Carl Schmitt which is cited in the previous chapter. They might have invoked a 1935 precedent from the Permanent Court of International Justice condemning Nazi decrees in Danzig that allowed courts to punish new crimes where they are 'deserving of penalty according to the fundamental conceptions of a penal law and sound popular feeling'. The Permanent Court said this was incompatible with the prohibition on retroactive punishment in the Constitution of the Free City, which was guaranteed by the League of Nations. The Nazi lawyer arguing before the Permanent Court contended that under the new legislation 'real justice will take the place of formal justice, and that henceforth the rule will be *nullum crimen sine poena* instead of *nullum crimen sine lege*'.[4]

The 1946 judgment of the International Military Tribunal spoke to the objections concerning the principle of legality. The Nazi defendants had a good argument that prosecution for crimes against peace violated the prohibition of retroactive criminal law. According to the Nuremberg judgment, 'it is to be observed that the maxim *nullum crimen sine lege* is not a limitation of sovereignty, but is in general a principle of justice'. The French version of the judgment is more qualified: '[*n*]*ullum crimen sine lege* ne limite pas la souveraineté des États; elle ne formule qu'une règle généralement suivie'. The judgment continues:

> To assert that it is unjust to punish those who in defiance of treaties and assurances have attacked neighbouring states without warning is obviously untrue, for in such circumstances the attacker must know that he is doing wrong, and so far from it being unjust to punish him, it would be unjust if his wrong were allowed to go unpunished ... [The Nazi leaders] must have known that they were acting in defiance of all international law when in complete deliberation they carried out their designs of invasion and aggression.[5]

In other words, the Tribunal admitted that there was a retroactive dimension to prosecution for crimes against peace, but said leaving such wrongs unpunished would be unjust. The *nullum crimen* rule was thus a relative one, subject to exception in light of circumstances. With respect to war crimes,

---

[3] 'Motion adopted by all defense counsel, 19 November 1945' (1948) 1 IMT 168–170.

[4] *Consistency of Certain Danzig Legislative Decrees with the Constitution of the Free City*, Series A/B No. 65 (1935), p. 52.

[5] (1948) 22 IMT 203, p. 462.

the Tribunal was able to point to some precedent supporting international prohibition of certain behaviour, including the Hague Convention of 1907.

CRIMES AGAINST HUMANITY AT NUREMBERG

The Nuremberg Tribunal did not directly address the retroactivity issue with respect to crimes against humanity. Possibly the matter was not considered in the final judgment because the Nazi defendants did not raise it explicitly in their pre-trial motion, which was confined to crimes against peace in keeping with the opinion by Carl Schmitt. At Tokyo, crimes against humanity barely figured in the proceedings because as a general rule the Japanese did not abuse their own citizens (at least, this was not alleged in the proceedings), unlike the Germans.

Perhaps, had the judges at Nuremberg felt compelled to speak to the point, they would have favoured the same logic with respect to crimes against humanity as they did for the other innovation, crimes against peace. Thus, the Nazis 'must have known that they were acting in defiance of all international law' when they perpetrated the atrocities and persecutions encompassed in the notion of crimes against humanity. But the analogy has its limits. International law had already clearly tackled the issue of aggressive war in the 1928 Kellogg-Briand Pact, even if it had not specifically indicated that individuals could be held criminally responsible. There could be no argument that waging aggressive war was not a matter of international concern any more than this could be said with respect to violations of the laws or customs of war. Yet there was nothing similar with respect to crimes against humanity, aside from the rather vague pronouncements concerning human rights in declarations such as the Atlantic Charter and the four freedoms speech of Franklin Roosevelt.

During preparations for the postwar trials, a criminal law concept that was usually labelled 'atrocities, persecutions and deportations' began to emerge. It was clearly understood that a gap needed to be filled. The existing law of war crimes was probably adequate to address outrages committed against civilians within occupied territories, but it said nothing with respect to a state's own citizens. At meetings of the United Nations War Crimes Commission in 1944, British and American negotiators indicated unease at the idea that war crimes prosecutions might innovate and hold Germans accountable for crimes committed against minority groups within their own borders. But a consensus developed that Nazi atrocities directed against Jews and others inside Germany itself could be subject to prosecution, although with the proviso that there must be a link to the aggressive war. Absent such a nexus with war, the Allied lawmakers said there could be no criminal liability for acts directed by a state against its own nationals.

In the final days of the London conference in late July 1945, the chief American negotiator Robert Jackson proposed that the category of 'atrocities, persecutions and deportations' be renamed 'crimes against humanity'. He told the conference that the idea originated with a prominent English legal academic. We now know this to have been Hersch Lauterpacht, who held the chair in public international law at the University of Cambridge. At about the same time, Raphael Lemkin was proposing a cognate term, 'genocide'. It is a remarkable coincidence that Lemkin had enrolled at the University of Lvov in 1919 just as Lauterpacht, who was three years his senior, was leaving the same university to pursue advanced studies in law in Vienna. There is no evidence that either of these personalities, both of whom made unique and lasting contributions to international criminal law, met in Lvov. Perhaps their paths crossed in the 1940s and 1950s, when Lemkin was the indefatigable campaigner for ratification of the Genocide Convention and Lauterpacht the British judge at the International Court of Justice.

Unlike Lemkin, who devised the term 'genocide', Lauterpacht never claimed to have invented the expression 'crimes against humanity'. Where did this term come from? Most scholarly writing points to the 24 May 1915 declaration of the British, French, and Russian governments about the Armenian atrocities. The version of that document in the United States archives, which originated in the French foreign ministry, spoke of 'these new crimes of Turkey against humanity and civilization'. The text in the Foreign Office, however, does not use the term. Reference is also made to the Martens clause in the Hague conventions, which speaks of 'the laws of humanity, and the dictates of the public conscience'.

VOLTAIRE COINED THE TERM

It seems that the notion of crimes against humanity was in wide circulation from at least the middle of the eighteenth century. The author of the expression may have been Voltaire. It was often used in France (sometimes as *crimes de lèse humanité*). Speaking of acts that were universally condemned, such as theft and murder, Voltaire said 'that which is approved in England and condemned in Italy, ought to be punished in Italy, as if it were one of the crimes against humanity'.[6] The great Italian philosopher

---

[6] Voltaire, *A Philosophical Dictionary: From the French of M. De Voltaire*, 1793, repr., London: W. Dugale, 1843, p. 293.

of criminal justice, Cesare Beccaria, a contemporary of Voltaire, suggested that excessive penalties could be an outrage against humanity, a crime against humanity or *soverchio rigore contro di un colpevole muove a sdegno l'umanità*.[7] The term was also being widely used in English at about the same time. For example, John Bowles wrote, with respect to atrocities committed in Ireland, that the French would attack England 'to punish us for outrages which have been too long unpunished, to carry vengeance into the midst of our country, and to punish Albion (Great Britain) for its long Catalogue of crimes against humanity'.[8] Henry Mann described the expulsion of the *Acadiens* from Nova Scotia as a 'crime against humanity; the conversion of an honest, industrious and thrifty peasantry into a host of penniless vagrants was as wrong and cruel as it was unnecessary'.[9] Referring to Napoleon Bonaparte, James Stephen addressed 'the numberless positive crimes against humanity, justice, and honour, by which Napoleon is disgraced, and it seems astonishing and is truly opprobrious to the moral taste of the age that he should still find any admirers'.[10]

Later in the nineteenth century, 'crimes against humanity' was a label regularly attached to slavery and the slave trade. For Condorcet, 'l'esclavage est regardé universellement dans les treize états comme un crime de lèse humanité, comme une tache à la gloire des amis de la liberté'. A pioneering American jurist, Henry Wheaton, wrote of public opinion 'stigmatizing the traffic as a crime against humanity'.[11] In 1846 the dismemberment of Poland by various European powers was condemned as 'crimes against humanity, and worthy of eternal reprobation'.[12] At the 1849 Peace Congress, presided over by Victor Hugo, a British statesman blamed those who provided loans for perpetrators of war atrocities, saying 'it is you who give strength to the arm which murders innocent women and helpless old age; it is you who supply the torch which reduces to ashes peaceful and inoffensive villages, and on your souls will rest the burden of these crimes against humanity'.[13]

---

[7] Cesare Beccaria, *Dei delitti e delle pene: coi commentari di varii insigni scrittori*, 1764, p. 240.

[8] John Bowles, *The Political and Moral state of Society, at the Close of the Eighteenth Century*, London: Woodfall, 1800.

[9] Henry Mann, *The Land We Live In or The Story of Our Country*, New York: The Christian Herald, 1806.

[10] James Stephen, *The Dangers of the Country*, Philadelphia: Samuel F. Bradford, 1807.

[11] Henry Wheaton, *History of the Law of Nations in Europe and America: From the Earliest Times to the Treaty of Washington, 1842*, New York: Gould, Banks & Co., 1845.

[12] Philip McGrath, 'The Petition of a Public Meeting holden at the Crown and Anchor Tavern Strand, the 25th day of March, 1846', in *Appendix to the Reports of the Select Committee of the House of Commons on Public Petitions*, 1846, p. 210.

[13] Edward Miall, *Report of the Proceedings of the Second General Peace Congress*, London: Charles Gilpin, 1849, p. 79.

By the early twentieth century, the term 'crimes against humanity' was being widely employed, often to describe atrocities associated with European colonialism in Africa and elsewhere. The Irish patriot Roger Casement invoked crimes against humanity to describe persecution of indigenous peoples in the Amazon basin. In 1903 Baron Descamps, who was later to preside over efforts at establishing an international criminal court within the League of Nations, claimed that 'the slave-trade has another character; it is the very denial of every law, of all social order. Man-hunting constitutes a crime of high treason against humanity.'[14] The British Parliamentary debates of 1907 report that 'the position of the native in the Congo today was a disgrace to civilization. The atrocities which had been committed and the annexation of the Congo to Belgium would only be another crime added to a crime against humanity as Belgium did in the Congo.'[15]

Thus, by 1915, when the three European powers invoked 'these new crimes of Turkey against humanity' with respect to atrocities against the Armenians, the term was already very familiar and in common usage. It did not yet have an agreed definition set out in a legal text. But then, at least in common law countries where crimes have been defined by case law, neither did murder and rape. What was new at Nuremberg was a genuine and determined attempt to hold individuals criminally accountable for such behaviour, even if it had not previously been codified in a formal sense. The idea that certain atrocities went beyond the sovereign authority of states, and attracted international condemnation, had been well anchored for many years. In other words, when Hersch Lauterpacht proposed the term 'crimes against humanity' to Robert Jackson in the English summer of 1945, it was not being cut from whole cloth.

STEADY STATE OR BIG BANG?

Explaining the universe, astronomers have traditionally considered two basic models, the 'steady state' and the 'big bang'. Under the steady state theory, the universe has always existed. We simply learn more about it as better and better telescopes enable us to peer deeper into its dark expanses. On the other hand, the big bang theory posits a universe that was created, and that continues to expand or, at some point, contract. This may

---

[14] Edouard Eugène François Descamps, *New Africa: An Essay on Government Civilization in New Countries, and on the Foundation, Organization and Administration of the Congo Free state*, S. Low, Marston and Company, 1903, p. 132.

[15] *The Parliamentary Debates (Authorized Edition)*, vol. 179, London: HM Stationery Office, 1907, p. 1225.

be a useful metaphor in understanding the temporal issues associated with international crimes. The discussion is of course not unrelated to the law vs morality debate, developed by Gustav Radbruch and, subsequently, in the celebrated Hart–Fuller exchanges in the *Harvard Law Review*. But those discussions were about obedience to immoral law rather than the legitimacy of retroactive criminal prosecution.

Steady state proponents adopt an approach that is inspired in some sense by natural law, although they often prefer to call it 'customary international law'. Their philosophy is reflected in a paragraph of the preamble to the 1948 Genocide Convention, where it is recognized that 'at all periods of history genocide has inflicted great losses on humanity'. The word genocide itself did not exist until 1944. But, as Paul Boghossian has noted, the term 'smallpox' was only devised in the 1820s, yet the disease had killed people long before that.[16] 'Murdering civilians was always a crime under customary international law' is how this idea is often expressed. In the seventeenth century, Grotius wrote about 'gross violations of the law of nature and of nations, done to other states and subjects'.[17]

Both sides in this debate surfaced in the aftermath of Nuremberg. General Assembly Resolution 95(I) of December 1946 confirmed the 'Nuremberg principles' as evidence that the London Charter and the judgment of the International Military Tribunal were declaratory of pre-existing international law.[18] Others were more willing to concede the point that some of the offences punishable by the International Military Tribunal amounted to retroactive application of law, but considered this was acceptable because the Nazi crimes could not go unpunished. This was the view taken in the Tribunal's judgment, cited earlier in this chapter. In support of the position, Hans Kelsen wrote:

Since the internationally illegal acts for which the London Agreement established individual criminal responsibility were certainly also morally most objectionable, and the persons who committed these acts were certainly aware of their immoral character, the retroactivity of the law applied to them can hardly be considered as absolutely incompatible with justice. Justice required the punishment of these men, in spite of the fact that under positive law they were not punishable at the time they performed the acts made punishable with retroactive force. In case two postulates of justice are in conflict with each other, the higher one prevails; and to punish those who were morally responsible for the international crime of the Second World War may certainly be considered as more important than to

---

[16] Paul Boghossian, 'The Concept of Genocide' (2010) 12 *Journal of Genocide Research* 69.
[17] Hugo Grotius, *On War and Peace*, II.20.XI, 247.   [18] GA Res. 95(I).

comply with the rather relative rule against *ex post facto* laws, open to so many exceptions.[19]

Along similar lines, the Dutch judge at the International Military Tribunal for the Far East ('Tokyo Tribunal'), B.V.A. Röling, said of the principle *nullum crimen sine lege* that

this maxim is not a principle of justice but a rule of policy, valid only if expressly adopted, so as to protect citizens against arbitrariness of course (Nullum crimen, nulla poena sine lege), as well as against arbitrariness of legislations (Nullum crimen, nulla poena sine praevia lege). Nor does this rule consider whether a certain act was criminally wrong at the moment it was committed, but only the question as to whether that act was or was not forbidden under penalty. As such, the prohibition of *ex post facto* law is an expression of political wisdom, not necessarily applicable in present international relations. This maxim of liberty may, if circumstances necessitate it, be disregarded even by powers victorious in a war fought for freedom. It is, however, neither the task nor within the power of the Tribunal to Judge the wisdom of a certain policy.[20]

Similarly, a United States Military Tribunal, in the trial of Nazi judges and prosecutors, said:

As a principle of justice and fair play, the rule in question will be given full effect. As applied in the field of international law that principle requires proof before conviction that the accused knew or should have known that in matters of international concern he was guilty of participation in a nationally organized system of injustice and persecution shocking to the moral sense of mankind, and that he knew or should have known that he would be subject to punishment if caught. Whether it be considered codification or substantive legislation, no person who knowingly committed the acts made punishable by [Control Council] Law 10 can assert that he did not know that he would be brought to account for his acts.[21]

These remarks were echoed years later, by the District Court of Jerusalem, in *Eichmann*:

It is indeed difficult to find a more convincing instance of just retroactive legislation than the legislation providing for the punishment of war criminals and criminals against humanity and against the Jewish People, and all the reasons justifying the Nuremberg judgments justify *eo ipse* the retroactive legislation of the Israel legislator. We have already referred to the decisive ground of the

---

[19] Hans Kelsen,'Will the Judgment in the Nuremberg Trial Constitute a Precedent in International Law?' (1947) 1 *International Law Quarterly* 153, at p. 165. For an endorsement of Kelsen's approach, see the reasons of Justice Peter Cory in *R* v *Finta* [1994] 1 SCR 701, at p. 874.

[20] Neil Boister and Robert Cryer (eds), *Documents on the Tokyo International Military Tribunal, Charter, Indictment and* Judgments, Oxford: Oxford University Press, 2008, at p. 700.

[21] *United States of America* v *Alstötter* et al. ('The Justice Case') (1951) 3 TWC 954 (United States Military Tribunal), at pp. 977–8.

existence of a 'criminal intent' (mens rea), and this ground recurs in all the Nuremberg judgments. The Accused in this case is charged with the implementation of the plan for the 'Final Solution of the Jewish Question'. Can anyone in his right mind doubt the absolute criminality of such acts?[22]

The International Military Tribunal is not without its critics, of course. At the International Military Tribunal for the Far East, Judge Pal of India objected strenuously on the retroactivity issue and eventually voted to acquit, although his concerns were with crimes against peace, not crimes against humanity.[23] Along similar lines, Kenneth S. Gallant has written recently that the famous statement of the Nuremberg Tribunal about *nullum crimen* being a principle of justice 'has a cynical ring to it. It implies that judges can and should ignore principles of justice in service of the sovereign powers that created their court.'[24]

Consideration of the progressive definition of crimes against humanity provides some insight into this process. The negotiators at the London Conference in June and July 1945, where the legal framework of the Nuremberg trial was mapped out, quite intentionally agreed to a narrow definition of crimes against humanity. Accordingly, only atrocities committed in association with the war would be punishable. Their approach was subsequently endorsed by the judges. The records of the Conference show that this was intended to insulate those who created the law from being prosecuted for crimes similar to those for which they planned to charge the Nazis (see the discussion of the drafting of the Charter of the Nuremberg Tribunal in Chapter 4, 'The Genocide Mystique'). Since Nuremberg, some have argued that this was a 'jurisdictional' limitation rather than a substantive one. The negotiators and the judges, it is said, were not defining crimes against humanity as such, given that these already existed under customary international law. Rather, the theory continues, they were limiting the scope of the concept solely for the purpose of circumscribing the jurisdiction of the International Military Tribunal. In other words, according to this view, a broader notion of crimes against humanity that encompassed atrocities committed in peacetime already existed in international law, although it had not been defined by treaty or in some other formal text. Perhaps, employing the steady state theory and principles of natural law, it had already existed.

Some problems with this approach present themselves, however. There was, in fact, no practice by states upon which to base a customary

---

[22] *AG Israel* v *Eichmann* (1968) 36 ILR 5 (District Court, Jerusalem), para. 27.
[23] Neil Boister and Robert Cryer (eds), *Documents on the Tokyo International Military Tribunal*, Oxford: Oxford University Press, 2008, at pp. 811–930.
[24] Kenneth S. Gallant, *The Principle of Legality in International and Comparative Criminal Law*, Cambridge: Cambridge University Press, 2009, at p. 1.

international law analysis. Unlike treaties, whose content and chronology is simple enough to establish, customary international law requires evidence of behaviour by states, as well as the recognition that these states understood the purported rules governing their behaviour to be mandatory. Whether or not this was the case can be determined based upon objective evidence, in contrast with a standard by which such behaviour must 'shock the conscience of humanity'. There are many classic examples of customary legal norms being identified with respect to the delimitation of fishing zones, the immunities of diplomats, and universal jurisdiction over crimes such as piracy. But where the prior existence of atrocity crimes is concerned, the claim rarely relies upon evidence of practice. In reality, it is little different from the argument of the Nuremberg judges that 'in such circumstances the attacker must know that he is doing wrong, and so far from it being unjust to punish him, it would be unjust if his wrong were allowed to go unpunished'. The difference is that Nuremberg's retroactivity problem was not answered by pointing to customary international law. Rather, the judges appeared to acknowledge that there were exceptions to the *nullum crimen* norm.

AN ACT OF CREATION

As explained above, there is plenty of evidence that the term 'crimes against humanity' was in common use long before 1945, although rarely by states. But there had been no prosecutions to indicate what the term actually meant in a strict criminal law sense. Moreover, on various occasions the negotiators at Nuremberg indicated that they were taking care to define crimes against humanity because it was a standard by which they too would be judged. They had already excluded themselves from the jurisdiction of the International Military Tribunal by specifying in the Charter that it was limited to 'the major war criminals of the European axis'. So there was no need to constrain the definition of crimes against humanity, because the victors could not be prosecuted by the Tribunal in any case. Yet the drafters of the Nuremberg Charter understood that they were completing an exercise in international lawmaking, whose results would be of general application, and not just defining the jurisdiction of a judicial institution. Robert Jackson wrote that this was a specific point of disagreement with Soviet negotiators, but one on which they eventually conceded.

Accordingly, the architects of the Nuremberg trial understood this as an act of creation—the big bang—rather than one of identifying a pre-existing universe—the steady state. Commenting on the Charter of the

Nuremberg Tribunal a few days after its adoption, Hersch Lauterpacht wrote to a legal officer in the Foreign Office that there would be no difficulty responding to the argument that punishing the crime of aggression was not retroactive in nature. He contrasted this with crimes against humanity, which he described as 'clearly an innovation'. Lauterpacht thought it a wise course for the four Powers who had created the International Military Tribunal 'frankly [to] admit that—notwithstanding the doctrine and the various historical instances of humanitarian intervention—all this is an innovation which the outraged conscience of the world and an enlightened conception of the true purposes of the law of nations impel them to make immediately operative'.[25] This is what they seem to have done.

In December 1945 the definition of 'crimes against humanity' adopted at the London Conference was employed in Control Council Law No. 10, but with some adjustments. In the latter text there is no nexus or link with armed conflict, a fact that is often invoked by supporters of the steady state or customary international law theory. In July 2010 the Extraordinary Chambers of the Courts of Cambodia cited Control Council Law No. 10 to bolster a claim that crimes against humanity perpetrated in the 1970s did not then require a link with armed conflict.[26] But Control Council Law No. 10 consisted of legislation enacted by the occupying powers operating, in effect, as the government of Germany. The premise of its drafters—who were the same as those who adopted the Nuremberg Charter—was that the lawmaking exercise was quite different from the one for the International Military Tribunal. Certainly it makes no sense that the same countries that resolutely insisted on a link between crimes against humanity and armed conflict in August 1945, when they adopted the Nuremberg Charter, and in October 1945, when they agreed to a minor amendment to the definition of crimes against humanity in order to leave no doubt about the matter, would have completely reversed their position in December 1945 in the Control Council Law No. 10. The definition in December is different because the four powers recognized that they were enacting national and not international law. It therefore furnishes an unconvincing precedent to support the steady state argument.

Today, nobody would contend that the link between crimes against humanity and armed conflict established at Nuremberg continues to apply. Proponents of the steady state theory consider that this is because it never existed, or at least that it did not exist prior to 1945. It simply took several

---

[25] Hersch Lauterpacht to Patrick Dean, 30 August 1945, FO 371/51034, cited in Elihu Lauterpacht, *The Life of Hersch Lauterpacht*, Cambridge: Cambridge University Press, 2010, at pp. 273–4.

[26] *Duch* (No. 001/18-07-2007/ECCC/TC), Judgment, 26 July 2010, para. 291.

decades for the reality of the international universe to become apparent. The big bang theory is different, in that it views international criminal law as a dynamic process, whereby new crimes are defined and old ones amended as a consequence of legal development, influenced by evolving values. Under the big bang theory, the nexus between armed conflict and crimes against humanity that existed at Nuremberg was part of the original understanding, and was only removed at some point subsequent to 1945.

One of the landmarks in this debate is the *Tadić Jurisdictional Decision* of the International Criminal Tribunal for the former Yugoslavia, rendered on 2 October 1995. There, the Appeals Chamber said, not without some ambiguity, that

the nexus between crimes against humanity and either crimes against peace or war crimes, required by the Nuremberg Charter, was peculiar to the jurisdiction of the Nuremberg Tribunal. Although the nexus requirement in the Nuremberg Charter was carried over to the 1948 [sic] General Assembly resolution affirming the Nuremberg principles, there is no logical or legal basis for this requirement and it has been abandoned in subsequent state practice with respect to crimes against humanity. Most notably, the nexus requirement was eliminated from the definition of crimes against humanity contained in Article II(1)(c) of Control Council Law No. 10 of 20 December 1945…[27]

The word 'peculiar' suggests the jurisdictional argument of the steady state theorists. But the judges also spoke of the 'obsolescence' of the armed conflict requirement, and said: 'It is by now a settled rule of customary international law that crimes against humanity do not require a connection to international armed conflict.' This implies that the law changed after 1945, a manifestation of the big bang theory. In a recent journal article, the late Antonio Cassese, who presided over the Appeals Chamber in *Tadić*, criticized a 2006 judgment of the European Court of Human Rights for its failure to note that in 1949 international law only contemplated crimes against humanity when committed in connection with war crimes or crimes against peace. He wrote that 'the indispensable link between those crimes and war had not yet been severed. It is only later, in the late 1960s, that a general rule gradually began to evolve, prohibiting crimes against humanity even when committed in time of peace.'[28]

---

[27] *Tadić* (IT-94-1-AR72), Decision on the Defence Motion for Interlocutory Appeal on Jurisdiction, 2 October 1995, para. 140.

[28] Antonio Cassese, 'Balancing the Prosecution of Crimes against Humanity and Non-Retroactivity of Criminal Law, The Kolk and Kislyiy v Estonia Case before the ECHR' (2006) 4 *Journal of International Criminal Justice* 410, at p. 413.

Professor Cassese's comment is certainly helpful in discerning the meaning of the discussion on this point in the *Tadić Jurisdictional Decision*. The reference to the late 1960s almost certainly points to the Convention on the Non-Applicability of Statutory Limitations to War Crimes and Crimes Against Humanity, adopted by the United Nations General Assembly in 1968. Article 1(b) of that treaty speaks of '[c]rimes against humanity whether committed in time of war or in time of peace as they are defined in the Charter of the International Military Tribunal, Nürnberg'. The Convention on the Non-Applicability of Statutory Limitations entered into force in 1970, but even today it only has a few more than fifty States Parties, which is not a particularly impressive score.

There is also evidence for this expanding universe in the work of the International Law Commission on the Code of Crimes Against the Peace and Security of Mankind. The Commission had been vexed by the link between crimes against humanity and armed conflict from the beginning of its activities, in 1949. At the start of its 1954 session, the members voted to remove the nexus with armed conflict. But in the days that followed, they had second thoughts. It seemed that without such a connection, it might be difficult to distinguish crimes against humanity, or at least a certain number of them, from ordinary crimes such as murder. They set to work devising another contextual element that might replace the nexus with armed conflict, and concluded their 1954 session by adding a link to state policy: 'Inhuman acts by the authorities of a state or by private individuals acting under the instigation or toleration of the authorities...'[29] The work of the International Law Commission on the Code is interesting, but the meanderings in the drafts over the years makes it a source for practically any proposition, and therefore of limited authority.

The 2006 European Court of Human Rights judgment in *Kolk and Kislyiy* v *Estonia* provides modest support for the international recognition of crimes against humanity committed in peacetime as early as 1949. The point does not seem to have been debated before the Court, however, and too much should not be read into this decision. It was convincingly criticized by Professor Cassese, as discussed above. Subsequently, in *Korbely* v *Hungary*, the Grand Chamber of the Court held that the nexus with armed conflict 'may no longer have been relevant by 1956'.[30] This time, the judgment proposed some authority in support, but the sources cited do not adequately reflect the complexity of the debate. It is striking that in its May 2010 ruling, in *Kononov* v *Latvia*, the Grand Chamber cited the Nuremberg

---

[29] Report of the International Law Commission covering the work of its sixth session, 3 June–28 July 1954, UN Doc. A/2693.

[30] *Korbely* v *Hungary*, no 9174/02 [GC], Judgment, 19 September 2008, para. 82.

Principles adopted by the International Law Commission in 1950 as authority for the content of customary international law.[31] Although the Grand Chamber reproduced virtually the entire text of the Principles, it omitted Principle VI(c) which states that crimes against humanity must be 'carried on in execution of or in connection with any crime against peace or any war crime'.

The European Court's pronouncement in *Korbely* was eventually cited by the Extraordinary Chambers of the Courts of Cambodia, in its first trial judgment as authority for the view that there was no nexus by the mid-1970s. Indeed, the Cambodia tribunal implied that there never was a nexus.[32] But *Duch* was the result of a guilty plea, without the important legal issue concerning the temporal issues associated with the definition of crimes against humanity being properly contested. Thus, a seemingly important judgment relies upon a flimsy authority that is itself based upon a misinterpretation. At first glance, the argument seems to have strong support, but it is like the giant with feet of clay.

Decades from now, this will no longer be of any practical interest. There can be no doubt that crimes against humanity perpetrated today do not require any connection with armed conflict. But other manifestations of the same type of debate may continue, to the extent that the flexible concept of crimes against humanity may expand to cover new types of atrocities. This may be the result of imaginative use of the residual category of crimes against humanity, 'other inhumane acts', or an expansive approach to the crime against humanity of persecution. For example, there would be little question that a prohibition of marriage among ethnic or religious minorities would satisfy the current definition. Article 7(1) of the Rome Statute of the International Criminal Court speaks of persecution 'on political, racial, national, ethnic, cultural, religious, gender as defined in paragraph 3, or other grounds that are universally recognized as impermissible under international law'. At present, it is probably unreasonable to consider a prohibition on same-sex marriage to constitute the crime against humanity of persecution. But this will change at some point in the future. The evolution may be marked not by an amendment to the text but by judicial decision, as judges conclude that the defendant 'knew or should have known' that the conduct was forbidden.

---

[31] *Kononov* v *Latvia*, no 36376/04 [GC], Judgment, 17 May 2010, paras 122, 207.
[32] *Kaing Guek Eav alias Duch* (001/18-07-2007), Judgment, 26 July 2010, para. 292.

GENOCIDE'S BEGINNINGS AS AN INTERNATIONAL CRIME

Outside the criminal courtroom, retroactivity issues present themselves in a more politicized context. Acts perpetrated deep in the past, when criminal prosecution is not an option because there are no living suspects, are denounced as international crimes. Sometimes the purpose is merely hortatory, although a subtext involving claims of compensation may lurk in the background. There seems to be a window of human history dating back a few hundred years, but not longer, when such claims are entertained. Nobody wastes much energy trying to argue that charges of crimes against humanity, war crimes, or genocide be sustained against the Romans for the rape of the Sabine women, or the Athenians for the massacre at Milos, or the religious leaders responsible for the Spanish inquisition.

On the other hand, claims based upon colonialism, racial discrimination, and the slave trade in recent centuries retain some salience. The Declaration adopted at the 2001 Durban Conference on Racism and Xenophobia states that 'slavery and the slave trade are a crime against humanity and should always have been so, especially the transatlantic slave trade...'. Of course, as has been explained above, there is nothing innovative about describing slavery and the slave trade as crimes against humanity, a label used in this context as early as the eighteenth century and perhaps even before. Incidentally, the words 'should always have been so' point to the evolving universe of the big bang rather than the static steady state theory by which such acts were always prohibited. Nobody was ever prosecuted for slavery and the slave trade as crimes against humanity prior to the contemporary period, however, nor is anyone alive to stand trial today for the atrocities of the nineteenth century and earlier. But there may be other consequences. These are unlikely to be financial, despite the hopes of some activists, but they may well bear political significance.

One of the best examples of such difficulties involves the crime of genocide. Unlike crimes against humanity, a notion that existed prior to the Second World War in the public conscience even in the absence of a legal definition and efforts at prosecution, the same cannot be said for genocide. The word itself was unknown until 1944. A big bang! Can we say that genocide was committed, for example, in 1915 with regard to the Turkish persecutions of the Armenian population? A recent study by Geoffrey Robertson, and in particular the documents that he obtained from the Foreign and Commonwealth Office pursuant to a freedom of information request, reveal British diplomats invoking the supposed non-retroactive application of the 1948 Genocide Convention as a rationale for failing to take a position on the description of the events. A draft answer prepared by bureaucrats in the Foreign Office said that 'additionally, the government's legal advisors have said that the 1948 UN Convention on genocide, which is in any event not retrospective in application, was drafted in response to the holocaust and whilst the term can be applied to tragedies that occurred subsequent to the holocaust, such as Rwanda, it cannot be applied retrospectively'.[33] The issue returned on 7 June 2006, when government spokesman Geoff Hoon replied to a parliamentary inquiry:

The fact is that the legal offence of genocide had not been named or defined at the time that the actual atrocities were committed. The UN Convention on Genocide came into force in 1948 so it was not possible at the time of the events that we are considering legally to label the massacres as genocide within the terms of the convention. I recognize that it is perfectly possible intellectually to try to apply the definitions of genocide from the convention to appalling tragedies that occurred in this case some 30 years before.[34]

The British government returned to the point in 2007, in a memorandum that said 'it is not common practice in law to apply judgments retrospectively'.[35] But these are no more than the mealy-mouthed efforts of bureaucrats and politicians to avoid tension with Turkish diplomats.

Although as a general rule international treaties do not operate retroactively (or retrospectively), there are exceptions. Indeed, most of the treaties dealing with international criminal prosecution have been given a retroactive effect. Examples include the war crimes provisions of the Treaty of Versailles, the Charter of the International Military Tribunal, and the instruments establishing the Special Court for Sierra Leone and the Special Tribunal for Lebanon.

The International Court of Justice has made a couple of tantalizing comments to the effect that there is no express temporal limitation in the Genocide Convention to prevent it from having a retroactive effect.[36] It is surely going much too far to suggest that the Court has unequivocally endorsed the position that the Convention applies to events prior to its

---

[33] 'Parliamentary Question Background Document Relating to a Written Question from Lord Buffen Tabled on 23 January 2001—Draft response for Baroness Scotland', cited in Geoffrey Robertson, *Was There an Armenian Genocide?*, 9 October 2009, para. 65.

[34] Hansard, 7 June 2006, Col. 136WH.

[35] Memorandum from the Russia, South Caucasus and Central Asia Directorate, FCO to Mr Murphy, titled 'HMG's position on the Armenian genocide claims', 2 July 2007, cited in Geoffrey Robertson, *Was There an Armenian Genocide?*, 9 October 2009, para. 79.

[36] *Application of the Convention on the Prevention and Punishment of the Crime of Genocide (Croatia v Serbia)*, Preliminary Objections, 18 November 2008, para. 123; *Application of the Convention on the Prevention and Punishment of the Crime of Genocide (Bosnia and Herzegovina v Serbia and Montenegro)*, Preliminary Objections [1996] ICJ Reports 617, para. 34.

adoption or entry into force. If it is accurate to ascribe a retroactive effect to the Convention, however, how far back in history can this go? Given that the Convention establishes jurisdiction of the International Court of Justice to adjudicate disputes between states arising from the Convention, including charges that genocide has been committed, could Turkey be sued on this basis with respect to the atrocities of 1915?

In its advisory opinion on reservations to the Genocide Convention, issued in 1951, the International Court of Justice wrote:

The origins of the Convention show that it was the intention of the United Nations to condemn and punish genocide as 'a crime under international law' involving a denial of the right of existence of entire human groups, a denial which shocks the conscience of mankind and results in great losses to humanity, and which is contrary to moral law and to the spirit and aims of the United Nations. The first consequence arising from this conception is that the principles underlying the Convention are principles which are recognized by civilized nations as binding on states, even without any conventional obligation.[37]

Obviously, if only a few months after the entry into force of the Convention the International Court of Justice considered that 'the principles underlying the Convention' were binding on states regardless of whether or not they had ratified the Convention, there is an evident implication that these principles applied well into the past, that is, before the entry into force and even before the adoption of the Convention. Reference is also made to the preamble of the Convention, which states that at 'all periods of history genocide has inflicted great losses on humanity'. These words are meant to apply to events before the Convention was adopted. There is also some state practice to confirm this perspective on the crime of genocide from a historic perspective. In its submissions to the International Court of Justice in 1951, the United States said:

The practice of genocide has occurred throughout human history. The Roman persecution of the Christians, the Turkish massacres of Armenians, the extermination of millions of Jews and Poles by the Nazis arc outstanding examples of the crime of genocide. This was the background when the General Assembly of the United Nations considered the problem of genocide.[38]

Nevertheless, paragraph 2 of the Convention's preamble refers to 'genocide' rather than to 'the crime of genocide'. Perhaps this was entirely inadvertent. Yet although 'genocide' may have inflicted great losses on

---

[37] *Reservations to the Convention on the Prevention and Punishment of the Crime of Genocide (Advisory Opinion)* [1951] ICJ Reports 16, p. 23.

[38] *Reservations to the Convention on the Prevention of Genocide (Advisory Opinion)* [1951] Pleadings, Oral Arguments, Documents 23, 'Written Statement of the Government of the United States of America', at p. 25.

humanity at 'all periods of human history', it does not necessarily follow that the *crime* of genocide was punishable under international law at all times.

INCORPORATION IN NATIONAL LAW

A large number of states have incorporated the crime of genocide within their own national legislation. They often give their legislation retroactive effect. It does not seem to be state practice to limit this retroactive effect to events subsequent to entry into force of the Convention. For example, Canada's Crimes Against Humanity and War Crimes Act, adopted in 2000, gives national courts jurisdiction over genocide committed in the past, without any temporal limitation. Although prosecutions for genocide by national jurisdictions are rare, even with respect to contemporary events, there is some evidence of proceedings for the crime of genocide directed at acts perpetrated prior to entry into force of the Convention.

There is no doubt that the term 'genocide' was employed in official and international legal contexts prior to the adoption of the Convention. Seven months after the November 1944 publication of Raphael Lemkin's book *Axis Rule in Occupied Europe*, where the term was introduced, 'genocide' was being used by the United States at the London Conference. Justice Robert Jackson, the head of the American delegation, made reference to 'Genocide or destruction of racial minorities and subjugated populations by such means and methods as (1) underfeeding; (2) sterilization and castration; (3) depriving them of clothing, shelter, fuel, sanitation, medical care; (4) deporting them for forced labour; (5) working them in inhumane conditions'.[39] The indictment of the International Military Tribunal, issued in October 1945, charged Nazi defendants with 'deliberate and systematic genocide, viz., the extermination of racial and national groups, against the civilian populations of certain occupied territories in order to destroy particular races and classes of people, and national, racial or religious groups, particularly Jews, Poles, and Gypsies'. The term was also used on several occasions by prosecutors during the trial.

On 11 December 1946 the United Nations General Assembly adopted Resolution 96(I) on the subject of genocide:

Genocide is a denial of the right of existence of entire human groups, as homicide is the denial of the right to live of individual human beings; such denial of the right of existence shocks the conscience of mankind, results in great losses to

---

[39] 'Planning Memorandum Distributed to Delegations at Beginning of London Conference, June 1945', in *Report of Robert H. Jackson, United States Representative to the International Conference on Military Trials*, Washington, DC: US Government Printing Office, 1949, pp. 64–68, at p. 68.

humanity in the form of cultural and other contributions represented by these human groups, and is contrary to moral law and to the spirit and aims of the United Nations.

Many instances of such crimes of genocide have occurred when racial, religious, political and other groups have been destroyed, entirely or in part.

The punishment of the crime of genocide is a matter of international concern.

The General Assembly, therefore

Affirms that genocide is a crime under international law which the civilized world condemns, and for the commission of which principals and accomplices—whether private individuals, public officials or statesmen, and whether the crime is committed on religious, racial, political or any other grounds—are punishable;

Invites the Member states to enact the necessary legislation for the prevention and punishment of the crime;

Recommends that international co-operation be organized between states with a view to facilitating the speedy prevention and punishment of the crime of genocide, and, to this end,

Requests the Economic and Social Council to undertake the necessary studies, with a view to drawing up a draft convention on the crime of genocide to be submitted to the next regular session of the General Assembly.

This Resolution began the process that concluded with the adoption of the Convention in 1948. Was the resolution intended to be declaratory of pre-existing international law or is it better described as evidence of the progressive development of international law? The preparatory work of the Resolution is ambiguous in this respect. The preamble states: 'Many instances of such crimes of genocide have occurred...' Perhaps this idea is the ancestor of paragraph 2 of the Convention's preamble. However, innovative criminal law legislation is almost always aimed at events that take place in the past but that have been previously unpunishable. Codification is generally a response to past conduct rather than an attempt to set out new standards of behaviour in the absence of prior transgressions. Thus, the preambular idea that genocide *has* occurred in the past is not necessarily authority for the view that it was already an international crime at the time the Convention was adopted.

The initial draft of General Assembly Resolution 96(I), which was apparently authored by Raphael Lemkin himself, said that 'the very serious crime of genocide when committed in time of peace lies within the exclusive territorial jurisdiction of the judiciary of every state concerned', in contrast with crimes that had already been made matters of international concern, such as piracy, and trade in women and children. The draft resolution was proposed by Cuba, India, and Panama. These three states, at any rate, do not seem to have thought that genocide was unquestionably an international crime in 1946. Yet in presenting the proposal to the General Assembly, the Cuban representative said 'that genocide was not a new crime but had been committed on a vast scale during the last World War'. The Cuban delegate continued that 'in deference to the rule of *non crimen sine lege*, ... Cuba therefore asked that genocide be declared an international crime'.[40]

Shortly afterwards, as work on the draft Genocide Convention began, a United Nations Secretariat document explained:

The chief legal and constitutional obstacle to the punishment of crimes against peace, war crimes, and crimes against humanity was, in the past, the opinion held by some that the rules against retroactive penal legislation, namely, the rules *nullum crimen sine lege* and *nulla poena sine lege*, made the punishment impermissible. It is one of the purposes of the draft convention to dissipate any doubt as far as the crime of genocide is concerned.[41]

This bolsters the suggestion that Resolution 96(I) was declaratory of existing international law, by which genocide was already a crime. Its purpose was not to create new law but rather to 'dissipate any doubts' because of the 'opinion held by some'.

Resolution 96(I) was almost immediately taken as authority for the existence of the crime of genocide prior to its adoption. In *Alstötter* et al. ('The Justice Case', made famous in the Stanley Kramer film *Judgment at Nuremberg*), an American Military Tribunal, delivering judgment on 3–4 December 1947 (that is, a year prior to adoption of the Convention), spoke of 'the crime of genocide' committed during the Second World War. The tribunal referred to General Assembly Resolution 96(I) as authority for the prosecution of Nazi atrocities. Speaking to the charge that this might constitute retroactive prosecution, the tribunal said 'we find no injustice to persons tried for such crimes. They are chargeable with knowledge that such acts were wrong and were punishable when committed.' The tribunal concluded that Oswald Rothaug, a Berlin prosecutor, 'participated in the national programme of racial persecution...He participated in the crime of genocide.' Another Berlin prosecutor, Ernst Lautz, was convicted of enforcing a law that comprised 'the established government plan for the extermination of those races. He was an accessory to, and took a consenting part in, the crime of genocide.'[42] Similarly, in *Greifeldt* et al. ('The RuSHA Case'), in a judgment

[40] Prevention and Punishment of Genocide, Historical Summary, 2 November 1946–20 January 1948, UN Doc. E/621.

[41] Ad Hoc Committee on Genocide, List of Substantive Issues to be Discussed in the Remaining Stages of the Committee's Session, Memorandum Submitted by the Secretariat, UN Doc. E/AC.25/11.

[42] *United States of America* v *Alstötter* et al. ('The Justice Case') (1951) 3 TWC 954 (United States Military Tribunal), at pp. 963, 983, 1128, 1156.

dated 10 March 1948, another American military tribunal referred to the 'crime of genocide'.[43] In both trials, the convictions were registered pursuant to Control Council Law No. 10, which did not use the word 'genocide'. But it is clear that the American Military Tribunals considered genocide to be a form of crime against humanity. Convictions for genocide were also recorded by courts in Poland in 1946 and 1947 with respect to Second World War atrocities.

A more direct link with the Genocide Convention itself is found in the *Eichmann* prosecution. The accused was charged pursuant to legislation enacted to give effect to Israel's obligations under the Convention. The Nazi and Nazi Collaborators (Punishment) Law, which was adopted in 1950 and was explicitly intended to apply retroactively, contained a provision entitled 'crimes against the Jewish people'. It was essentially identical to the definition of genocide in article 2 of the Convention except that it did not apply generally to national, ethnic, racial, and religious groups, but only to 'the Jewish people'. Eichmann was convicted on this basis for acts perpetrated between 1941 and 1945.

All of these prosecutions by national courts, which were applying legislative provisions that they considered to be derived from international law, concerned acts that occurred prior to the entry into force of the Genocide Convention. Indeed, most of the punishable acts took place even before the word genocide had been invented. There is therefore considerable precedent for the proposition that the crime existed prior to 11 January 1951, when the Genocide Convention entered into force. The judgments do not, however, provide an adequate response to the question as to whether the crime of genocide existed under international law before the Second World War.

There is no judicial authority for prosecution of the crime of genocide prior to the Nazi atrocities. This is a question that may never be answered by a court of criminal justice, and one that is probably already entirely theoretical. Criminal prosecution is confined to living human beings who were above the age of criminal responsibility when the acts took place, and who are physically and mentally fit to stand trial. It seems unlikely that there will ever be genocide trials of individuals for acts perpetrated before the Second World War. For the same reason, related or ancillary issues to the existence of the crime of genocide, such as the absence of statutory limitation and the availability of universal jurisdiction, may be relevant to acts

---

[43] *United States of America* v *Greifelt* et al. ('The RuSHA Case') (1951) 5 TWC 88 (United States Military Tribunal), at p. 253.

perpetrated in recent decades but are irrelevant to events that took place ninety years ago.

Evidence of actual prosecution may be helpful here. We can say that genocide existed as an international *crime* because it was prosecuted as such when committed during the Second World War. There is, of course, the objection that this might violate the maxim *nullum crimen sine lege*. But perhaps that is a separate question. That the prosecutions took place and the convictions were registered is authority for the existence of the crime. That this may have been retroactive criminal prosecution is a complaint about fairness, but it does not imperil the claim that the crime was already part of the law. There may be jurisdictions that would refuse to prosecute genocide committed prior to a certain date out of concern for the principle of legality. This is a jurisdictional rather than a substantive matter.

Unless one adopts the view that the crime of genocide is based in natural law and that it therefore existed from the beginning of human society—the steady state theory—it must be acknowledged that at some point in the past it cannot be accurate to speak of the *crime* of genocide. In other words, despite the preambular reference in the Genocide Convention to 'all periods of history', genocide *became* punishable under international law at an identifiable moment in time. The *crime* of genocide appears to predate the 1948 Convention; it also precedes the 1946 General Assembly Resolution and it can even be shown that it existed before the word itself was invented, in 1944. But just how far back can we go? One solution is to rely upon the more solid charge of crimes against humanity, where the case for the concept's relevance early in the twentieth century and even before seems stronger in some respects. Because the notion of crimes against humanity had a well-recognized usage and meaning, by comparison with 'genocide', the argument for retroactive application seems more viable. But here we encounter the genocide mystique, a matter developed in detail in Chapter 4. For some of the victims and their heirs and successors, it is inadequate to base claims upon crimes against humanity rather than genocide.

HUMAN RIGHTS LAW AND THE PRINCIPLE
OF LEGALITY

In place of the rather flexible approach at Nuremberg, and perhaps somewhat in reaction to it, international human rights law proposes a seemingly intransigent prohibition of retroactive prosecution unless it can be shown that the crime existed under international law. Concern about the fate of the Nuremberg precedent weighed heavily on states engaged in the process of transforming the rather laconic provisions of the Universal Declaration of Human Rights into treaties. Two drafting projects were underway in the months following the adoption of the Declaration in December 1948: the European Convention on Human Rights and the Covenant on Human Rights. The European Convention moved more quickly to completion, and was concluded in November 1950. The Covenant took much longer, being split into two instruments along the way. Only the first, the International Covenant on Civil and Political Rights, adopted in 1966, is relevant to this chapter.

In 1949 and 1950 the Western European states that prepared the European Convention of Human Rights chose to incorporate article 11(2) of the Universal Declaration—it became article 7(1) of the Convention— but added a paragraph, article 7(2), so as much more explicitly to shield the Nuremberg jurisprudence from challenges based upon the principle of legality: 'This article shall not prejudice the trial and punishment of any person for any act or omission which, at the time when it was committed, was criminal according to the general principles of law recognized by civilized nations.' According to a Chamber of the European Court of Human Rights, in a July 2008 judgment, the drafting history of the European Convention shows that the purpose of article 7(2) was to shelter laws that, 'in the wholly exceptional circumstances at the end of the Second World War, were passed in order to punish war crimes, treason and collaboration with the enemy'. The implication is that without paragraph 2, Nuremberg would run afoul of paragraph 1. The Court says that paragraph 2 'does not in any way aim to pass legal or moral judgment on those laws'.[44]

The drafters of the International Covenant on Civil and Political Rights adopted a provision that differs slightly from article 7(2) of the European Convention, but that is of similar effect and that was inspired by the same considerations: 'Nothing in this article shall prejudice the trial and punishment of any person for any act or omission which, at the time when it was committed, was criminal according to the general principles of law recognized by the community of nations.' Thus, two of the major human rights instruments reflect a large degree of deference towards the approach of the Nuremberg Tribunal, while implicitly acknowledging that it did not, strictly speaking, faithfully respect the *nullum crimen* principle.

The European Court of Human Rights has often reflected the same malleable approach to *nullum crimen* that was adopted by the International Military Tribunal and that was endorsed by the likes of Hans Kelsen, B.V.A. Röling, and Hersch Lauterpacht. It has tended to reject the militant positivism proposed by the Nuremberg defendants. For example, the Court has held that

---

[44] *Kononov* v *Latvia*, no 36376/04, Judgment, 24 July 2008, para. 115(b), citing *X* v *Belgium*, no 268/57 [1960] *Yearbook* 241; *Touvier* v *France*, no. 29420/95 (1997) 88 DR 148; *Papon* v *France (no. 2)* (dec.), no. 54210/00, ECHR 2001-XII (extracts).

uncodified crimes may be prosecuted providing they are sufficiently foresee-able and accessible. This is not really all that different from the remarks of the war crimes tribunal, cited above: 'the accused knew or should have known that in matters of international concern he was guilty of participation in a nation-ally organized system of injustice and persecution shocking to the moral sense of mankind'. It is an approach that might seem to lean to the natural law or 'steady state' approach, in its fealty to morality as a basis for human conduct. But on closer scrutiny, it seems compatible with either theory. Even if law is not written down, this does not mean it did not begin at some point in time. The existence of the norm is explained by evolving values and their attendant prohibition. These are foreseeable and accessible to a potential offender. We do not need abstract and eternal morality to get this result.

Cases from the United Kingdom dealing not with international crimes but with the ordinary crime of 'spousal rape' provide important authority here.[45] This concept had not traditionally been part of the common law, which defined the crime of rape as an act perpetrated by a man against a woman other than his wife. In the 1980s common law judges in England started to find defendants guilty of raping their wives. The convicted men petitioned the European Court of Human Rights, arguing that the law had been changed without them being properly informed. The Court dismissed the applications, saying the criminal prohibition of rape, even with respect to a spouse, was both foreseeable and accessible. The Court was persuaded in its opinion by the fact that the crime in question was offensive to 'human dignity and human freedom'. In other words, it might well have applied the non-retroactivity rule in a stricter fashion had the case concerned a more technical or administrative offence that did not engage core values.

The liberal approach to *nullum crimen* taken by the European Court appears to have influenced judges at the ad hoc international criminal tribunals. In one of the more detailed treatments of this issue, a Trial Chamber of the International Criminal Tribunal for the former Yugoslavia was asked to declare that the concept of superior responsibility as a mode of liability amounted to retroactive law. It turned to the case law of the European Court of Human Rights, noting that article 7 of the Convention 'allows for the "gradual clarification" of the rules of criminal liability through judicial interpretation'. It said that it was 'not necessary that the elements of an offence are defined, but rather that general description of the prohibited conduct be provided',[46] citing in support several rulings of the European Court, including one of the spousal rape decisions, which it

---

[45] *CR* v *United Kingdom*, Ser. A, No. 335-B, para. 41: *SW* v *United Kingdom*, Ser. A, No. 335-B, para. 36.

[46] *Hadžihasanović* et al. (IT-01-47-PT), Decision on Joint Challenge to Jurisdiction, 12 November 2002, para. 58.

quoted *in extenso*. Subsequently, the Appeals Chamber of the Special Court for Sierra Leone relied upon this passage in its discussion of *nullum crimen* in the child soldier case.[47]

A year after the *Hadžihasanović* jurisdictional motion, the Appeals Chamber of the International Criminal Tribunal for the former Yugoslavia invoked the words of the International Military Tribunal to the effect that *nullum crimen* was 'first and foremost a "principle of justice"'. Also citing the spousal rape cases of the European Court, the Appeals Chamber said:

> This fundamental principle 'does not prevent a court from interpreting and clari-fying the elements of a particular crime'. Nor does it preclude the progressive development of the law by the court. But it does prevent a court from creating new law or from interpreting existing law beyond the reasonable limits of acceptable clarification. This Tribunal must therefore be satisfied that the crime or the form of liability with which an accused is charged was sufficiently foreseeable and that the law providing for such liability must be sufficiently accessible at the relevant time, taking into account the specificity of international law when making that assessment.

The Appeals Chamber referred again to the European Court's position that the concepts of 'foreseeability' and 'accessibility' of a norm will greatly depend on 'the content of the instrument in issue, the field it is designed to cover and the number and status of those to whom it is addressed'. On the specificity of international criminal law, the Court returned to Nuremberg, and the words of the United States Military Tribunal in the *Alstötter* case, explaining the difficulties of applying the *ex post facto* rule to such prosecutions.[48]

As noted earlier, even if it is valid, the *nullum crimen* objection does not undermine the conclusion that the crime of genocide existed prior to 11 January 1951, or that crimes against humanity were prohibited during the 1930s and even before. Perhaps the *nullum crimen* norm was thinner in the 1940s, and it is thicker today. Case law of the European Court of Human Rights and the International Criminal Tribunal for the former Yugoslavia echoes the philosophy of the judges at Nuremberg, to the extent that the prosecutions concern crimes that strike at human dignity. The subject of retroactivity loses little of its fascination as the years go by, perhaps because it unleashes debates about the nature of law in general, and because it touches upon the fundamental fairness of the proceedings.

---

[47] *Norman* (SCSL-2004-14-AR72(E)), Decision on Preliminary Motion Based on Lack of Jurisdiction (Child Recruitment), 31 May 2004, para. 25.

[48] *Milutinović* et al. (IT-99-37-AR72), Decision on Dragoljub Ojdanić's Motion Challenging Jurisdiction—*Joint Criminal Enterprise*, 21 May 2003, paras 37, 38, 68.

3

VICTORS' JUSTICE? SELECTING
TARGETS FOR PROSECUTION

In his opening address at the Nuremberg trial, the American Prosecutor Robert Jackson said: 'That four great nations, flushed with victory and stung with injury stay the hand of vengeance and voluntarily submit their captive enemies to the judgment of the law is one of the most significant tributes that Power has ever paid to Reason.'[1] Jackson's colleague on the United States Supreme Court, Harlan Fiske Stone, was less enthusiastic. He called the International Military Tribunal a 'high grade lynching party'. Nuremberg has its enthusiasts, including the present author, but it also has its detractors. One of the most persistent charges is that the Nuremberg trial constituted 'victors' justice'. Far from 'stay the hand of vengeance', say critics, the Nuremberg trial was a vindictive exercise with little resemblance to a fair trial.

The victors' justice complaint can actually be divided into three somewhat distinct issues. The first issue concerns the legal norms being applied, particularly the crimes of which the Nazis were accused. Although war crimes had some pedigree, the other two categories, crimes against humanity and crimes against peace, were being prosecuted for the first time. This opened up the allegation that the trials amounted to *ex post facto* justice. The issue of retroactivity is addressed in detail in the previous chapter (Chapter 2, '*Nullum Crimen Sine Lege*').

The second issue concerns the overall fairness of the proceedings. There is a lingering sense that due process rights generally recognized as minimum guarantees were not fully respected. A very early ruling of the International Criminal Tribunal for the former Yugoslavia said that in devising their Rules of Procedure and Evidence, 'the Judges were conscious of the need to avoid some of the flaws noted in the Nuremberg and

---

[1] (1947) 2 IMT 99.

Tokyo proceedings'.[2] But this is like modern-day architects criticizing the Parthenon because it doesn't have ramps for the disabled and proper emergency exits. It is wrong to assess trials in 1945 and 1946 by human rights standards that prevail five or six decades later. On balance, the proceedings certainly met the standards of the time.

The third issue concerns the selectivity of the Tribunal. It was directed at Nazi perpetrators alone, despite the fact that there was much evidence that some of the crimes over which the Tribunal exercised jurisdiction had also been perpetrated by those who had established the institution. War crimes and other atrocities perpetrated by the victors, ranging from the Katyń massacre to the dreadful bombings of cities in Germany and Japan, including the nuclear destruction of Hiroshima and Nagasaki, and the more quotidian breaches of international law associated with brutal armed combat such as murdering prisoners or the issuance of orders not to take them, were not addressed as part of postwar accountability and they remain unpunished to this day. At the Tokyo Tribunal the Indian judge, Radhabinod Pal, openly challenged the one-sided nature of the proceedings in his lengthy dissenting opinion. For Judge Pal, the European allies in the Pacific conflict were just as egregious as the Japanese. He voted to acquit.[3]

At Nuremberg, the judges were not immune to these concerns. For example, answering charges that two German admirals, Dönitz and Raeder, had ordered that unrestricted submarine warfare be conducted, defence lawyers produced evidence that the American admiral in the Pacific theatre had ordered the same thing, and that similar instructions had been given by the British Admiralty. What amounted to indiscriminate attacks on merchant ships was a violation of the Washington Naval Protocol of 1936. The Nuremberg judgment treated it as a war crime. But in light of the evidence that the Allies had done the same thing, the judges refused to impose a sentence upon the Nazi admirals for this particular crime. It is often reported that the Nazi admirals were acquitted on the submarine warfare count,[4] but careful reading of the judgments shows this not to be the case.

There can be little doubt that when the Nuremberg Charter was being crafted, the four powers (the United Kingdom, France, the United States,

---

[2] *Tadić* (IT-94-1-T), Decision on the Prosecutor's Motion Requesting Protective Measures for Victims and Witnesses, 10 August 1995, para. 21.

[3] Neil Boister and Robert Cryer (eds), *Documents on the Tokyo International Military Tribunal*, Oxford: Oxford University Press, 2008, at pp. 811–930.

[4] Eg David Luban, 'The Legacies of Nuremberg', in Guénaël Mettraux (ed), *Perspectives on the Nuremberg Trial*, Oxford: Oxford University Press, 2008, pp. 638–72, at p. 660.

and the Soviet Union) understood that they were establishing an international legal regime that would, in the future, apply to themselves as well, as is explained more fully in Chapter 2. 'If certain acts and violations of treaties are crimes, they are crimes whether the United States does them or whether Germany does them. We are not prepared to lay down a rule of criminal conduct against others which we would not be willing to have invoked against us,' said Robert Jackson, the American Prosecutor. For this reason, the founders of the Nuremberg Tribunal carefully limited the scope of crimes against humanity to acts associated with aggressive war. This is the so-called nexus by which peacetime acts were not subject to prosecution as crimes against humanity. It was a careful, cynical choice intended to insulate the four 'great' powers from criminal liability for the racist, colonialist, and repressive policies of their own regimes. But the orientation of the Court was also ensured by other more structural measures.

The jurisdiction of the Nuremberg tribunals was defined in such a way as to make prosecution of any military or political leaders of the Allies a legal impossibility. Article 1 of the Charter of the International Military Tribunal confirmed that the institution's mandate was 'the just and prompt trial and punishment of the major war criminals of the European Axis'. The wording of the Charter of the Tokyo Tribunal was slightly different, referring to 'the major war criminals in the Far East', but without specifying which side they were on. In any event, those who created the two tribunals could also count on the cooperation of the prosecutors, who were their employees. Not only did they appoint them, they could also dismiss them. There seemed to be no particular unease with the idea that the prosecutors would consult with the governments that named them about important decisions during the trial. For added certainty, the Americans named General William J. Donovan as Deputy Prosecutor. Donovan was then the head of the major United States intelligence agency, the forerunner of the CIA. One of the reasons he was there was to ensure that indictments were not issued against senior Nazis with whom the Americans had made deals in the final months of the war. The Soviets had a 'Special Government Commission for Directing the Nuremberg Trials', chaired by Andrey Vyshinsky. It gave instructions to their Prosecutor on matters such as the handling of the Katyń forest massacre issue.[5] It seems likely that the British and French prosecutors received political instructions as well. The extent to which the four Nuremberg prosecutors were controlled

---

[5] For some of the documents, see: Anne M. Cienciala, Natalia S. Lebedeva, and Wojciech Materski (eds), *Katyn, A Crime without Punishment*, New Haven and London: Yale University Press, 2007, at pp. 326–9.

by the governments for whom they worked is not fully known. It makes a fascinating subject for future archival research by legal historians.

When the modern generation of international criminal tribunals was established in the 1990s, it was often said that the alleged distortion in prosecutorial policy by which only one side would be brought to justice, believed to be an unavoidable consequence of political involvement in the international judicial process, was being addressed and corrected. The International Criminal Tribunal for the former Yugoslavia, created in May 1993, was held out as a progressive development over Nuremberg because it was spawned by the Security Council, acting in the name of the 'international community', rather than by one or more of the victors. At the time, in any event, there were no victors in the Balkan wars.

There were certainly important structural improvements. The Statutes of the ad hoc Tribunals contain provisions specifying that the Prosecutor is to act independently, and is to take instructions from no government. The Statutes vary slightly in mode of appointment. Prosecutors are elected by the United Nations Security Council or appointed by the Secretary-General to a three or four-year term. Nothing indicates the grounds for which the Prosecutor is subject to dismissal, perhaps only an oversight but more likely a discreet message that in fact he or she may be removed at any time at the pleasure of the Security Council or the Secretary-General. The method of appointment of the judges is also an improvement on Nuremberg and Tokyo. At the Yugoslavia and Rwanda Tribunals they are elected from a list proposed by the Security Council. The actual process is not pretty, with much political horse trading among member states that is not always properly focussed on the competence and integrity of the candidates. Nevertheless, there is an acceptable degree of transparency, something that was lacking in the 1940s, when the judges were simply appointed by the four powers that established the Tribunal.

An early decision of the Yugoslavia Tribunal said:

[t]he Nuremberg and Tokyo trials have been characterized as 'victor's justice' because only the vanquished were charged with violations of international humanitarian law and the defendants were prosecuted and punished for crimes expressly defined in an instrument adopted by the victors at the conclusion of the war. Therefore, the International Tribunal is distinct from its closest precedents.[6]

This was true, but only up to a point. As at Nuremberg, the jurisdiction of the ad hoc Tribunal was carefully delineated by those who had created it. The Tribunal could only prosecute serious international crimes 'committed

---

[6] *Tadić* (IT-94-1-T), Decision on the Prosecutor's Motion Requesting Protective Measures for Victims and Witnesses, 10 August 1995, para. 21.

on the territory of the former Yugoslavia since 1991'. The jurisdiction of the other three ad hoc tribunals, for Rwanda, Sierra Leone, and Lebanon, is limited in a similar manner. It may be worth recalling that those who effectively control the establishment of the United Nations tribunals, namely the permanent members of the Security Council, are essentially the same countries that set up the Nuremberg court (with the addition of China). In 1945 they were called the 'great powers', whereas today they are the 'permanent five'. Same product, different packaging. In 1945 they claimed to act on behalf of 'civilized nations'; today, they prefer a more modern and politically palatable term, the 'international community'. The essence remains largely equivalent. Targets for prosecution are chosen on the basis of a number of complex political calculations, premised as much on strategic national interests as on an abstract fidelity to principles of justice. To be sure, any one of the five can always veto the establishment of an international justice mechanism that comes too close to home. For this reason, criminal tribunals for Israel, Burma, or Sri Lanka have never been seriously entertained.

TAKING SIDES AT THE AD HOC TRIBUNALS

When the International Criminal Tribunal for the former Yugoslavia was created, in 1993, significant military intervention by armies of the major powers was not contemplated. To some American senators, it came as a surprise that the 1999 Kosovo bombing undertaken by NATO forces, mainly by American forces, was technically within the jurisdiction of the court. These were acts perpetrated on the territory of the former Yugoslavia since 1991 and therefore were comprised within the Tribunal's jurisdictional framework set out in article 1 of the Statute. Responding to pressure from civil society organizations, Prosecutor Carla Del Ponte opened an investigation and, unusually, published a report of the findings. Her office concluded that acts attributed to the NATO forces were not sufficiently prohibited by international law as to provide a reliable basis for launching a formal prosecution. The explanation was unconvincing, mainly because the Prosecutor's report only responded to specific allegations and did not, on its own initiative, propose that further investigations be carried out (this is further discussed in Chapter 6). Privately, many at the Tribunal said the Prosecutor had little choice because the Security Council would have shut down the entire operation if even serious consideration was given to prosecuting Americans, or other NATO nationals. In the Security Council, the permanent representative of Russia, Sergei Lavrov, complained:

When it comes to reports of violations committed by the Federal Republic of Yugoslavia, the Tribunal immediately issues indictments and gets down to work, as, for example, in the case of the situation in Kosovo. However, if questions arise—for instance, concerning the actions of the North Atlantic Treaty Organization (NATO)—the Tribunal, even in the face of such obvious facts as the deaths of innocent civilians, the destruction by air strike of civilian targets, finds no grounds for launching an investigation. We are appalled by the Tribunal's failure to act in response to ongoing ethnic cleansing against Serbs and other national minorities in Kosovo.[7]

To be sure, in theory the ad hoc tribunals have been authorized to prosecute all of the warring parties in the various conflicts, perhaps with the exception of Lebanon, where the remit is narrowest. The Special Tribunal for Lebanon is only mandated to deal with a handful of specific incidents relating to a political assassination, one that figures as a small piece in a far greater and much protracted conflict. The International Criminal Tribunal for the former Yugoslavia held trials of Croats, Bosniacs, and Kosovars, as well as the Serbs against whom it was largely focussed, albeit unofficially. Nobody was happy. The Serbs complained that they were bearing the brunt of the prosecutions, while the others grumbled that they were victims of a misguided attempt to make the institution look balanced. The Special Court for Sierra Leone probably manifests the best effort at addressing atrocities committed on all sides. Rather than reflecting a different philosophical perspective, its attempt to address perpetrators from the various combatant factions may well have been due to the difficulty in distinguishing the conduct of various participants. It was easy to be even-handed in Sierra Leone because all parties to the conflict behaved so badly.

The problem has presented itself most acutely at the International Criminal Tribunal for Rwanda. The Statute of the Tribunal, and the documents associated with its establishment, make clear that its purpose is to address the genocide of 1994, rather than the panoply of atrocity crimes perpetrated in Rwanda and in the sub-region both before and after that tragic three-month period. In 1999 a judge of the Tribunal refused to confirm a genocide charge against an accused who had murdered the Prime Minister and several Belgian soldiers. He would only authorize counts of war crimes and crimes against humanity. The Prosecutor, Louise Arbour, chose to withdraw the case. It seemed that she considered prosecuting charges other than genocide was a distraction from the Tribunal's mission. Her application to withdraw said:

the judicial proceedings instituted by the Prosecutor should be within the framework of a global policy aimed at shedding light on the events that occurred in Rwanda in 1994 and highlighting the complete landscape of the criminal acts

---

[7] UN Doc. S/PV.4161, paras 7–8.

perpetrated at the time, and that such objective would not be achieved through the prosecution of a single count indictment the factual elements of which relate solely to the murders of the former Prime Minister and ten UNAMIR Belgian soldiers.[8]

Later, the Prosecutor agreed to accept a few plea bargains whereby genocide charges were dropped in exchange for an acknowledgement of responsibility for crimes against humanity. But this was really an expedient enabling some quick convictions to be registered, freeing up the resources of the Office of the Prosecutor for other cases.

For many years, the Prosecutor of the International Criminal Tribunal for Rwanda was urged to deal with the 'flip-side' crimes perpetrated by the largely Tutsi forces who vanquished the *génocidaires* and who have held power in Kigali since 1994. There is much evidence to suggest their responsibility for serious international crimes, although not for genocide. Prosecutor Carla Del Ponte, who held office from 1999 to 2003, was keen on pursuing this, but her successor, Hassan Jallow, showed much less interest. Critics charge that his reluctance manifests a complacent relationship with the current Rwandan authorities, with whom cooperation is essential for the Tribunal to conduct its activities. But it may well reflect a genuine and sincere belief that the mission of the Tribunal is to address the 1994 genocide. Moreover, Prosecutor Jallow may feel that the pressure to prosecute the Tutsi military leaders is itself driven by a political constituency rather than some well-meant and altruistic vision of a court that deals with all sides in a conflict. He has been harshly criticized, notably by the NGO Human Rights Watch, on this account. In a letter from the organization to Prosecutor Jallow, Human Rights Watch said: 'It would be a failure of justice—not merely victor's justice—if you do not vigorously investigate and prosecute senior RPF officials because they are currently senior officials or military leaders in Rwanda.' Moreover, '[f]ailure to do so will taint perceptions of the Tribunal's impartiality and undermine its legitimacy for years to come'.[9]

Over the years, advocates for one conflict or another have come to the United Nations and argued: 'You set up a tribunal for Yugoslavia and Rwanda, why don't you do it for our conflict?' The answer was rarely more than a diplomatic shrug of the shoulders. There was no rhyme or reason to the intervention of the Security Council. It operated when there was

---

[8] *Ntuyahaga* (ICTR-98-40-T), Decision on the Prosecutor's Motion to Withdraw the Indictment, 18 March 1999.

[9] 'Kenneth Roth to Hassan Jallow', 14 August 2009. See also: Human Rights Watch, 'Rwanda: Tribunal Risks Supporting "Victor's Justice": Tribunal Should Vigorously Pursue Crimes of Rwandan Patriotic Front', 1 June 2009.

consensus among its permanent members. That meant, in particular, that it was inactive when the strategic interests of a permanent member or, for that matter, the behaviour of the permanent member itself, were threatened in some way. The Special Tribunal for Lebanon provides a striking example here. The Security Council directed the establishment of an international court to prosecute the assassins of Rafiq Hariri, a former prime minister of the country and friend of Presidents Bush and Chirac, but did nothing the following year when brutal armed conflict between Israel and Hezbollah devastated much of the country. In 1990 the United States and the United Kingdom launched an initiative to establish a tribunal aimed at Saddam Hussein for the invasion of Kuwait. But nobody seriously entertained the idea of a Security Council-created tribunal when the United States and the United Kingdom invaded Iraq in 2003, contrary to the very prohibition of aggression that they had invoked against the Iraqi president thirteen years earlier. When the permanent members feel threatened, the best hope of international justice still remains an unofficial initiative such as the toothless 'tribunal' set up in the late 1960s by two of the world's great philosophers, Bertrand Russell and Jean-Paul Sartre, to deal with American atrocities in Vietnam.

SELECTING 'SITUATIONS' AT THE INTERNATIONAL CRIMINAL COURT

The International Criminal Court is not created by the Security Council and is, to some extent, immunized against control by the five permanent members. It is a treaty-based institution governed by its States Parties, all of whom are equal in principle. The most important manifestation of this independence from the Security Council is the so-called *proprio motu* Prosecutor. In contrast with all of the predecessors at earlier international criminal tribunals, the Prosecutor of the International Criminal Court has the authority to designate what are called 'situations'. A situation is distinct from a 'case', the term used to describe the stage in the proceedings when an individual defendant has been identified. At the previous tribunals, the 'situation' was really the definition of the institution's jurisdiction. The Second World War, the conflicts associated with the break-up of Yugoslavia, the Rwandan genocide, terrorism in Lebanon, and the civil war in Sierra Leone are all 'situations'. The prosecutors of these ad hoc institutions were generally free to select individual accused persons or 'cases' as long as they remained within the 'situation'. But they could not stray outside this perimeter. Any attempt to do so would have resulted in dismissal of a case by the judges on jurisdictional grounds. Besides, such a 'runaway prosecutor' would quickly have been replaced with one prepared to respect the terms of his or her engagement.

The Rome Statute of the International Criminal Court contemplates three ways of identifying a situation for prosecution. The first two are broadly similar to what has prevailed in previous models of international justice: referral by a State Party or by the Security Council. But the Prosecutor of the International Criminal Court is also empowered to designate a 'situation' even when States Parties and the Security Council are silent. Yet even when a State Party or the Security Council refers a situation, the Prosecutor still has the power to refuse to proceed if he or she judges that this is not in 'the interests of justice'. This authority to refuse to proceed is as unprecedented as the power of the Prosecutor to launch an investigation.

The Prosecutor's power to proceed is limited only by the jurisdictional provisions of the Statute, which confine the Court's scope to the territory of States Parties and to their nationals, and to acts perpetrated subsequent to 1 July 2002 when the Statute entered into force. Thus, the Prosecutor is enabled with the authority to investigate and prosecute war crimes attributable to British troops in Iraq, because Britain is a State Party to the Rome Statute. He or she may also proceed with respect to war crimes committed by American troops in Afghanistan, which is a State Party to the Rome Statute, because there is jurisdiction over all crimes committed on Afghan territory. But the Prosecutor cannot initiate investigations of Sri Lankan generals in relation to the destruction of the Tamil Tigers in 2009 because Sri Lanka has not joined the Court. Exceptionally, the Prosecutor can also act where a state that has not joined the Court has acknowledged its jurisdiction in accordance with article 12(3) of the Statute. Côte d'Ivoire has made such a declaration, as has the Palestinian Authority (the validity of the latter declaration has been a matter of some debate, because only a 'state' can take this step).

If the independent Prosecutor of the International Criminal Court is not subject to the political whims of the five permanent members of the Security Council, or the states that created the Court, on what does he or she base decisions about the selection of 'situations' and the refusal to proceed upon 'complaints' from States Parties or the Security Council? One view might be that the Prosecutor should investigate and prosecute *all* situations in which crimes subject to the jurisdiction of the Court have been perpetrated where national justice systems have failed to act effectively. This would certainly be the logic of a victim-oriented approach. Why should one victim of a crime against humanity be less or more entitled to international justice than another? Some observers have seriously entertained such an interpretation, pointing to the requirement, in article 15(3) of the Rome Statute, that the Prosecutor 'shall' proceed with an investigation if, acting upon a complaint, he or she determines that there is a reasonable basis a crime within the jurisdiction of the Court has been committed.

In a national justice system, this would assuredly be the expectation. Thinking in this respect is often coloured by analogies with domestic courts, where the idea of a politicized prosecutor is quite repulsive. At the national level in a functional justice system displaying the attributes of the rule of law all serious crimes against the person will be prosecuted. Case law of international human rights tribunals has established this as an entitlement of victims that flows from treaty norms.[10] Yet a mechanistic extrapolation based upon the model of national prosecution to the context of international criminal tribunals is fundamentally defective because there can be no serious prospect that all perpetrators of serious international crimes will be brought to justice by such institutions. The tribunals, and their budgets, were never conceived to deal with *all* crimes within their jurisdiction. By nature, they are selective.

Indeed, this selectivity is also apparent at the national level where international crimes are concerned. States may recognize an obligation to prosecute the totality of serious crimes against the person, including war crimes and other international crimes, but only to the extent that they are perpetrated on their territory. They show no inclination to extrapolate this general principle when such crimes are committed elsewhere, even if the suspect is within their grasp. Under universal jurisdiction, where an international crime is concerned states are free to prosecute perpetrators in their custody despite the fact that the act was committed abroad. But in practice they rarely do this. Prosecutions under universal jurisdiction generally focus on crimes committed in areas where the state has historically had national interests, often in its former colonies. Furthermore, states that actually exercise universal jurisdiction often require a form of internal political authorization before a prosecution may be undertaken for such crimes. They do not generally entrust to an independent prosecutor the decision about whom to prosecute for international crimes committed outside their own territory.

THE LAW OF GRAVITY

Since the Rome Statute entered into force in July 2002, the International Criminal Court has been in a position to exercise jurisdiction over many

---

[10] For example, *MC* v *Bulgaria*, no. 39272/98, Judgment, 4 December 2003, paras 102–107.

tens of thousands of cases. Yet after nearly a decade of activity, it has only actually proceeded with trials against a small number of individuals, all of them nationals of the Democratic Republic of the Congo and Kenya. Partly, this is a resource issue. With an annual budget of about €100 million, the number of major trials that the Court can undertake is seriously constrained. Perhaps the International Criminal Court has under-performed by comparison with the other international criminal tribunals. But even the most efficient and expeditious of them, the International Military Tribunal at Nuremberg, only managed to judge twenty-two individuals in a trial that lasted nearly a year. International justice, and especially the International Criminal Court, can only aspire to deal with a handful of the crimes that are committed. Choices must be made. On what basis, however?

The Rome Statute provides little if any guidance here. It would probably have been impossible for States Parties to reach agreement on the criteria to be employed. A subsequent instrument, the Rules of Procedure and Evidence, which was negotiated by the States Parties, did nothing to fill the void. Even before Luis Moreno-Ocampo took office as first Prosecutor of the International Criminal Court, lawyers in his office had prepared draft regulations that attempted to codify the process by which 'situations' would be selected among the many deserving possibilities. These draft regulations naively approached the matter of selection of situations in a manner that suggested the Prosecutor would proceed with everything that was admissible. There was to be a complex procedure, involving 'evaluation teams' and a 'draft investigation plan', leading to a decision by the Prosecutor. Nevertheless, nothing indicated the grounds on which the Prosecutor would make the determination. There was an intriguing reference to his or her 'inherent powers'. But the Prosecutor did not adopt the draft. Years later, he proclaimed a new and much streamlined version of the Regulations that vaguely referred to the 'seriousness of the information', 'jurisdiction, admissibility (including gravity), as well as the interests of justice'. These were the factors to be assessed in identifying the 'situations' that the Prosecutor would target. The Regulations said that in assessing gravity, 'various factors including their scale, nature, manner of commission, and impact' were to be taken into account.[11] They might just as well have said, like the American judge who was famously asked to define pornography: 'The Prosecutor, in his wisdom, will know an appropriate situation when he sees it.'

The word gravity was used only once in the 2003 draft regulations. Presumably at the time, nobody in the Office of the Prosecutor thought

---

[11] Regulations of the Office of the Prosecutor, ICC-BD/05-01-09, Regulation 29.

that the concept of 'gravity' was very significant in the selection of situations or of cases. The term 'gravity', which appears in the Statute in two places relevant to the selection of cases and situations, had not figured in any significant manner in the early pronouncements of the Office of the Prosecutor. Up to that time, academic writers on the Rome Statute had generally failed to view the concept of 'gravity' as being particularly relevant to the exercise of prosecutorial discretion. The two major Commentaries on the Rome Statute published at the time virtually ignored the matter.

That changed in late 2005, when the Prosecutor discovered the gravity criterion in order to explain his decision to proceed against the leaders of the Lord's Resistance Army in Uganda rather than against those of the government forces. When the first arrest warrants were issued by the Court, the Prosecutor found himself criticized by human rights NGOs, notably Human Rights Watch and Amnesty International, for only charging suspects on one side of the Ugandan civil war. In reply, the Prosecutor invoked 'gravity' and said that the Lord's Resistance Army had killed many more people than the soldiers of the Ugandan People's Defence Forces. In this context, he seemed to be talking about the selection of cases, rather than of situations. Or was he saying that the 'situation' of the Lord's Resistance Army was more serious than the 'situation' of the Ugandan People's Defence Forces, in effect relating the 'situation' to the identification of opposing combatant groups in a civil war? It was not really clear.

Within a few months the Prosecutor used the same gravity argument to resist entreaties that he investigate the conduct of British troops in Iraq. Probably many of the complainants felt strongly that the war was unlawful. They would not have understood or appreciated the distinction between the legality of the initiation of the war (*jus ad bellum*) and the conduct within it (*jus in bello*), something addressed in more detail in Chapter 8 ('Crimes Against Peace'). At the time, the Court could not and still cannot prosecute the crime of aggression. But there was no shortage of evidence that British soldiers had been engaged in various atrocities, including murder of civilians, and these were war crimes in the classic sense. Because the United Kingdom was a State Party to the Rome Statute, the Court had jurisdiction over war crimes perpetrated by British nationals. Furthermore, the allies of the United Kingdom, the Americans, were also suspected of important violations. However, neither the United States nor Iraq were States Parties to the Rome Statute. The Prosecutor could not investigate or proceed with charges against Americans for acts perpetrated on the territory of a non-party state. Some complaints suggested that the British could also be prosecuted as accomplices for war crimes committed by the Americans because they were part of a joint criminal enterprise.

In February 2006 the Prosecutor announced his decision not to proceed with an investigation into war crimes committed in Iraq by nationals of States Parties to the Rome Statute. He acknowledged that there was a reasonable basis to believe that crimes within the jurisdiction of the Court had been perpetrated. The Prosecutor referred to evidence that there had been four to twelve victims of wilful killing and a limited number of victims of inhuman treatment, totalling in all less than twenty persons. The sum of these violations, he reasoned, was 'of a different order' than the number of victims in other situations being investigated or analysed by the Office of the Prosecutor, notably Northern Uganda, the Democratic Republic of the Congo and Darfur. He said each of the latter situations involved thousands of wilful killings as well as intentional and large-scale sexual violence and abductions. The explanation was unconvincing, because any reasonable observer knows that since the invasion by the United Kingdom and the United States in 2003, and largely as a consequence, Iraq has been the scene of massive human rights violations. At a minimum, tens of thousands of innocent civilians have been killed and perhaps millions have been displaced. By setting specific acts attributable to British troops of which he had evidence, rather than the war as a whole, alongside general reports of victimization in other conflicts in central Africa, the Prosecutor was comparing apples and oranges. Or rather, he was comparing cases to situations.

The fallacy of the comparison between Iraq and central Africa became clear within a matter of days, when Moreno-Ocampo announced the arrest of the Court's first prisoner, Thomas Lubanga. A Congolese warlord, Lubanga was not charged with the massive murders, abductions, and sexual violence that the Prosecutor had cited in his comparison with the British conduct in Iraq. Lubanga was accused only of the recruitment of child soldiers within the context of a civil war. Was that more serious than the murder and ill-treatment of civilians by British soldiers engaged in a war of aggression?

Many suspected that Moreno-Ocampo was actually trying to steer clear of a confrontation with one or two major powers. Sometimes, people around the Court would mutter such excuses under their breath, as if it was an embarrassing secret. Perhaps they hadn't suspected that much of the world is familiar with the double standards by which the south is judged differently than the north. All that the Prosecutor's decision did was confirm suspicions that the Court was not the politically neutral body its proponents had bragged about. In addition to being an influential member of the Court, the United Kingdom is also a permanent member of the Security Council. In contrast, Uganda and the Democratic Republic of the

Congo were soft targets for the Court's activities. And they were compliant ones, in a sense, to the extent that the Prosecutor appeared to be interested only in rebel groups rather than government forces.

The contrived reasoning about gravity also kept the Prosecutor sweet with the Americans, who would not have been keen on prosecutions relating to the behaviour of their principal military ally in the Iraq invasion. Indeed, it was at about this time that the United States began to warm to the International Criminal Court. Years later, the Wikileaks website published a revealing confidential document, written in July 2003, from an American diplomat assessing the Prosecutor's attitude towards Iraq. 'Ocampo has said that he was looking at the actions of British forces in Iraq—which...led a British ICTY prosecutor nearly to fall off his chair', said the dispatch. 'Privately, Ocampo has said that he wishes to dispose of Iraq issues (ie Not to investigate them.)'

The *proprio motu* authority of the Prosecutor to launch investigations on his own initiative was held out as the crown jewel in the Rome Statute. It was this power that distinguished the Court from its predecessors, and promised to shelter it from the stigma of 'victors' justice'. Surprisingly, then, the Prosecutor did not in fact select a situation in the formal sense of exercising his own authority pursuant to article 15 of the Statute until late 2009, more than six years after taking office. He applied to the Pre-Trial Chamber for authorization to open an investigation into the post-electoral violence in Kenya. By then, there were four active situations, in Northern Uganda, the Democratic Republic of the Congo, the Central African Republic, and the Sudanese province of Darfur. The first three had been referred to the Court by States Parties in accordance with article 14. The fourth resulted from a Security Council resolution, pursuant to article 13(b) of the Rome Statute. In other words, the initial situations before the Court largely resembled the Nuremberg approach and that of the ad hoc tribunals, in that they had been designated by governments, or by an inter-governmental body, the Security Council.

THE 'INTERESTS OF JUSTICE'

Even if the Security Council or a State Party refers a situation to the Court, the Prosecutor is not required to proceed. If this occurs, he or she may be called upon to justify the decision before a Pre-Trial Chamber in accordance with article 53 of the Statute. Nothing of the sort has happened as yet. One of the grounds that the Prosecutor may invoke for refusal is that investigation or prosecution would be contrary to the 'interests of justice'. There have been attempts to parse the meaning of these words, including a rather prolix position paper issued at the instigation of human rights NGOs. The latter wanted the Prosecutor to rule out the possibility of resisting prosecution in the event of a political settlement involving amnesty.

The claim that the 'interests of justice' do not provide a basis for declining to prosecute when amnesties have been granted as part of a peace process is surely reading too much into the text of article 53. The purpose of the reference to 'interests of justice' is to endow the Prosecutor with discretion. Given the range of views of states on such issues as amnesties, about which the Rome Statute is silent, it would have been impossible to devise a formula to guide such discretion (see Chapter 7, 'No Peace without Justice? The Amnesty Quandary'). The words 'interests of justice' are often used in legal texts when it proves impossible to provide more definitive guidance in the exercise of a particular power or right. It is a way in which lawmakers say 'We can't do any more here than trust that a wise person will know to do the right thing.' That is also the function of 'interests of justice' in article 53 of the Rome Statute.

Thus, the Prosecutor of the International Criminal Court has been given extraordinary and largely unfettered powers that hitherto were the prerogative of bodies such as the four-power conference that created the Nuremberg Tribunal and the United Nations Security Council responsible for establishing the various ad hoc tribunals. He or she can decide where to prosecute and where not to prosecute, when to turn on the tap of international justice and when to turn it off. Currently, the 'gravity' criterion remains central to the Prosecutor's explanation for decisions about the selection of situations. But the Prosecutor's career at the Court is confined to a single nine-year term. Future prosecutors may view this differently, and dwell upon other criteria to account for their own subjectivity.

By way of example, in 1997 a conference on transitional justice in the former Yugoslavia held in Strasbourg considered the advisability of establishing a truth and reconciliation commission. The various experts and stakeholders at the meeting largely agreed that this was to be desired. A few days later, the Prosecutor of the International Criminal Tribunal for the former Yugoslavia, who had been represented at the Strasbourg meeting, issued a statement that was harshly critical of the initiative. Louise Arbour could not see the feasibility of a truth commission working in parallel with the International Tribunal. Shortly thereafter, Arbour's predecessor as Prosecutor, Richard Goldstone, published an op-ed in the *International Herald Tribune* praising the proposed commission. The only point here is that reasonable people like Louise Arbour and Richard Goldstone may reach radically different conclusions on important issues concerning the operation of international justice. It will be no different if successive prosecutors at the International Criminal Court choose to act in the 'interests of justice'.

The 'interests of justice' is a nebulous and intangible notion, ideally suited to camouflage the real reasons behind choices about whether or not to proceed in situations. The results are ultimately the product of the Prosecutor's own personal determinations. This is not to suggest that the Prosecutor's selection of situations is purely arbitrary or capricious. All of the situations he has agreed to prosecute to date are certainly 'serious'. But this can also be said of other situations where he is inactive and, seemingly, uninterested. In one sense or another, these choices reflect the political judgements, prejudices, predispositions, and leanings of the individual to whom they are entrusted. Furthermore, the prosecutorial choices are not simply about some triage between situations that are serious and those that are not. The Prosecutor of the Court also conducts a ranking among situations already deemed 'serious'. In 2006 he appeared to decide that murder and torture of civilians by a foreign army following an illegal invasion was not as serious as the recruitment of child soldiers by a rebel militia. Others might be inclined to reverse the order.

As an experiment, ask every individual in a room full of people to write the single 'situation' that they think is most deserving of international justice on a slip of paper. Inevitably, the responses will vary greatly. If victims of atrocities are present, they will almost invariably select the situations that concern them. Understandably, victims cannot easily make such choices with objectivity. But even those who are more detached will probably indicate the countries, regions, and types of crime that, for one reason or another, often related to their personal interests and experiences, are closest to their hearts: Iraq, Gaza, Sri Lanka, Colombia, North Korea, child soldiers, sexual violence, cluster munitions, hate propaganda. Each situation has its merits, each manifests gravity, and each has a decent claim to be at the top of the list. But why is the individual determination made by the Prosecutor of the International Criminal Court any more legitimate than that of one of the individuals in this casual survey?

AN INCOMPLETE DEBATE ABOUT POLITICAL DIRECTION

The first six 'situations' investigated by the Prosecutor concern geographically contiguous countries in central Africa: Uganda, Sudan, Central African Republic, Democratic Republic of the Congo, Kenya, and Libya. Is it really conceivable that an objective application of the gravity criterion, as proposed in materials from the Office of the Prosecutor, leads inexorably to this result? Is it simply a coincidence, the unintended conjuncture of the objective application of selection criteria built around an inchoate notion of 'gravity'? Can this be explained reasonably as a purely judicial determination flowing from application of the Rome Statute and the Regulations of the Office of the Prosecutor? There must surely be a strong presumption that some sort of policy determination is involved, absent any convincing explanation to the contrary.

Certainly, many states, especially States Parties in the global north, and particularly the non-party state that has become one of the keener supporters of the Court in recent years, the United States of America, seem very comfortable with the Prosecutor's focus on central Africa. There has been much interest in the apparent warming of the United States to the Court, which many attribute to the more enlightened orientation of the administration that replaced George W. Bush. Actually, the process was underway well before the 2008 election. It seems to be as much related to the fact that the Court's priorities correspond to the strategic interests of the United States as it is to the more progressive multilateralism of President Obama and Secretary of State Clinton.

The first Prosecutor of the Court, Luis Moreno-Ocampo, has regularly insisted that his actions and decisions are based on judicial and not political factors. But if this is really the case, then a better explanation for the choice of situations for prosecution must be advanced. The 'gravity' language strikes the observer as little more than obfuscation, a laboured attempt to make the determinations look more judicial than they really are. The seriousness of the situations in central Africa is unquestioned. Yet there are many serious situations over which the Court can exercise jurisdiction elsewhere in the world. Nor are these observations meant to cast aspersions on the good faith of those involved in these determinations. They have undoubtedly convinced themselves that they have found a legalistic formula enabling themselves to do the impossible, namely, to take a political decision while making it look judicial.

Quietly, and despite the rhetoric about the absence of political considerations in the selection of situations, the Prosecutor does in fact draw upon a coterie of advisers based in what is called the 'Jurisdiction, Complementarity and Cooperation Unit'. Possibly external experts are also consulted from time to time. It is an entirely opaque process, shrouded in the language of denial and the myth of the irrelevance of political factors. The problem here is not only transparency but also accountability. By contrast, the Security Council, which is responsible for the political triggering and guidance of the ad hoc tribunals, operates somewhat in the open. Its members are responsible for their choices not only to the international community as a whole but also to their national political constituencies.

The enormous discretion of the Prosecutor is restrained by the Rome Statute in a couple of ways. First, decisions to initiate prosecutions and to block them are subject to review by a three-judge Pre-Trial Chamber. The legal parameters to be followed by the judges are as oracular as those of the Prosecutor. In practice, it appears unlikely that judges will second-guess the exercise of the discretion of the Prosecutor, as long as it remains within reasonable bounds. After all, they are not asked to make assessments of prosecutorial priorities, merely to confirm that they have been made appropriately and are not entirely arbitrary. The judges are not charged with making the best determination of the selection policy of the Court, only with endorsing the validity of those situations that are chosen by the Prosecutor.

Second, a decision to prosecute, in either a 'situation' or a 'case', may be blocked by resolution of the United Nations Security Council, pursuant to article 16 of the Statute. Here, we return to nakedly political considerations. But the Security Council's authority is itself closely circumscribed. It must act by resolution, and this means one of the permanent five can obstruct the process by means of the veto. The Security Council must renew any resolution on an annual basis. The United States has already shown itself to be remarkably adept at manipulating the article 16 procedure, invoking it in 2002 and 2003 on spurious grounds, and then threatening to veto its use where it provided a solution to a genuine problem facing the Court in 2008.

The provisions in the Rome Statute concerning the relationship between the Prosecutor and the Security Council were probably the most contentious of the entire negotiations. The United Nations International Law Commission initially prepared the working draft statute that formed the basis of discussions. Finalized in 1994, its conception was of a court that was similar to the existing models—the Nuremberg tribunal and the International Criminal Tribunal for the former Yugoslavia—in the sense that the selection of situations was entirely subject to the control of the political body responsible for the establishment of the institution. The proposed court would only be able to operate in situations that had been designated by the Security Council or by a member state. But even if a member state were to assign a situation to the court, this could not go ahead if the matter was already being considered by the Security Council. Given that virtually every potential situation that might merit prosecution would be a crisis of sufficient proportions to have already engaged the Security Council, in practice this meant that the Council was the gatekeeper of the proposed court.

When the debate about the draft statute shifted from the conservative International Law Commission to the more intoxicating atmosphere of the General Assembly, ideas began to circulate whose consequence was to weaken the control over the court by the Security Council in terms of the designation of situations. Some of this was nurtured by post-Cold War euphoria and the political opportunities generated by the new unipolar world order. Important countries that were excluded from the inner circle of the United Nations, such as Germany, Canada, South Africa, and Argentina, exploited the chance to attempt indirectly the long-awaited reform of the Security Council that had been unattainable directly through amendment of the Charter of the United Nations. This became merged with very seductive discourse about establishing a purely judicial institution at the international level, one whose prosecutorial policy would be based upon objective criteria rather than political interests. From this alchemy, the independent prosecutor was born.

THE INDEPENDENT PROSECUTOR AND
THE ROME STATUTE

Over the four years of negotiations that culminated in the Rome Conference at which the Statute of the International Criminal Court was adopted the concept of the independent Prosecutor gained purchase. It was enshrined as one of the central policy planks of the 'like-minded caucus' that was so influential in the process. As this debate continued to evolve, the theory of the independent Prosecutor operated as a kind of Trojan horse for the campaign to weaken the grip of the Security Council. The principle of prosecutorial independence was consistent with general views on the mission of impartial criminal justice, although there was little serious reflection about the distinctions between the way this worked at the domestic level and the added complexities on the international plane. Nevertheless, it operated very effectively to challenge the vision of a court whose Prosecutor would be subject to direction from the Security Council. It seems that no alternative to the Security Council was considered as a source of policy orientation for the Prosecutor in the determination of appropriate 'situations'. Many states wanted to remove the Security Council from the picture, and the most effective way to do so was chanting the mantra about political control being incompatible with a judicial institution. A more subtle and refined approach, which would acknowledge the imperative of some type of direction to the Prosecutor but from a source other than the Security Council, never emerged.

The challenge of political guidance may be one factor that explains the lacklustre performance of the Court in its first decade of activity. The ad hoc tribunals, and Nuremberg and Tokyo before them, succeeded not only because of the political forces that established them but also because of the political consensus that supported their work. The most famous of the cases directed against former heads of state, Milošević and Taylor, were only able to proceed because of widespread political backing in the regions affected by the conflicts for the idea that international justice be done. In the most celebrated case to come before the International Criminal Court, of Sudanese President Omar Al-Bashir, such support has been weak in the part of the world where it is most needed.

The International Criminal Court continues to plod along, consistently failing in the targets that it has itself set. A year after taking office, the Prosecutor proposed a budget that was based upon the proposition that '[i]n 2005, the Office plans to conduct one full trial, begin a second and carry out two new investigations'.[12] A flow chart derived from the Prosecutor's forecasts indicated that the first trial before the Court would be completed by August 2005.[13] He became somewhat less ambitious in 2006, when a three-year strategic plan proclaimed the expectation that the Court would complete two 'expeditious trials by 2009, and ... conduct four to six new investigations'.[14] Actually, the first trial only began in early 2009, and was nowhere near completion by the end of the year. The second started in November 2009. In February 2010 a new three-year strategic plan said the Court would finish the three trials then under-way or about to begin, and start 'at least one new trial'. In addition, the Prosecutor said he intended to continue ongoing investigations in seven cases, and conduct 'up to four new investigations of cases'.[15] In fact, by early 2011 not even one trial was close to completion. Even assuming the goals proclaimed in 2010 are achieved—an unlikely prospect, given a pattern of unfulfilled aspirations—that will mean that in its first nine years of operation the International Criminal Court will have completed trials of four people, started the trial of another individual, and investigated cases involving eleven individuals, for a total of sixteen. Given that holding trials is the core activity of the Court, these mistaken projections reflect an unrealistic assessment of the difficulties facing the institution. It is submitted in this chapter that the lack of political direction to the Prosecutor has contributed significantly to making the work of the Court

---

[12] Draft Programme Budget for 2005, ICC-ASP/3/2, para. 159.   [13] Ibid., p. 49.
[14] Report on Prosecutorial Strategy, 14 September 2006, p. 3.
[15] Prosecutorial Strategy, 2009–12, 1 February 2010, p. 2.

so difficult and frustrating. Precisely for this reason, at least in part, the International Criminal Court does not compare well with the perform-ance of the other international criminal tribunals.

WHO'S AFRAID OF VICTORS' JUSTICE?

What does all of this have to do with 'victors' justice'? It has been the label attached to international trials allegedly tainted with the politics of those who established them. The critique suggests that matters improved some-what at the ad hoc tribunals, compared with Nuremberg and Tokyo. Only with the International Criminal Court, and its *proprio motu* Prosecutor, has the problem been solved, goes the explanation. But has it? In reality, what we have at the International Criminal Court is a political determination, only with less transparency, not more. This is not to suggest that the Prosecutor receives instructions from some clandestine committee of political advisers and foreign intelligence agencies. However, he or she is certainly compelled to select situations where objective, judicial criteria alone do not suffice as guidance. The discretion of the Prosecutor of the International Criminal Court in selecting situations on his or her own initiative (article 15), and in accepting or rejecting selections that have already been referred by the Security Council or by States Parties (in accordance with article 53), has an inherently political dimension.

The quest for the judicial international prosecutor—one who is above politics, and who is modelled on domestic prosecutors where all serious crimes against the person are addressed regardless of political consider-ations—is as elusive as the search for the end of the rainbow. For this rea-son, the Rome Statute is incomplete. The Prosecutor does, in fact, make political choices. He or she does not seriously consider for prosecution all admissible situations that fall within the jurisdiction of the Court. Some, like Iraq, are set aside because they concern powerful states, although the justification for this gets dressed up in unconvincing language about com-parative 'gravity'. Others are selected where they seem to represent a con-sensus of some states, but not all. Prosperous states in the global north seem pleased enough that prosecutorial energy is devoted to central Africa. When African states complain that they are being unfairly targeted, the answer is that the determinations are based upon 'gravity' and that they respond to objective criteria. This is about as persuasive as the sugges-tion that the United Nations Human Rights Council focusses on all serious country situations involving human rights violations, or that the United Nations Security Council deals in an even-handed manner with all threats to international peace and security. The only difference is that the Councils of the United Nations are avowedly political bodies and they make no pretence to the contrary.

Many war crimes committed by the Allied forces during the Second World War went unpunished. Decades before the Second World War, international law had attempted to outlaw aerial warfare altogether. Probably the turning point was the infamous attack on the Basque city, Guernica, immortalized in the great mural by Picasso that hangs today in Madrid's Reina Sophia gallery. Thus began a gradual descent into violations of the laws and customs of war, sometimes rationalized in the name of reprisal. It eventually led to use of the atomic bomb at Hiroshima and Nagasaki, and the fire storms that cremated uncounted civilian inhabitants of Dresden, Hamburg, and Tokyo.

There are also many reports that Allied soldiers murdered German prisoners, something that, then as now, is a violation of the laws of war. Following the Malmédy massacre in December 1944, when eighty-four American soldiers were executed by German forces during the Battle of the Bulge, an order was issued that SS troops and paratroopers were not to be taken prisoner and were to be shot on sight. In the Abbaye Ardenne case, the commander of an SS armoured unit, Kurt Mayer, was charged with killing Canadian prisoners. He led evidence showing that during the invasion of Normandy the Allied forces including the Canadians had issued written orders not to take prisoners. The Canadian force commander commuted Meyer's sentence from execution to life imprisonment because he was certain that his own soldiers had perpetrated similar acts.

The Katyń forest massacre is only one of the many examples of atrocities perpetrated by the Soviets as they fought the Nazis for survival. It is discussed in detail in this volume in Chapter 6, 'History, International Justice, and the Right to Truth'. With the war ending, and victory virtually assured, Soviet soldiers committed large-scale rapes of German civilians, a war crime by any definition and one apparently perpetrated with official consent or indifference. After the political changes in eastern and central Europe associated with the end of the Cold War, a few prosecutions were attempted against anti-Nazi fighters for their behaviour during the war. Probably more are still to come in the Baltic states, Slovenia, and elsewhere, although the temporal window for prosecution of the ageing men and women suspected of such crimes is quickly closing. But there is no question of holding leaders and senior officials accountable. In any event, few if any remain alive. In a European Court of Human Rights case arising from the war crimes trial of a Latvian partisan, *Kononov* v *Latvia*, Russia intervened in the proceedings to argue, essentially, that only Nazis could commit war crimes. Its claim that anything else amounted to retroactive prosecution (see Chapter 2, *'Nullum Crimen Sine Lege'*) was dismissed by the Grand Chamber of the Court.

Lawyers for the Nazi defendants raised the matter of Allied war crimes on behalf of SS *Einsatzgruppen* leaders in one of the subsequent proceedings held by the Americans in the Nuremberg courtroom after the big trial had finished. They argued that it was not a war crime to murder civilians, because the Allies had done the same when they indiscriminately bombed German population centres. The judges responded:

> Thus, as grave a military action as is an air bombardment, whether with the usual bombs or by atomic bomb, the one and only purpose of the bombing is to effect the surrender of the bombed nation. The people of that nation, through their representatives, may surrender and, with the surrender, the bombing ceases, the killing is ended. Furthermore, a city is assured of not being bombed by the law-abiding belligerent if it is declared an open city. With the Jews it was entirely different. Even if the nation surrendered they still were killed as individuals.[16]

Actually, the purpose of the bombing might better be described as terrorizing the civilian population. There can be no doubt that today such massacres of civilians would be viewed as a war crime. What the judges were really doing was resisting the argument of moral equivalence.

All serious crimes ought to be addressed by courts of criminal justice, and these Second World War atrocities perpetrated by the victors are no exception. That they have been left virtually unpunished is much to be regretted. But lamenting the impunity of Allied war crimes during the Second World War does not inexorably lead to the conclusion that the Nuremberg and Tokyo tribunals were distorted because they did not punish both sides. One can, as did the judges in the *Einsatzgruppen* case, argue that the Allied crimes were not comparable to those of the Nazis. In particular, to the extent that the core crime of the prosecutions was aggression, it seems obvious enough that it is the aggressor and not the victim of aggression who will be the focus of international justice. But that is not really the heart of the argument by the judges in *Einsatzgruppen*. Their logic was one of relative gravity. They obviously disagreed with the modern-day Nazi supporters in Germany and elsewhere who claim: Auschwitz + Dresden = 0. But while courts are free to make assessments of relative gravity, as did the *Einsatzgruppen* judges, this is a decision that may be better left to other forums. Such determinations require the wisdom that comes from political rather than judicial assessments.

---

[16] *United States of America* v *Ohlendorf* et al. (*'Einsatzgruppen* case') (1948) 4 TWC 411 (United States Military Tribunal), at p. 467.

THE INTRACTABLE CHALLENGE OF
BALANCED PROSECUTIONS

Those who espouse the victors' justice critique of Nuremberg and Tokyo might turn their attention to describing what balanced justice at the end of the Second World War ought to have looked like. Would the victors' justice stigma be removed if there had been a trial of twenty-four American leaders, and twenty-four British leaders, and twenty-four Soviet leaders, along with the twenty-four Nazi defendants? If not twenty-four, how many? How big a sample, how much symbolism, is required to beat back the charge of victors' justice? This is not a question that lawyers or judges can answer. It is a matter for determination at the political level.

The Prosecutor of the International Criminal Tribunal for Rwanda has been frequently taken to task for his apparent refusal to launch trials for atrocities perpetrated by the Rwandese Patriotic Army forces during and after the 1994 genocide. Different arguments are advanced. One contention is that the Tribunal will not fulfil its mission of transitional justice, including reconciliation between the two ethnic groups of the Rwanda conflict, until both sides are brought to justice. Another holds that the alleged massacres committed by Tutsi troops as they fought for power against the genocidal regime in Rwanda are just as evil and deserving of prosecution as the crimes the Tutsi were fighting to stop. The first theory earns support among well-meaning but somewhat naive enthusiasts for transitional justice. They seem to operate more on the basis of the personal intuitions of Western intellectuals and activists than hard, empirical evidence. The second finds its constituency among revisionists and deniers with their own political agenda, be it in Rwanda or Germany.

That even-handed prosecution of both sides—whatever that might look like—is important or necessary for reconciliation is an interesting hypothesis but no more than that. Do the wounds left by massive crimes such as the genocides in Nazi-occupied Europe or Rwanda heal better if the victims or those who liberate them acknowledge a part in the wrongdoing? It does not seem verifiable that where both sides are not prosecuted, justice cannot be done, or that its purported benefits in terms of reconciliation are diminished. The Nuremberg trial probably contributed to a shared narrative, one common to victor and vanquished alike, that enhanced the building of a democratic, pluralist, and largely peaceful modern Europe. A Nuremberg-like trial of the victors might well have done more harm than good in terms of reconciliation, acknowledgement of the truth, and justice for the victims.

The debates continue. Such challenges are inherent in international prosecution, which is both selective and political by nature. There is no solution that relies exclusively on judicial standards. For these reasons, justice in such areas cannot be the preserve of the courts, in the way that it is at the domestic level. Inevitably, it is a mixture of the judicial and the political. The challenge for those involved in the judicial wing of this process is to ensure the greatest legitimacy without at the same time encouraging the myth that what they are doing is devoid of a political dimension.

4

THE GENOCIDE MYSTIQUE

'When *I* use a word, it means just what I choose it to mean—neither more nor less', said Humpty Dumpty.

'The question is whether you *can* make words mean so many different things', said Alice.

Lewis Carroll, *Through the Looking Glass*, Ch. 6

In January 2011, as political violence in Abidjan took scores of lives, the permanent representative of Côte d'Ivoire to the United Nations warned of imminent genocide. Newsrooms around the world chattered about the provocative allegation and soon the ambassador was featured on the front pages of the major international media. Journalists called upon academic experts qua pundits, asking for informed comments on whether there was a genuine threat of genocide. Like physicians in a hospital emergency room who are afraid to turn away a notorious hypochondriac 'just in case this time the illness really is serious', there was a reluctance to dismiss the claim as frivolous. After all, isn't political violence coupled with signs of ethnic or tribal hatred a tell-tale indicator of genocide, a 'precursor', to use the preferred jargon? Well, yes. Except that such warning signs of genocide can be found practically everywhere there is political tension and conflict. Sounding the alarm every time a few dozen people are massacred in the course of a political conflict is like a doctor sending for a battery of sophisticated tests every time a patient sneezes. But as Côte d'Ivoire's diplomat learned, if he didn't already know it, invoking the spectre of genocide is certainly an effective way to get attention.

Months earlier, there had been another spectacular example of the ability of a genocide charge to stir debate and excite the media. A consultant to the United Nations Office of the High Commissioner for Human Rights had prepared a draft report on atrocities committed in the Democratic Republic of the Congo over the best part of a decade that began in 1995.

The report described the terrible ethnic violence that has afflicted the eastern region of the country, and particularly the Kivu provinces. Much of this was the aftermath of the Rwandan genocide. The thrust of the report was to show a pattern of terrible crimes perpetrated by the many participants in the conflict, including forces backed by the current Rwandan government. The report was fast and loose on the specifics, describing in detail many distinct incidents but then extrapolating a pattern of relatively small episodes into mind-boggling numbers whereby hundreds of measurable casualties soon re-emerged as hundreds of thousands and even millions.

It also considered the legal ramifications. Certainly many of the atrocities amounted to war crimes and crimes against humanity, using well-accepted definitions and established judicial precedents. These were uncontroversial observations, but hardly the stuff to excite journalists, who have long documented the sad tale of atrocities in the region. A conclusion that war crimes had been committed systematically over many years in the Democratic Republic of the Congo would have been largely ignored by international media, who have heard this all many times before. The same applies to policy-makers in governments and at United Nations headquarters in New York.

To make sure that the report didn't remain an obscure footnote, the magic word, genocide, was added to spice up the charges.

Several incidents listed in this report, if investigated and judicially proven, point to circumstances and facts from which a court could infer the intention to destroy the Hutu ethnic group in the DRC in part, if these were established beyond all reasonable doubt. The scale of the crimes and the large number of victims, probably several tens of thousands, all nationalities combined, are illustrated by the numerous incidents listed in the report (104 in all). The extensive use of edged weapons (primarily hammers) and the apparently systematic nature of the massacres of survivors after the camps had been taken suggests that the numerous deaths cannot be attributed to the hazards of war or seen as equating to collateral damage. The majority of the victims were children, women, elderly people and the sick, who were often undernourished and posed no threat to the attacking forces. Numerous serious attacks on the physical or mental integrity of members of the group were also committed, with a very high number of Hutus shot, raped, burnt or beaten. If proven, the incidents' revelation of what appears to be the systematic, methodological and premeditated nature of the attacks listed against the Hutus is also marked: these attacks took place in each location where refugees had allegedly been screened by the AFDL/APR over a vast area of the country. The pursuit lasted for months, and on occasion, the humanitarian assistance intended for them was allegedly deliberately blocked, particularly in the Orientale province, thus depriving them of resources essential to their survival. Thus the apparent systematic and widespread attacks described in this report reveal a number of inculpatory elements that, if proven before a competent court, could be characterized as crimes of genocide.[1]

In reality, these observations might describe scores of conflicts in various parts of the world: ethnic violence, killing of civilians, victimization of women and children, blocking of humanitarian assistance. Of course, the report was not saying this actually amounted to genocide, merely that it 'could' be. The claim would have to be 'investigated and judicially proven'. Then, a court might be able to 'infer' the criminal intent, if 'established beyond all reasonable doubt'. It was like seeing a child with a black eye and then speculating that it might result from parental neglect or abuse. There was an added sting in the draft report: the suggestion that Rwandan government troops and their allies were responsible suggested that the victims of an unchallenged genocide—that of the Rwandan Tutsi in 1994—were guilty of the same crime themselves.

Prior to its release to the public, there was much quarrelling in the High Commissioner's office about the wisdom of including the genocide allegation in the report. Concerned that cooler heads might remove the provocative reference when the report was published, a partisan of the genocide thesis opted for a pre-emptive strike. The draft was leaked to the French newspaper *Le Monde*, some of whose readers might constitute a receptive audience for the charge that the Kigali regime was itself a villain. The High Commissioner was pushed into a corner. If she removed the references to genocide, it would look as if she had bowed to pressure from the Rwandan government, which was understandably outraged. Finally, several paragraphs were added to the report that toned down but did not completely eliminate the genocide charges. Like Côte d'Ivoire's ambassador to the United Nations, with the frivolous warning of genocide in Abidjan, the consultant and his allies within the Office of the High Commissioner had succeeded in giving a dramatic buzz to what was really a rather pedestrian analysis of already well-known and well-documented events.

It was not the first time that a charge of genocide had been used to humiliate those who had themselves once been the victims of the crime. In 1982, when Israeli armed forces sealed off two Palestinian refugee camps located in Beirut so that racist extremists could massacre the inhabitants of Sabra and Shatilla, the United Nations General Assembly labelled the crime genocide. More recently, there were charges, although nothing as substantial as a General Assembly resolution, alleging that Israel had

---

[1] Report of the Mapping Exercise documenting the most serious violations of human rights and international humanitarian law committed within the territory of the Democratic Republic of the Congo between March 1993 and June 2003, August 2010, para. 31 (unofficial translation from the French, references omitted).

committed genocide during the war in Gaza in late 2008 and early 2009, which is known as 'Operation Cast Lead'. The genocide definition is hardly applicable to either situation, but the accusation has great demagogic effect. Perhaps it is thought to convey a sense of shame or chastisement that may deter Israeli Jews and Rwandan Tutsi from violations of human rights and the laws of armed conflict.

Another contemporary manifestation of this phenomenon is the charge directed at the Sudanese government for its handling of the civil war in Darfur. The claim grew legs in late 2004 when the Bush administration, including the President himself, raised the stakes by suggesting that the Khartoum government was responsible for genocide in the suppression of secessionist movements within Darfur province. It was election time in the United States, and this devastating accusation against Islamic Sudan resonated with the Christian right in the United States as well as with other constituencies. A blue-ribbon panel of United Nations experts, chaired by the eminent jurist Antonio Cassese, quickly concluded that genocide was not the right word. The charges against the Sudanese regime and its militia should be described as crimes against humanity and war crimes, it said. But that did not deter the United States and many NGOs based in that country. They continued to speak of genocide in Darfur. Eventually, the Prosecutor of the International Criminal Court became afflicted with the same syndrome. He insisted on charging the President of Sudan with genocide, arguing as late as 2009 and 2010 that this was an ongoing crime, despite regular United Nations reports confirming that the civil war had long abated and that targeted killings of civilians could be counted in the tens or perhaps hundreds, at most.

In 2008 former president Jimmy Carter visited Darfur as part of a fact-finding delegation of elder statesmen and international personalities. Carter, by then in his eighties, rather bravely got into a shoving match with Sudanese soldiers. There could be no doubt about the seriousness he attached to the ongoing human rights crisis in Darfur. At one point, he answered a journalist's question about genocide by saying that this was not the right term, and that crimes against humanity was the more accurate nomenclature. Soon Carter was being blasted in the neo-conservative press for trivializing the 'genocide' in Darfur. But a few days later when the President of the United States, George Bush, opposed a congressional resolution condemning the genocide of the Armenians, the usually shrill voices of the right-wing media were silent.

The word 'genocide' itself has a strange, mysterious effect. For victims, it presents itself as a badge of honour, the only adequate way to describe their suffering or that of their ancestors. Those who question whether the word is appropriate in given circumstances are sometimes dismissed as 'deniers'. That term was first used in the 1960s to describe anti-Semitic ideologues who argued that the Holocaust did not take place, or who grossly distorted the number of victims, or in other ways attempted to trivialize the scope of the Nazi crimes against the Jewish people. But the concept has spread to other 'genocides', where neither the facts nor the law are as clear. Countries such as Switzerland have legislation that threatens prosecution for denying 'genocide' in general, wherever it may take place. The European Union has a framework directive, which is in effect an instruction to adopt domestic legislation, requiring enactments to repress the crime of:

denying or grossly trivializing crimes of genocide, crimes against humanity and war crimes...directed against a group of persons or a member of such a group defined by reference to race, colour, religion, descent or national or ethnic origin when the conduct is carried out in a manner likely to incite to violence or hatred against such a group or a member of such a group.

Repulsive as some manifestations of this phenomenon may be, the unintended but likely consequence may be to stifle debate and discussion about historical and contemporary events and their legal designation.

THE RHETORICAL POWER OF THE G-WORD

The word 'genocide' entered the language in the mid-1940s. It had been devised to describe Nazi atrocities, specifically the attempted destruction of the Jews of Europe. By 1948 it had a widely accepted legal definition, set out in article II of the Convention on the Prevention and Punishment of the Crime of Genocide:

...any of the following acts committed with intent to destroy, in whole or in part, a national, ethnical, racial or religious group, as such:
  (a) Killing members of the group;
  (b) Causing serious bodily or mental harm to members of the group;
  (c) Deliberately inflicting on the group conditions of life calculated to bring about its physical destruction in whole or in part;
  (d) Imposing measures intended to prevent births within the group;
  (e) Forcibly transferring children of the group to another group.

The Convention was adopted in Paris on 9 December 1948 at the third session of the United Nations General Assembly. It was the result of lengthy negotiations within United Nations bodies. The Convention entered into force slightly more than two years later, on 12 January 1951, after obtaining the requisite twenty ratifications. But despite its importance in the general scheme of international human rights treaties, and a willingness to accept many of its provisions as declaratory of customary international law, it still only has about 140 States Parties, a comparatively low number by contrast with other human rights treaties. Many of those states that are still not parties were formerly colonies, and probably their absence from the list is explained by the fact that they have never bothered to ratify some pre-independence treaties. There is nothing to suggest that the fifty-odd states that are not parties to the Genocide Convention have any significant disagreement with its provisions. Many of those who are not parties to the 1948 Convention have ratified the Rome Statute of the International Criminal Court. It contains an identical definition of the crime of genocide to that of the 1948 Convention.

Genocide is, first and foremost, a legal concept. Like many other terms—murder, rape, theft—it is also used in other contexts and by other disciplines, where the meaning may vary somewhat from that of criminal law. Some historians and sociologists employ the term genocide to describe a range of atrocities involving killing large numbers of people. But even at the legal level, it is imprecise to speak of a single, universally recognized meaning of genocide. Although the text of article II of the Convention is generally accepted, like most legal definitions its language is subject to various interpretations. Important controversies remain about the scope of the concept even within the framework of what is a concise and carefully worded definition. The crime of genocide has been incorporated within the national legal systems of many countries, where domestic legislators have imposed their own views on the term, some of them varying slightly or even considerably from the established international definition. As a result, even in law, it is correct to speak of several definitions or interpretations of the concept of genocide.

The term itself was invented by a lawyer, Raphael Lemkin. A Polish Jew, Lemkin found asylum from the Nazis in the United States. Most of his family perished during the Holocaust. Lemkin intended to fill a gap in international law as the discipline then stood in the final days of the Second World War. Even before leaving Poland in 1939 Lemkin had been engaged at an international level in attempts to codify new categories of international crimes involving atrocities committed against vulnerable civilians and groups. Lemkin's famous proposal, contained in a chapter entitled 'Genocide' in his 1944 book *Axis Rule in Occupied Europe*, called for the 'prohibition of genocide in war and peace'. Lemkin insisted upon the relationship between genocide and the growing interest in the protection of peoples and minorities that had been manifested in several treaties and declarations adopted following the First World War. He noted the need to

revisit international legal instruments, pointing out particularly the inad-
equacies of the Regulations annexed to the fourth Hague Convention of
1907, which were 'silent regarding the preservation of the integrity of a
people'. According to Lemkin:

the definition of genocide in the Hague Regulations thus amended should consist
of two essential parts: in the first should be included every action infringing upon
the life, liberty, health, corporal integrity, economic existence, and the honour
of the inhabitants when committed because they belong to a national, religious,
or racial group; and in the second, every policy aiming at the destruction or the
aggrandizement of one of such groups to the prejudice or detriment of another.[2]

Lemkin's engagement prompted the United Nations General Assembly
to recognize genocide as an international crime in December 1946 (this
is discussed in Chapter 2, 'Nullum Crimen Sine Lege'). He actively participated in the negotiations leading to adoption of the 1948 Convention on
the Prevention and Punishment of the Crime of Genocide. Following the
Convention's adoption, Lemkin campaigned ceaselessly for its ratification
until his death, in 1959. The definition in the Convention was considerably
narrower than he probably would have liked, particularly because of its
exclusion of various acts of persecution of national minorities falling short
of outright physical extermination. At the same time, Lemkin felt strongly
that the protected groups contemplated by the Convention should remain
confined to those of a national, ethnic, racial, or religious nature.

Genocide is closely related to another category of international law,
crimes against humanity. Whereas article II of the Convention protects
four enumerated groups, crimes against humanity contemplates 'any identifiable group or collectivity on political, racial, national, ethnic, cultural,
religious, gender...or other grounds that are universally recognized as
impermissible under international law', according to the definition in
the Rome Statute of the International Criminal Court. Moreover, genocide is essentially confined to the physical destruction or extermination
of a group, as contrasted with crimes against humanity which, according
to article 7 of the Rome Statute, extend to various forms of 'persecution',
meaning 'the intentional and severe deprivation of fundamental rights contrary to international law'. Many of the punishable acts that Lemkin had
hoped to include in the definition of genocide but that were excluded from
the Convention are comprised within crimes against humanity.

---

[2] Raphael Lemkin, *Axis Rule in Occupied Europe: Laws of Occupation, Analysis of Government,
Proposals for Redress*, Washington, DC: Carnegie Endowment for World Peace, 1944, at pp. 90–93.
On Lemkin, see: William Korey, *An Epitaph for Raphael Lemkin*, New York: Jacob Blaustein Institute
for the Advancement of Human Rights, 2001; John Cooper, *Raphael Lemkin and the Struggle for the
Genocide Convention*, Basingstoke: Palgrave Macmillan, 2008.

The narrowness of the definition has been a source of great frustration over the years, and there have been frequent calls for amendment. Nevertheless, when presented with the ideal occasion to make the long-awaited changes to the definition, participants at the Rome Conference on the International Criminal Court, in 1998, left the 1948 text intact. There were a few modest suggestions, but these did not gain any traction during the negotiations. When Cuba proposed that it be expanded to include social and political groups, one by one the delegates at the Rome Conference rose to express their satisfaction with the fifty-year-old text of the Convention and the reluctance of their governments to consider any amendment whatsoever. This was not because international lawmakers were in a particularly conservative mood. At the very moment they chose to preserve unchanged the historic definition of genocide, radical innovations were being made to the definitions of the other two categories of international atrocity, crimes against humanity, and war crimes.

The relatively restrictive definition of genocide has also prompted some individual experiments, especially in the academic literature of the social sciences and humanities. Various scholars advance a definition they call 'my own', as if the English language (and other languages) permits such indulgence. It is striking that the authoritative *Oxford English Dictionary* offers a single definition. It is virtually identical to the text of article II of the 1948 Convention: 'The (attempted) deliberate extermination of an ethnic or national group.'

GENOCIDE AND CRIMES AGAINST HUMANITY

The legal concept of genocide was forged in the crucible of post-Second World War efforts to prosecute Nazi atrocities. Its development took place in conjunction with that of other international crimes, especially crimes against humanity, with which it bears a close but complex relationship. The development and history of genocide as a legal concept cannot be properly understood without considering the parallel existence of crimes against humanity.

Initially, the Allies had only planned to prosecute the Nazis for committing 'war crimes', in a manner similar to what had been proposed at the end of the First World War. They set up a body that was accordingly named the United Nations War Crimes Commission. Revelations about the scale and depravity of the behaviour of the Nazis soon compelled a more ambitious and innovative scheme. As American Prosecutor Robert Jackson later explained, in his opening address at the Nuremberg trial, '[t]he wrongs which we seek to condemn and punish have been so calculated, so malignant and so devastating, that civilization cannot tolerate their being ignored because it cannot survive their being repeated'.

The immediate preparations for the Nuremberg trial were made at the London Conference, which convened over several weeks from mid-June to early August 1945. There were two contenders for the legal characterization of the atrocities committed against civilian populations, including those perpetrated against German nationals: genocide and crimes against humanity. The definitions of both genocide and crimes against humanity were still, at this stage, somewhat embryonic and unsettled. As noted above, genocide had been introduced by Lemkin in his famous book in November 1944. In a planning memorandum, Robert Jackson employed the word 'genocide'. It was evident that the neologism had already entered the language. It was also used in the indictment and by the prosecutors in their speeches during the trial. Nevertheless, the negotiators at the London Conference opted for the term 'crimes against humanity' in the Charter of the International Military Tribunal. 'Crimes against humanity' was proposed by Robert Jackson as a more eloquent term for what the negotiators at the London Conference had been calling 'atrocities, persecutions and deportations'. Unlike the freshly minted term 'genocide', 'crimes against humanity' had been part of the language for nearly two centuries, albeit in a colloquial rather than a legal sense (see the discussion about the history of the term in Chapter 2, *Nullum Crimen Sine Lege*). The crime against humanity of extermination was probably viewed at the time as a synonym for genocide. Lemkin himself later wrote that '[t]he evidence produced at the Nuremberg trial gave full support to the concept of genocide'.[3]

Crimes against humanity, as defined at Nuremberg, were subject to a very serious limitation. They were confined to atrocities committed in association with aggressive war. This was quite intentional on the part of those who drafted the legal provisions governing prosecutions, especially the four great powers, the United States, the United Kingdom, France, and the Soviet Union. Indeed, extending international law from classic war crimes involving battlefield offences and various forms of attacks upon civilians in an occupied territory so that it would also cover atrocities perpetrated by a government against its own civilian population was not only novel and unprecedented, it was also threatening to the very states who were organizing the prosecution. The distinctions were candidly set out by

---

[3] Raphael Lemkin, 'Genocide as a Crime in International Law' (1947) 41 *American Journal of International Law* 145, at p. 147.

the head of the United States delegation, Robert Jackson, during a session of the London Conference on 23 July 1945:

It has been a general principle of foreign policy of our Government from time immemorial that the internal affairs of another government are not ordinarily our business; that is to say, the way Germany treats its inhabitants, or any other country treats its inhabitants is not our affair any more than it is the affair of some other government to interpose itself in our problems. The reason that this program of extermination of Jews and destruction of the rights of minorities becomes an international concern is this: it was a part of a plan for making an illegal war. Unless we have a war connection as a basis for reaching them, I would think we have no basis for dealing with atrocities. They were a part of the preparation for war or for the conduct of the war in so far as they occurred inside of Germany and that makes them our concern.[4]

Speaking of the proposed crime of 'atrocities, persecutions, and deportations on political, racial or religious grounds', which would shortly be renamed crimes against humanity, Justice Jackson indicated the source of the preoccupations of his government:

[O]rdinarily we do not consider that the acts of a government toward its own citizens warrant our interference. *We have some regrettable circumstances at times in our own country in which minorities are unfairly treated.* We think it is justifiable that we interfere or attempt to bring retribution to individuals or to states only because the concentration camps and the deportations were in pursuance of a common plan or enterprise of making an unjust or illegal war in which we became involved. We see no other basis on which we are justified in reaching the atrocities which were committed inside Germany, under German law, or even in violation of German law, by authorities of the German state.[5]

There is little doubt that the British, the French, and the Soviets had similar concerns. As a result, the definition of crimes against humanity in article VI(c) of the Charter of the International Military Tribunal requires that atrocities be committed 'in furtherance of or in connection with any crime within the jurisdiction of the International Tribunal'. The four powers were reasonably confident that by attaching such a condition to crimes against humanity, they could convict the Germans without exposing themselves to liability under international law. This vision of crimes against humanity was confirmed in the final judgment. The International Military Tribunal made a distinction between prewar persecution of German Jews, which it characterized as 'severe and repressive', and German policy during the

---

[4] 'Minutes of Conference Session of 23 July 1945', in *Report of Robert H. Jackson, United States Representative to the International Conference on Military* Trials, Washington, DC: US Government Printing Office, 1949, at p. 331.

[5] Ibid., p. 333 (my emphasis).

war itself, for which convictions were registered. Although the judgment frequently referred to events during the 1930s, none of the accused was found guilty of an act perpetrated prior to 1 September 1939, the day the war broke out.

Following the judgment at Nuremberg, there was considerable outrage about the restriction upon the concept of crimes against humanity that the London Conference had imposed and that the Nuremberg judgment had confirmed. A member of the Nuremberg prosecution team, Henry King, later described meeting Raphael Lemkin in the lobby of the Grand Hotel in Nuremberg in October 1946, a few days after the International Military Tribunal completed its work:

When I saw him at Nuremberg, Lemkin was very upset. He was concerned that the decision of the International Military Tribunal (IMT)—the Nuremberg Court—did not go far enough in dealing with genocidal actions. This was because the IMT limited its judgment to wartime genocide and did not include peacetime genocide. At that time, Lemkin was very focussed on pushing his points. After he had buttonholed me several times, I had to tell him that I was powerless to do anything about the limitation in the Court's judgment.[6]

Lemkin rushed back from Nuremberg to New York, where the United Nations General Assembly was holding its first session. On his prompting, India, Cuba, and Panama proposed a resolution that they said would address a shortcoming in the Nuremberg trial by which acts committed prior to the war were left unpunished. This launched a process that concluded two years later with the adoption of the Convention on the Prevention and Punishment of the Crime of Genocide. Proposals to make reference to crimes against humanity as a related concept, or as some kind of broader umbrella under which the crime of genocide was situated, were rejected by the drafters of the Convention so as not to create any confusion about the fact that genocide could be committed in time of peace as well as in wartime. This could not be said with any certainty about crimes against humanity at the time precisely because of the Nuremberg precedent.

The acknowledgement of genocide as an international crime by the General Assembly of the United Nations in 1946, and its codification in the 1948 Convention, can be understood as a reaction to the narrow approach to crimes against humanity in the Nuremberg judgment of the International Military Tribunal. It was Nuremberg's failure to recognize the international criminality of atrocities committed in peacetime that

---

[6] Henry T. King Jr, 'Origins of the Genocide Convention' (2008) 40 *Case Western Reserve Journal of International Law* 13, at p. 13.

generated the first initiatives at recognizing and defining the crime of
genocide. Had Nuremberg affirmed the reach of international criminal law
into peacetime atrocities, the Genocide Convention might never have been
adopted. Lemkin himself, whose personal role cannot be underestimated,
might well have turned his attention to other priorities, and not hastened
to New York in an effort to repair the defects in the Nuremberg judgment.
The term 'genocide' might then have become a popular or colloquial label
used by journalists, historians, and social scientists but one absent from
legal discourse.

The major powers, who had imposed the wartime limitation or nexus
on crimes against humanity when they crafted the legal framework of the
Nuremberg trial, were hardly going to retreat on this point a few years
later when the Genocide Convention was being negotiated. A mere ter-
minological change, from crimes against humanity to genocide, could
not then result in agreement by which such crimes could be punishable in
peacetime as well as in wartime. Obviously, the only way to secure consensus on peacetime genocide was to narrow the concept from the much
broader notion of crimes against humanity, which includes acts of persecution directed against a range of groups. From this point on, we can no
longer speak of genocide and crimes against humanity being largely syn-
onymous. Henceforth, genocide was defined considerably more narrowly
than crimes against humanity, as acts directed against a limited enumeration of protected groups that consisted of physical destruction or extermination. Nevertheless, unlike crimes against humanity it required no
connection with armed conflict.

In the decades that followed Nuremberg, international criminal law
presented a woefully incomplete normative framework. On the one hand,
there was the Genocide Convention with its relatively robust obligations
to which states could be bound by treaty. Under article IX, they were subject to the International Court of Justice for breaches of the Convention.
The crime could be committed in time of peace as well as in wartime. But
genocide was defined very narrowly, restricted to four categories of groups
and to a limited range of punishable acts. In effect, the intentional extermination of the group in question was required. On the other hand were
crimes against humanity. They were much broader in scope, covering 'any
civilian population' as well as a range of behaviour delineated with vague
terms like 'persecution' and 'inhumane acts'. But crimes against humanity
had no treaty basis. Any attempt at prosecution or litigation would rest
on the less certain foundation of customary international law. Even more
troublesome, there was great doubt as to whether crimes against humanity
could be prosecuted when perpetrated in peacetime.

By the 1990s, with the adoption of the Rome Statute, the huge impunity gap was filled as the system became more comprehensive and coherent. Essentially, this flowed from the recognition that crimes against humanity could be committed in peacetime. International lawmakers chose to expand crimes against humanity but leave genocide alone. Genocide remained important in a rhetorical sense, but its legal significance diminished as crimes against humanity filled the void.

THE EXCLUSION OF POLITICAL GROUPS

The definition of genocide in the 1948 Convention applies to 'national, ethnical, racial and religious groups'. The concept is broadly analogous to what, at the time the Convention was adopted, were considered by international law as 'national minorities'. This was clearly the perspective of Raphael Lemkin and one of the other international experts who assisted the United Nations in preparing the first draft of the Convention, Vespasian Pella. In the initial draft of General Assembly Resolution 96(I), proposed in late 1946 and apparently drafted by Lemkin himself, the concept of genocide was meant to apply to 'national, racial, ethnical or religious groups'. The terminology is essentially identical to what appears in the final version of the Convention. It is the formulation that has had wide acceptance ever since it was adopted in 1948. But the final text of the 1946 resolution spoke of genocide as a crime 'committed on religious, racial, political or any other grounds'. Nothing in the records of the General Assembly indicates why the words 'political or any other' were added.

It has become a bit of an urban legend that political groups were excluded from the Convention at the behest of the Soviet Union. The Soviets purportedly schemed to exclude political groups out of unease that massacres of the Kulaks, purges of their regime's opponents, and wartime executions like the Katyń massacre might fall within the scope of genocide. The drafting history shows a far more complex debate on this subject, and a fairly large consensus for exclusion of political groups. The United States, for example, ostensibly switched its position in a spirit of compromise. Actually, it had long planned to drop political groups from the Convention, and had privately reassured Lemkin of this. As for the Soviets, they and their allies in Eastern and Central Europe actually abstained in the vote to remove political groups from the Convention. The resolution by which political groups were excluded was adopted by a large majority.

We do not have the same difficulty at all with national, ethnic, racial, and religious groups. Their identification is not without its own problems, of course. The distinction between the definition of the group and the motive for its destruction was present throughout the negotiations of the Genocide Convention. One of the early drafts, for example, referred to destruction of 'a national, racial, religious or political group, on grounds of the national or racial origin, religious belief, or political opinion of its members'. Critics of this formulation felt that reference to the motive of the destruction would make prosecutions too difficult. Because some countries were reluctant to part with the concept, an enigmatic compromise was reached and the words 'as such' were inserted. We can conceive of the destruction of an ethnic or racial group on political grounds, and often the *génocidaire* will attempt to rationalize racist massacres by claiming that the victims were subversives or rebels, opposed to the regime or to the majority. In Turkey, in 1915, the Ottomans argued (and continue to argue) that the Armenians were dangerous allies of their Russian enemies. The murders and the forced displacements that threatened the survival of the Anatolian Armenians were explained as wartime measures undertaken in the interests of national security. In much the same way, Nazi defendants in war crimes trials have argued that they shipped Jews to Auschwitz out of concerns that they would rise as a fifth column and help the approaching Soviet armies. In one notorious case of a universal jurisdiction prosecution, Canadian courts actually swallowed this argument.[7] But in contrast with such claims, we do not see anything analogous with respect to political groups, that is, a political group massacred on racial grounds.

Although most national legislators have abided by the enumeration of groups in the 1948 Convention, some national laws reflect the view that the prohibition of genocide is about protecting groups in a more general sense. References to political groups can be found in the laws of Bangladesh and Ethiopia, for example. The French genocide provision speaks about groups whose identification is based upon 'arbitrary criteria'. Perhaps the most far-reaching provision is found in the laws of Costa Rica, which describe genocide as 'a national, ethnic, racial, religious, political or trade union group or any identifiable group based on gender, sexual orientation, culture, social status, age, disability or health'. Have they left anything out?

It is often argued that the decision by the drafters to omit political groups from the Genocide Convention was illogical or arbitrary. Why are some groups protected and not others? Isn't it true that political groups have also been victims of terrible atrocities? The argument is compelling but it is not without difficulty. The first is the notion of 'political group', a rather casual formulation whose concrete application raises real problems. The examples of attempted atrocities directed against 'political groups' are

----

[7] *R* v *Finta* [1994] 1 SCR 701.

often in reality cases of killings based upon political grounds. This is not exactly the same thing. In Cambodia, one of the features of the genocide museum at Tuol Sleng is a room filled with eyeglasses, apparently collected from the victims who were deemed 'intellectuals' and therefore hostile to the regime. But the murder of members of a class of individuals who are branded as subversive is not necessarily the destruction of a political group. Intellectuals being what they are, the bespectacled individual victims of the Khmer Rouge probably had a range of political views, and some may even have been sympathetic to the ideology of those who killed them. Such massacres can readily be described as 'political' in a general sense, but they hardly respond to a legal concept of 'political group'. Indeed, most of the discussions on this issue manifest great vagueness about the scope of the term 'political group'.

Underpinning the concept of genocide is the idea that the survival of national, ethnic, racial, and religious groups is not only a right of the victims themselves but also a value of profound importance to humanity as a whole. We view the existence of such groups as being important in and of itself, in much the same way as we lament the disappearance of endangered species and the extinction of plants and animals. There is something enriching about this diversity, of benefit to us all. Certainly, we would not dare suggest that some national, ethnic, racial, and religious groups are illegitimate, or that their disappearance is not to be lamented. Who would say the same thing about political groups? The world would surely be a better place if some political groups were to be totally eliminated. That is not to justify the extermination of their members, of course. But it suggests one component of the difference between political groups and national, ethnic, racial, and religious groups.

Ultimately, this is about a vision of the purpose of the Genocide Convention, and of the concept of genocide more generally. Is the prohibition of genocide aimed at protecting the survival of groups, or is it about addressing what, for want of a better term, can be called racism? Terms like 'racial group' are not defined in the Genocide Convention. But international law provides a useful definition of 'racial discrimination' that goes much beyond 'race'. According to article 1 of the International Convention for the Prevention of All Forms of Racial Discrimination, 'the term "racial discrimination" shall mean any distinction, exclusion, restriction or preference based on race, colour, descent, or national or ethnic origin which has the purpose or effect of nullifying or impairing the recognition, enjoyment or exercise, on an equal footing, of human rights and fundamental freedoms'. The only thing left out, by comparison with the enumeration in the Genocide Convention of 'national, ethnical, racial and religious groups', is religion. Probably that is because when the Convention on Racial Discrimination was adopted, in 1965, it was expected that a companion instrument dealing with religious persecution would soon be concluded. There would be little chance of misunderstanding if an attack on a group designated by religion were labelled racism.

CULTURAL GENOCIDE AND ETHNIC CLEANSING

Initial drafts of the Genocide Convention classified the crime using three headings: physical, biological, and cultural. In the final text, the classification disappeared. But so did any agreement that cultural genocide belonged in the Convention at all. Indeed, votes were taken that confirmed its exclusion altogether. Cultural genocide bears similarities with a concept that today we call 'ethnic cleansing', in that the physical extermination of the group is not required. Nothing in a literal reading of the Convention indicates that such expulsions were explicitly excluded, but this is what the proceedings in the 1948 General Assembly debates reveal. At one point Syria proposed that a sixth paragraph be added to article II. The Syrian amendment read: 'Imposing measures intended to oblige members of a group to abandon their homes in order to escape the threat of subsequent ill-treatment.'[8] Syria clearly had the ethnic cleansing associated with the recent creation of the state of Israel in mind. The amendment was defeated, but not principally because of sympathy with the plight of the Palestinians. Rather, the major powers were uncomfortable that the expulsions of ethnic Germans in central and eastern Europe that they had recently endorsed in the Potsdam agreement might fall within the genocide net. In effect, they were still saying that forced population transfers were not in principle contrary to international law, a position that fortunately seems no longer tenable. The German courts have prosecuted 'ethnic cleansing' as a form of genocide. In *Jorgic* v *Germany* a Chamber of the European Court of Human Rights held that while the prevailing interpretation of genocide excludes ethnic cleansing, there is sufficient support for the idea to prevent a defendant claiming he was being punished for a crime that didn't exist in violation of the principle of legality.

The Convention definition of genocide refers to the 'intent to destroy' without further precision. The five punishable acts that follow consist of a combination of physical, biological, and cultural attacks. For example, the fifth act of genocide in the definition, forcibly transferring children

---

[8] UN Doc. A/C.6/234.

from one group to another, quite evidently does not involve their physical destruction. Rather, the elimination of a group is contemplated by destroying the cultural memory and the national language, through assimilation at a very young age. A literal reading of the definition can therefore support an interpretation whereby the concept of 'intent to destroy' is broad enough to extend to acts of 'ethnic cleansing' or of cultural genocide falling short of physical destruction. This view is supported by some isolated judgments and dissenting opinions.[9] But the *travaux préparatoires* of the Convention make it clear enough that forcible transfer of children was to be the sole exception to the general rule by which cultural genocide was excluded.

OBJECTIVE AND SUBJECTIVE IDENTIFICATION

Eichmann was the first prosecution using a text derived from article II of the Convention. Identification of the victim group did not pose any legal difficulties. Israeli law avoided discussion about the nature of the 'groups' by simply reformulating the Convention's definition of genocide so as to refer to 'crimes against the Jewish people'. Nothing in the trial record suggests that Eichmann ever challenged the fact that the victims of Nazi atrocities were the 'Jewish people'. Judicial debate about the scope of the expression 'national, ethnical, racial and religious' only really began in the 1990s, with the prosecutions before the ad hoc tribunals. Initially the judges at the International Criminal Tribunal for Rwanda did not find this to be very straightforward. They could not decide to which of the four categories the Tutsi victims belonged. They were especially uncomfortable with the adjective 'racial', which since 1948 has fallen somewhat into disfavour as a scientific concept. Invoking some relatively isolated comments by delegates during the drafting of the Convention, they said that what had been meant in article II was to protect all 'stable and permanent' groups. This interpretative expansion of the definition met with little enthusiasm, either from other judges at the tribunals or from academic commentators. Years later, a United Nations Commission of Inquiry nodded in approval and even suggested that the 'stable and permanent' gloss on the convention had been so widely accepted as to become customary international law,[10] but it exaggerated the extent of the authorities. Eventually, judges

---

[9] *Krstić* (IT-98-33-A), Partially Dissenting Opinion of Judge Shahabuddeen, 19 April 2004; *Blagojević* (IT-02-60-T) Judgment, 17 January 2005; *Jorgić* v *Germany* (App. no. 74613/01), Judgment, 12 July 2007, para. 47.

[10] Report of the International Commission of Inquiry on violations of international humanitarian law and human rights law in Darfur, UN Doc. S/2005/60, para. 501.

of the International Criminal Tribunal for Rwanda took judicial notice of the fact that the Tutsi, as well as the Hutu and the Twa, were ethnic groups within Rwanda at the time of the 1994 genocide.[11]

The 'stable and permanent' hypothesis was the result of a search for objective meaning to the nature of the protected groups. But how can any objective meaning for 'racial group' be determined when the term itself is largely abandoned in favour of more nuanced understandings of human diversity (and similarity) resulting from DNA research, for example. The better approach is to focus on the subjective dimension. Generally, it is the perpetrator of genocide who defines the individual victim's status as a member of a group protected by the Convention. The Nazis, for example, had detailed rules establishing who was Jewish and who was not. It made no difference whether the individual, perhaps a non-observant Jew of mixed parentage, denied belonging to the group. Jews did not voluntarily agree to wear the yellow star. As Jean-Paul Sartre wrote: 'Le juif est un homme que les autres hommes tiennent pour juif.'[12]

At the International Criminal Tribunal for Rwanda, judges concluded that the Tutsi were an ethnic group because they were so described on government-issued official identity cards. A Trial Chamber of the International Criminal Tribunal for the former Yugoslavia wrote that:

> the relevant protected group may be identified by means of the subjective criterion of the stigmatization of the group, notably by the perpetrators of the crime, on the basis of its perceived national, ethnical, racial or religious characteristics. In some instances, the victim may perceive himself or herself to belong to the aforesaid group.[13]

And sometimes the victim may not.

A PRETEXT FOR INTERVENTION?

In December 2008 a report entitled *Preventing Genocide* was published by a task force chaired by two former American cabinet ministers, Madeleine K. Albright and William S. Cohen. The task force was sponsored by Washington-based think tanks. The report spoke of the 'unmatched rhetorical power' of the term 'genocide'. In order to capitalize on this, the report proposed that the term be used to cover 'mass atrocities' as well as genocide, avoiding 'legalistic arguments that have repeatedly impeded timely and effective action'. There was a whiff of gunpowder in the proposal,

---

[11] *Kajelijeli* (ICTR-98-44A-T), Judgment, 1 December 2003, para. 241.
[12] Jean-Paul Sartre, *Réflexions sur la question juive*, Paris: Gallimard, 1954, pp. 81–4.
[13] *Brdanin* (T-99-36-T), Judgment, 1 September 2004, para. 683 (references omitted).

which urged military responses to genocidal threats and mooted the idea that where this was not authorized by the Security Council the United States might act on its own.

One feature of the genocide mystique is use of the concept to justify military intervention. In 1999 the term was employed occasionally, and at least once by President Bill Clinton, in order to legitimize the bombing of Serbia despite the fact that there was no blessing from the United Nations Security Council for military action. Following the Kosovo intervention, the Canadian government backed an initiative whose objective was to give an *ex post facto* justification to the use of force outside the framework of the Charter of the United Nations. The International Commission on Intervention and State Sovereignty argued that the use of force in order to prevent genocide was acceptable in violation of the Charter to the extent that the United Nations Security Council was deadlocked. The argument was seductive. How could the world stand by and let genocide take place because of some inconvenient prohibition on the use of force in the Charter, a document adopted more than half a century ago? States that were not friendly to the protection of human rights would veto prompt action, it was argued, with China and Russia being the standard examples (not everyone is aware that the main practitioner of the Security Council veto is the United States). The International Commission proposed a concept that it entitled 'responsibility to protect'. For some, this was nothing more than repackaging the old idea of 'humanitarian intervention'. The 'responsibility to protect' idea gained momentum and, in 2005, it was blessed by the Summit of Heads of State and Government convened on the sixtieth anniversary of the Charter of the United Nations.

The Outcome Document of the 2005 Summit recognized a right to intervene when genocide (as well as crimes against humanity, war crimes, and ethnic cleansing) was being committed, but conditioned this upon approval by the appropriate organs of the United Nations. Enthusiasts for military intervention were disappointed because they had hoped to carve out an exception to the Charter's prohibition on the use of force in situations where genocide was threatened. At the 2010 Review Conference of the International Criminal Court, United States diplomats tried, but without success, to establish a limit on the scope of the crime of aggression whereby acts intended to prevent genocide would not be deemed manifest violations of the Charter of the United Nations. While there is recognition of a duty of collective intervention to prevent genocide, there is little willingness to allow judgments about whether it is actually taking place to be left to individual states or groups that sit outside the structures of the United Nations.

Part of the problem is concern about the tendency to enlarge the scope of the term 'genocide'. Taken narrowly, the imperative for intervention seems hard to dispute. Another Auschwitz could never be countenanced. But politicians use the word 'genocide' loosely, without precision, and do this quite intentionally. When Albright and Cohen speak of genocide, they do not cleave to the strict wording of the Convention, or for that matter the definition in the *Oxford English Dictionary*. Rather, it is an amorphous notion of atrocity, suspiciously well suited to providing a pretext for the use of military force when this appears opportune.

In the aftermath of the Rwandan genocide, there was great determination to avoid the inertia of the United Nations should the events ever recur. Many were enamoured of intervention in Serbia aimed at the prevention of ethnic cleansing in Kosovo. But there was an adjustment to this early enthusiasm for action not authorized by the Charter of the United Nations in 2003, when Iraq was attacked by the United States and the United Kingdom. Fans of the 1999 NATO campaign directed at Serbia lost their stomach for such intervention when they saw its more perverse dimension. In Iraq, human rights concerns were trotted out as a Plan B explanation, once the fraud of the weapons of mass destruction allegations became clear. After all, hadn't Saddam Hussain committed genocide against the Kurds, Bush argued? Didn't this make invasion a moral imperative anyway, said Blair? Few were convinced. The consequence was that when the United Nations came to codify the notion of responsibility to protect in 2005, any hint that the use of force might be justified on humanitarian grounds in the absence of Security Council authorization was defeated. Still, the idea returns again and again, as it did in the efforts of the United States at the Kampala Conference.

A PEREMPTORY NORM (*JUS COGENS*)

Sometimes, the arguments are coiffed in a potent Latin expression, *jus cogens*. In English, the translation is 'peremptory norm'. There is general agreement that the prohibition of genocide is a norm of *jus cogens*. Like many domestic legal regimes, international law is made up of both codified law, in the form of treaties, and judge-made law, which consists of rules developed by the courts that are derived from the consistent practice of states. This is generally referred to as 'customary international law'. As a rule, the uncodified legal norm can always be overridden by a written text. In effect, legislators may decide to leave customary law alone or to change it. When they do, the new written rule prevails. But this is not the case with *jus cogens*, a norm that no treaty or convention can displace.

How this works in practice is a bit mysterious. Although the International Court of Justice used the term '*jus cogens*' on a couple of occasions in 2006 and 2007, it is not at all clear what the purpose or legal effect of the concept actually may be. Nobody has come up with a good example of a treaty or convention that runs counter to the prohibition of genocide, and where the *jus cogens* norm respecting genocide could outrank the treaty. It is a theoretical notion, with little or nothing in the way of realistic examples of its operation. Still, *jus cogens* seems to have some occult power, a bit like the golden dust that emanates from the magic wand of a fairy godmother. Thus, because the prohibition of genocide is a *jus cogens* principle, some contend that the Charter of the United Nations may be set aside if it appears to stand in the way of effective intervention.

The argument goes back to Raphael Lemkin, who said this flowed from recognition by the United Nations of genocide as an international crime in a resolution adopted by the General Assembly two years before the Convention was finalized: 'By declaring genocide a crime under international law and by making it a problem of international concern, the right of intervention on behalf of minorities slated for destruction has been established. This principle is already accepted by the UN and does not need any specific confirmation by treaty.'[14] The difficulty here is that intervention to prevent genocide cannot be unilateral. The idea that such intervention can somehow take place in breach of the provisions of the Charter of the United Nations, which subjects it to Security Council permission, is hard to sustain. After all, the resolution to which Lemkin referred and the 1948 Convention that resulted from it were both adopted by United Nations organs acting within the framework of the Charter. How could they possibly have been intended to contradict, amend, or override the Charter?

It cannot be gainsaid that there will be situations of 'mass atrocity', if not genocide, that call out for decisive international action, perhaps up to and including the use of force, but where there is not sufficient unanimity for action within the Security Council. Nourished by *jus cogens*, it is argued that human suffering and the danger that the crime of crimes will be committed means the rules of the Charter of the United Nations cannot stand in the way of the use of force. The scenarios used as examples are generally hypothetical and ultimately unrealistic. When the Security Council declined to intervene in Rwanda in 1994, the problem was not deadlock or the use of the veto by one of the five permanent members. Rather, this was a matter of political will for which few members of the Security Council at the

---

[14] Raphael Lemkin, 'Genocide as a Crime Under International Law' (1947) 41 *American Journal of International Law* 145.

time, and none of the permanent members, are without blame. Sometimes, as in Kosovo in 1999, the threat of intervention without a Security Council resolution is used to avoid diplomatic obstacles and to short-circuit negotiations. Russia insisted that attempts at peaceful solution of the Kosovo debacle be pursued. Frustrated by a failure to get their way in negotiations, some states with powerful armies turned their backs on diplomacy and claimed they were entitled to act anyway, because genocide was threatening. In 1999 the matter of intervention was never put to a vote in the Security Council. In 2003 the United States and the United Kingdom first sought a vote to bless military action in Iraq, but when they could not get the necessary majority they claimed they did not need one.

Could a situation arise where genocide takes place but the Security Council refuses to budge, probably because the key strategic interests of one of its permanent members leads to the threat or the actual use of the veto? Of course this is possible. What needs to be understood is that there is a conflict of norms, and that the imperative of preventing genocide runs headlong into the prohibition on the use of force without Security Council consent. In treaty law, the answer is not very complicated. The Charter of the United Nations must prevail. But is this simply an inconvenient technical matter, to be resolved by claiming that the *jus cogens* prohibition of genocide in effect trumps the Charter's limits on the use of force? The prohibition of the use of force to settle disputes is a fundamental value of the international community. Arguably, it too is *jus cogens*, a norm as potent and essential to the contemporary world order as the protection of the fundamental human rights of minorities from extermination.

Since 1945 the prohibition on the use of force has contributed to the effective prevention of world wars, and made the second half of the twentieth century considerably more peaceful than the first. Admittedly there have been terrible conflicts in the six decades since 1945, but nothing to compare with the two conflagrations that engulfed the planet in the first half of the twentieth century. Cherif Bassiouni has estimated the deaths attributable to armed conflict in the years since 1945 at about 92 million. That means an average of approximately 1.4 million every year or slightly less than 4,000 per day. It is an extraordinary and terrifying figure, a rather cold statistic that conceals within it imponderable personal tragedies at the individual level. But juxtapose the numbers with the Second World War, when somewhere between 62 to 78 million people perished in slightly fewer than six years, with most of the killing concentrated in four years. That's an average of 10 to 13 million per annum, or between 28,000 and 35,000 *every single day*. When the two world wars are taken together, the total number of deaths is somewhere between 78 and 94 million, roughly equivalent to the figure for the entire period since 1945. The comparison is even more dramatic when note is taken of the world population in the first half of the twentieth century of around 2 billion, compared with seven million in 2011. In other words, the world is a far, far safer place today than it was before the United Nations was established. The Charter's prohibition on the use of force without Security Council approval deserves some of the credit for this. It should not be discarded lightly.

DISAPPOINTED VICTIMS

There was much anguish when the International Court of Justice, applying article II of the Convention in the *Bosnia* v *Serbia* case, dismissed attempts to broaden the definition of genocide by interpreting the words 'to destroy' so as to encompass the notion of 'ethnic cleansing'. The Court said that 'ethnic cleansing', which it described as the 'deportation or displacement of the members of a group, even if effected by force', was not necessarily equivalent to destruction of that group, and that destruction was not an automatic consequence of such displacement.[15] The Court was hardly alone in its relatively conservative approach to interpreting the definition. There had been similar manifestations of this resistance to broadening the scope of the definition of genocide in judgments of the International Criminal Tribunal and in the initiatives of the Prosecutor. It appears that there was debate within the Office of the Prosecutor itself as to whether 'genocide' was the appropriate legal term to characterize atrocities widely described as 'ethnic cleansing', as the former press officer of the tribunal, Florence Hartmann, explained in her indiscreet memoir.[16]

Just as the crime of genocide emerged in international law as a reaction to the limitations on crimes against humanity, more recently the law on crimes against humanity has evolved to such an extent that it can certainly now cover acts of ethnic cleansing and cultural genocide, even when committed in peacetime. As a result, there is no impunity gap, and there is little or no pressure in a legal sense for the expansion of the definition of genocide by interpretation. Important political prerogatives and much symbolism remain associated with the label genocide. Many victims are deeply disappointed when their own suffering is acknowledged as 'mere' crimes against humanity. They do not fully appreciate the validity of the legal distinctions, which are the result of a complex historical debate.

---

[15] *Application of the Convention on the Prevention and Punishment of the Crime of Genocide (Bosnia and Herzegovina* v *Serbia and Montenegro)* [2007] ICJ Reports 43, para. 190.

[16] Florence Hartmann, *Paix et Châtiment*, Paris: Flammarion, 2007.

At the 2011 Conference of the International Association of Genocide Scholars, held in Buenos Aires, survivors of Argentina's 'dirty war' which took place between 1976 and 1982 spoke of being tortured in one of the country's 500 illegal detention sites. They were fortunate, in a sense, because perhaps 30,000 of their comrades had been murdered by the dictatorship. Many were dropped into the ocean from planes, while others were dumped in mass graves. The attacks of the Argentine regime were directed against political opponents, members of various left-wing organizations rooted in labour and student movements. 'Crimes against humanity' is the appropriate label for such atrocities. After more than two decades of impunity, justice is finally being done in Argentina. Hundreds of perpetrators have being convicted and sentenced to lengthy prison terms. But unsatisfied with the use of crimes against humanity as the legal characterization, lawyers and academics have tried to brand the acts of the dictatorship as genocide. At the 2011 Conference victims spoke of their unhappiness at the reluctance of the courts to convict perpetrators of genocide. What should have been a moment of satisfaction and relief for the victims was turned into disappointment because they were convinced—wrongly—that only genocide will describe their suffering appropriately.

The Genocide Convention continues to fascinate jurists, politicians, journalists, and human rights activists. For most of its first fifty years, it lived in a state of tension with crimes against humanity. There was much frustration with the narrowness of the definition of genocide. Schwarzenberger famously remarked that the Genocide Convention was 'unnecessary when applicable and inapplicable when necessary'.[17] Frank Chalk and Kurt Jonassohn wrote that 'the wording of the Convention is so restrictive that not one of the genocidal killings committed since its adoption is covered by it'.[18] Many, therefore, have argued for a dynamic interpretation of the concept of genocide. This would enlarge the protection to political and social groups and apply to a broader range of acts. But what they proposed, in reality, was equivalent to crimes against humanity without the nexus to armed conflict.

In early 1945 genocide and crimes against humanity were cognates, terms devised to describe the barbarous acts of the Nazi regime. Though not identical in scope—it was impossible to say with precision because the process of codification had not been completed—they neatly overlapped and could be used more or less interchangeably to describe the great crime

---

[17] Georg Schwarzenberger, *International Law*, Vol. I, 3rd edn, London: Stevens & Sons, 1957, at p. 143.
[18] 'The Conceptual Framework', in Frank Chalk and Kurt Jonassohn (eds), *The History and Sociology of Genocide*, New Haven and London: Yale University Press, 1990, pp. 3–43.

of the era, the attempted extermination of Europe's Jewish population. By late 1946 an important rift developed that was not repaired for many years. In 1995 the Appeals Chamber of the International Criminal Tribunal for the former Yugoslavia declared that the nexus between crimes against humanity and armed conflict no longer existed. That this view was shared by states found its confirmation in the adoption of article 7 of the Rome Statute, which defines crimes against humanity and makes no mention of any contextual requirement of armed conflict. At what point prior to the mid-1990s it can be said that the nexus disappeared is a matter of some debate, something discussed in Chapter 2, *'Nullum Crimen Sine Lege'*. The point is that the cause of the rupture between the two concepts whose linkage was not disputed at Nuremberg, namely the requirement in the judgment of the International Military Tribunal that crimes against humanity be committed in association with armed conflict, is no longer of any relevance. Perhaps it is time to heal this family squabble and reunite or at least harmonize these two concepts.

The absence of a crimes against humanity convention to parallel the Genocide Convention is being addressed in initiatives by academics and elder statesmen of the international human rights movement. Under the leadership of Professor Leila Sadat of Washington University of St Louis, a draft treaty has been prepared.[19] It addresses many of the same issues covered by the Genocide Convention, such as jurisdiction for national prosecutions, obligations of mutual legal assistance, and the non-availability of certain defences such as superior orders. The draft provisions reflect more modern approaches to these matters. The models for the text are contemporary instruments such as the International Convention for the Protection of All Persons from Enforced Disappearance. With a sophisticated and thoughtful draft, it is hoped that diplomats will pick up the baton and bring the treaty through to adoption.

Even without a crimes against humanity convention, most of the obligations set out in the Genocide Convention already apply to crimes against humanity, either through other legal instruments or as a result of customary obligation. One significant distinction is article IX, the compromissory clause by which the International Court of Justice is given jurisdiction over disputes arising between parties to the Convention. That provision has been invoked several times but with very limited results. It is totally superfluous for the many states that have accepted the jurisdiction of the Court more generally, through the optional clause in the Statute of the

---

[19] Leila Nadya Sadat (ed), *Forging a Convention for Crimes Against Humanity*, New York: Cambridge University Press, 2011.

International Court of Justice, because disputes concerning the Convention can be addressed by the Court regardless of article IX. For that matter, charges of crimes against humanity could also be litigated before the Court as a matter of customary international law, although this has never been done.

The distinction between genocide and crimes against humanity is still of great symbolic significance, of course. This is the core of the genocide mystique. It is tempting to suggest, as some have argued, that we eliminate altogether the distinctions between genocide and crimes against humanity. David Scheffer has proposed they be folded into a new category of 'atrocity crimes'. The Albright-Cohen report preferred to lump everything under the word 'genocide', thereby retaining the word's 'unmatched rhetorical power'. Concerned about how the term may be abused, Noam Chomsky has written in his foreword to *The Politics of Genocide*: 'As for the term "genocide", perhaps the most honourable course would be to expunge it from the vocabulary until the day, if it ever comes, when honesty and integrity can become an "emerging norm".'[20] Each of these approaches has strengths and weaknesses. At a minimum, it would be helpful it genocide's proper place, nestled within the broader concept of crimes against humanity and reserved exclusively for the clearest cases of intentional extermination of national, ethnic, racial, and religious groups, were better understood and appreciated.

---

[20] Noam Chomsky, 'Foreword', in Edward S. Herman and David Petersen, *The Politics of Genocide*, New York: Monthly Review Press, 2010, pp. 7–12, at p. 12

5

MENS REA, ACTUS REUS, AND THE ROLE OF THE STATE

Criminal law classically describes offences as being composed of two elements: the *mens rea* and the *actus reus.* The *mens rea* is the guilty mind and the *actus reus* is the guilty act. The words come from a Latin maxim that holds there to be no punishable act that is not the result of a guilty mind. It is not a crime merely to think guilty thoughts. If it were, we would need larger prisons and most of us would be in them. Guilty thoughts must be linked to an act. An act that is not the result of a guilty mind is not a crime. Nature—wild animals, high tides, sunspots—may cause harm, but this is not of interest to criminal law in the absence of the involvement of a guilty mind. As a result of legal presumptions, some humans are inherently incapable of having a guilty mind: young children and the insane, for example. But even intentional human behaviour that causes harm to society and perhaps real harm to victims may not necessarily be the product of a guilty mind.

Criminal justice systems occasionally recognize offences that may be committed in the absence of a guilty mind, although such crimes are very much the exception and they are rarely particularly serious. At the level of international criminal law, this low end of the intent spectrum rarely arises. The closest that international law comes to acts that are punishable without a guilty mind is the prosecution of commanders for the acts of their subordinates, when the superior 'had reason to know' that atrocities might be perpetrated by those under his or her control. Superior responsibility, as it is known, is set out in article 28 of the Rome Statute of the International Criminal Court as well as in the relevant instruments of the ad hoc tribunals. This looks like a negligence standard of *mens rea* to most criminal lawyers, although judges have gone to great pains to suggest that the threshold is higher. Negligent individuals have guilty minds, too, although their culpability is often viewed as being less serious than that of those who act intentionally and with planning or premeditation. But again, there are exceptions, and negligent behaviour is sometimes more egregious than intentional conduct. For example, some might consider the negligent operator of a motor vehicle whose carelessness results in the death of others to be guiltier than the person who knowingly assists in the euthanasia of a dying relative who has lost all quality of life.

The statutes of the Nuremberg and Tokyo tribunals, and of the ad hoc tribunals established by the United Nations, do not contain any general formulation concerning *mens rea* and *actus reus*. Case law of these bodies has developed a sophisticated canvas of principles, amongst them the well-accepted proposition that no crime can be committed without a guilty mind. Judgments of the tribunals are often divided into discussions of the material and psychological elements. The Rome Statute of the International Criminal Court is the first instrument of its kind to attempt a definition of these terms. Actually, the Statute only defines *mens rea*. Negotiators at the Rome Conference found it too difficult to agree upon the general scope of the *actus reus*, primarily because they could reach no common understanding of crimes of omission. According to article 30 of the Rome Statute, entitled 'mental element',

1. Unless otherwise provided, a person shall be criminally responsible and liable for punishment for a crime within the jurisdiction of the Court only if the material elements are committed with intent and knowledge.
2. For the purposes of this article, a person has intent where:
   (a) In relation to conduct, that person means to engage in the conduct;
   (b) In relation to a consequence, that person means to cause that consequence or is aware that it will occur in the ordinary course of events.
3. For the purposes of this article, 'knowledge' means awareness that a circumstance exists or a consequence will occur in the ordinary course of events. 'Know' and 'knowingly' shall be construed accordingly.

The words 'unless otherwise provided' suggest the possibility of a crime that can be committed without intent and knowledge. Some believe that this exception was included in order to shelter the prosecution of a negligent commander from defence arguments that he did not know subordinates were committing punishable acts. It might also help knock out the hypothesis of someone charged with recruiting child soldiers claiming he or she did not know the victims were under age. The Elements of Crimes, a document that complements the Rome Statute, requires proof either that the perpetrator 'knew or should have known that such person or persons were under the age of 15 years'.

The 'unless otherwise provided' expression may also apply to the definitions of international crimes that contain specific references to the nature of intent and knowledge that is required for a conviction. The definition of genocide, for example, requires that certain acts be committed 'with intent to destroy, in whole or in part, a national, ethnical, racial or religious group, as such'. The definition of crimes against humanity, on the other hand, speaks of acts 'committed as part of a widespread or systematic attack directed against any civilian population, with knowledge of the attack'. The former focusses on intent, the latter on knowledge. Often there is no reference to either intent or knowledge in definitions of international crimes. The judge is required to explain this aspect as part of the exercise of interpreting and applying the law. In the case of war crimes, an individual may not be convicted who is unaware of the existence of an armed conflict. But although international law distinguishes between crimes committed in international and non-international armed conflicts, judges will not require evidence that the accused person knew the type of war in which he or she was involved.

There is much misunderstanding about the nature of evidence establishing knowledge and intent. In both national and international justice systems, as a general rule the *mens rea* is not actually proven, in the sense that the prosecutor provides testimony or other evidence to rebut the claim that the act was perpetrated in ignorance or by accident. Only when the accused person actually raises this as a defence is evidence likely to be led in response, such as when an artillery captain claims that he had aimed at a military objective but hit a school or hospital by mistake. Usually, courts simply presume that individuals behave with knowledge of the obvious and that they intend the logical consequences of their acts.

What have sometimes been called the contextual elements of international crimes are usually what sets them apart from ordinary crimes. This justifies their existence as offences of concern to the international community as a whole. For example, the definitions of genocide, war crimes, and crimes against humanity all contain the act of murder (or killing) in their enumerations of punishable acts. The concept of homicide is well known to national criminal justice systems and has posed little difficulty before international courts. But for killing to be deemed genocide, it must be accompanied by the 'intent to destroy' a protected group. For it to be a crime against humanity, the court must be convinced that the perpetrator had knowledge that the murder was part of a widespread or systematic attack on a civilian population. The higher an accused sits in the hierarchy, the more obvious it may be that he or she had the guilty intent or knowledge. Evidence will tend to focus on the existence of orders, or at least the presumption that they were issued, coupled with the conduct of subordinates, giving the appearance of a concerted plan. In the case of the crime of aggression, international law goes a step further by requiring that the offender necessarily 'be a person in a position effectively to exercise control over or to direct the political or military action of a state'. Vice versa, low-ranking or marginal offenders become difficult to distinguish from ordinary criminals. In any case, they are of little interest to international prosecutors who must channel their limited resources to maximum effect.

CRIMES OF STATE

'Crimes against international law are committed by men, not by abstract entities, and only by punishing individuals who commit such crimes can the provisions of international law be enforced', reads the judgment of the International Military Tribunal.[1] This oft-cited phrase expresses a vital idea, but it may also have contributed to some misconception about the nature of international crimes. The Nuremberg court made the statement in answer to the claim that the Nazi leaders were not responsible because they were acting in the interests of the state. Where the famous pronouncement about 'abstract entities' may mislead is in suggesting that the state's role is irrelevant or secondary to the discussion about crimes under international law.

Article 6 of the Charter of the International Military Tribunal defines the subject-matter jurisdiction of the institution. In three distinct paragraphs it lists the core offences, namely crimes against peace, war crimes, and crimes against humanity. Often overlooked are the words in the introductory paragraph of article 6 that require offenders to have been 'acting in the interests of the European Axis countries'. This implies a gloss on the statement that 'crimes against international law are committed by men'. The offenders must be acting in the interest of a state. Even summary perusal of the judgment issued on 30 September and 1 October 1946 makes it clear just how pivotal the plan or policy of the Nazi state was to the prosecution.

Until the ad hoc tribunals began their work, in the mid-1990s, international criminal justice had concerned itself with leaders—politicians, generals, bankers, judges—who belonged to or were associated with the highest levels of the state apparatus. The issue of whether the crimes with which they were charged had a link to state policy did not really arise. It was implied in all aspects of the prosecution. No judges ever asked whether an individual accused, acting in isolation, could commit crimes against

---

[1] *France* et al. v *Göring* et al. (1946) 22 IMT 411, at p. 466.

humanity or war crimes. Invariably, those who were on trial before the international tribunals had acted as part of a large-scale plan or policy where a state stood at the centre. No accused ever pleaded innocence on the grounds that he or she had no connection with the state. Quite the contrary: defendants tended to argue that they could not be convicted as individual offenders because they were acting on behalf of a state. This was the argument to which the 'abstract entities' statement of the International Military Tribunal was a response.

One of the important steps in the establishment of the International Criminal Tribunal for the former Yugoslavia was a December 1992 speech by United States Secretary of State Lawrence Eagleburger in which he 'named names' of persons suspected of crimes against humanity. He explained that his government had provided details to the Commission of Experts 'whose decision it will be to prosecute or not'. Eagleburger had previously served as United States ambassador to Belgrade, and had been considered sympathetic to the Serbs, but by August 1992 his views had evolved and he began calling for a war crimes tribunal. 'We know that crimes against humanity have occurred, and we know when and where they occurred,' Eagleburger said, speaking to a conference on the Balkan conflict. 'We know, moreover, which forces committed those crimes, and under whose command they operated. And we know, finally, who the political leaders are and to whom those military commanders were—and still are—responsible.'[2] The list included the Bosnian Serb leaders, Karadžić and Mladić, who would figure in the early indictments of the Tribunal, as well as Serbian President Slobodan Milošević. Most of the names were familiar to those who had followed the conflict.

But the names of the first defendants to stand trial at the Tribunal— Dusko Tadić, Dražen Erdemović, Goran Jelisić, Dragoljub Kunarac—were nowhere to be found on Eagleburger's list. Eagleburger surely was unaware of their existence when he made the famous speech. They were insignificant individuals, guilty of participation in mass atrocity but far from the ranks of the leaders who had directed and driven the conflict. Kunarac led a fifteen-man reconnaissance unit, while the others appeared to command nobody but themselves. They were perverse, bigoted individuals of no consequence, the kind of thugs and hooligans one finds loitering around railway stations or street corners in sketchy neighbourhoods. By the year 2000 the Security Council had learned its lesson. When it proposed the third international criminal tribunal, the Special Court for Sierra Leone, the statute included

---

[2] Elaine Sciolino, 'U.S. Names Figures it Wants Charged with War Crimes', *New York Times*, 17 December 1992, p. 1.

instructions to the Prosecutor to focus on 'those who bear the greatest responsibility'. There would be no prosecutions at the Special Court of the Sierra Leonean equivalents of Tadić, Erdemović, Jelisić, and Kunarac.

It could not be presumed that there was a connection between the crimes perpetrated by Tadić, Erdemović, Jelisić, and Kunarac and a plan or policy of the Serb regime in Bosnia (or in Serbia), in contrast with the situation in the Nazi or Japanese leadership prosecutions at Nuremberg and Tokyo. They were simply too low in the hierarchy. Apparently in order to address this impediment to prosecution, judges developed a theory that international crimes did not require evidence of a state plan or policy. Intriguingly, at about the same time, international lawyers involved in drafting the Rome Statute and the accompanying Elements of Crimes were doing exactly the opposite, namely clarifying the plan or policy element of international crimes and ruling out the idea that they were the work of isolated madmen.

In the early years of its activities, the Office of the Prosecutor of the International Criminal Tribunal for the former Yugoslavia was especially cautious in charging the crime of genocide with respect to atrocities committed during the 1992–5 war in Bosnia and Herzegovina. Only a few indictments contained reference to genocide. One of these came to trial in 1999. It involved a severely disturbed Serb racist, Goran Jelisić. He had been the main executioner in the Luka camp, in northwest Bosnia, during a two-week killing spree in early 1992 shortly after the outbreak of the war. Jelisić was shown to have systematically killed Muslim inmates, as well as some Croats, totalling fewer than twenty individuals. The victims comprised the Muslim community leaders. Jelisić was charged with genocide both as an accomplice and as a principal perpetrator, in addition to crimes against humanity. He agreed to plead guilty to crimes against humanity, but the Prosecutor was not satisfied. Possibly as a test case so that she could clarify the applicability of the crime of genocide to the entire conflict, the Prosecutor insisted that trial proceed on the genocide count and rejected a proposed plea bargain.

Examining the evidence at the close of the prosecution's case, presiding Judge Claude Jorda and his colleagues concluded that the existence of any organized plan or policy of a state or similar entity to destroy in whole or in part the Bosnian Muslims had not been proven. Therefore, Jelisić could in no way be an accomplice to genocide because genocide was never committed by others. That is, there was insufficient evidence of the perpetration of genocide in Bosnia in the sense of some planned or organized attack on the Muslim population, noted the Trial Chamber.[3] This was the first significant

---

[3] *Jelisić* (IT-95-10-T), Judgment, 14 December 1999, para. 98.

confirmation in a decision of the Tribunal that judges were uncertain as to whether or not they should apply the concept of genocide to the 'ethnic cleansing' that had devastated the former Yugoslavia during the wars of the 1990s.

After dismissing the charge of complicity in genocide, the Trial Chamber turned to whether Jelisić might have committed genocide on his own, as an isolated perpetrator rather than as an accomplice. The Trial Chamber said this was 'theoretically possible', namely that an individual, acting alone, could commit the crime—a kind of Lee Harvey Oswald of genocide. In the end, Jelisić was also acquitted as a principal perpetrator. However, the Trial Chamber's approach has become authority for the entirely speculative and hypothetical proposition that genocide may be committed by a single, isolated individual without any requirement of an organized plan or policy of a state or similar entity.[4] The position of the Trial Chamber was confirmed on appeal and has been reaffirmed in subsequent decisions.

To be entirely accurate, nobody has ever actually been convicted of genocide in the absence of evidence that he or she was part of some broader plan or policy of a state or state-like entity. At the Yugoslavia Tribunal, the handful of genocide convictions have all related to the Srebrenica massacre, which was apparently organized and coordinated at the highest levels of the Bosnian Serb military and political leadership. For example, in the *Krstić* case, a Trial Chamber of the International Criminal Tribunal for the former Yugoslavia concluded that 'the Bosnian Serbs devised and implemented a plan to execute as many as possible of the military aged Bosnian Muslim men present in the enclave'.[5] The central issue, in terms of the guilt of General Krstić, was whether or not he had knowledge of the plan. The judges paid deference to the view in *Jelisić* that a plan was not a required element of the crime, but then proceeded to identify one nevertheless. In the Srebrenica prosecutions the Trial Chambers and the Appeals Chamber have concluded that the mass killings of Bosnian men were part of an 'execution plan' formulated by a state or state-like entity. All of the other genocide prosecutions at the International Criminal Tribunal for the former Yugoslavia, including that of Jelisić, have led to acquittals or abandonment of the charge of genocide. In one case, the Prosecutor agreed to drop genocide charges against one of the leaders of the Bosnian Serbs in exchange for her agreement to plead guilty to crimes against humanity and war crimes. At the International Criminal Tribunal for Rwanda the issue has never really arisen. All knowledgeable observers understand that

---

[4] Ibid., para. 100.
[5] *Krstić* (IT-98-33-T), Judgment, 2 August 2001, para. 87; also: ibid., para. 427.

the Rwandan genocide indisputably involved a plan or policy emanating from the state or, at the very least, from a powerful clique within it.

Shortly after the famous theory of the lone *génocidaire* emerged in *Jelisić*, the Tribunal considered an analogous issue with respect to crimes against humanity. Dragoljub Kunarac, Radomir Kovač, and Zoran Vuković were charged with a range of appalling sexual attacks on Muslim women in Foca, including what appears to have been the operation of a brothel for Serb soldiers. Kunarac led a fifteen-member 'reconnaissance unit' to which Kovač belonged. Vuković, who had been a waiter and driver before the war, belonged to another unit. They were duly convicted of rape as a war crime and a crime against humanity. On appeal, they argued that the Prosecutor not only had failed to establish any connections that suggested the crimes of the three men were related and that they interacted, it also did not establish that there was any general plan to commit sexual crimes against Muslim women. The suggestion was that these were isolated, opportunistic offences perpetrated by deranged misogynists profiting from the chaos of war. Certainly the evidence did not demonstrate much more, although the prosecution relied upon a widespread perception that rape had been used as a weapon of war and that there was something concerted about these sexual assaults.

The Appeals Chamber responded to the defence argument by stating that there was no requirement of a plan or policy under customary international law with respect to crimes against humanity. It noted that it had reached the same conclusion with respect to genocide in the *Jelisić* case. It was merely being consistent. In *Jelisić* the Appeals Chamber had provided no explanation for its finding. In *Kunarac* et al., however, there was an attempt to justify the Chamber's conclusions. The Appeals Chamber's discussion of this important point was summary at best. Most of the explanation was confined to a footnote.

Some writers have suggested that there is no plan or policy element because this is not stated explicitly in the definitions, either of genocide or of crimes against humanity. This is certainly the case for the Statute of the International Criminal Tribunal for the former Yugoslavia. But the Appeals Chamber had never previously been very inhibited about developing concepts that did not seem to be clearly stated in the written text. For example, it discovered the notion of common purpose complicity, which it dubbed 'joint criminal enterprise', in the words of article 7(1) of its Statute despite the fact that the laconic text of the provision says nothing of the sort. In the case of joint criminal enterprise, the Appeals Chamber cited article 25 of the Rome Statute as evidence confirming its expansive interpretation of its own Statute. But later, when it addressed the state policy element of crimes against humanity, the Appeals Chamber simply ignored an inconvenient passage in the Rome Statute's definition.

MISREADING THE AUTHORITIES AT THE YUGOSLAVIA TRIBUNAL

In the famous footnote in *Kunarac* et al. the Appeals Chamber of the International Criminal Tribunal for the former Yugoslavia noted that there had been 'some debate in the jurisprudence of this Tribunal as to whether a policy or plan constitutes an element of the definition of crimes against humanity'. The footnote is nearly 500 words in length, and references a number of authorities, as footnotes do. Detailed explanation is not provided to justify or explain the references, but this is normal enough. Footnotes are supposed to be obvious. But when the authorities cited in the reference are scrutinized, it is not at all apparent how they assist the Appeals Chamber in its conclusion that a state plan or policy is not an element of crimes against humanity.

The footnote begins by referring to the first codification of crimes against humanity in article VI(c) of the Charter of the International Military Tribunal, and to the judgment of the Tribunal in the cases of Streicher and von Schirach. Indeed, article VI(c) of the Charter of the International Military Tribunal, does not explicitly establish a state plan or policy as an element of crimes against humanity. However, the introductory paragraph or *chapeau* of article VI of the Charter specifies that accused persons must have been 'acting in the interests of the European Axis countries, whether as individuals or as members of organizations'. Moreover, the so-called nexus which requires that crimes against humanity be committed 'in connection with any crime within the jurisdiction of the Tribunal' has the effect of linking them to acts which are themselves associated with a state plan or policy, namely war crimes and crimes against peace. The possibility that crimes against humanity might apply to what are today called 'non-state actors' probably never even crossed the minds of those who drafted the Charter of the International Military Tribunal.

It is of course true that Nazi propagandist Julius Streicher was convicted of crimes against humanity by the International Military Tribunal despite the conclusion that 'the evidence fails to establish his connection with the conspiracy or common plan to wage aggressive war as that conspiracy has been elsewhere defined in this Judgment'.[6] However, Streicher was a *gauleiter*, a position of some importance in the Nazi regime. Moreover,

---

[6] *France* et al. v *Göring* et al. (1946) 22 IMT 411, at p. 547.

his crimes consisted essentially of being a propagandist for Nazi policy. It seems to be reading a lot into the judgment to assert, as did the Appeals Chamber, that his conviction is authority for the view that there is no state plan or policy element with respect to crimes against humanity. Von Schirach is the other example of a Nuremberg defendant invoked by the *Kunarac* Appeals Chamber. Since the 1920s von Schirach had been leader of the Hitler Youth. During the war, he was *gauleiter* of Vienna, and it was for atrocities committed during the Nazi occupation of Austria that he was convicted of crimes against humanity by the Nuremberg Tribunal. The convictions of these two at Nuremberg may support the position that a perpetrator of crimes against humanity need not be an 'insider' in the plan. It cannot buttress the argument that crimes against humanity do not require the existence of a plan, something of which there can be no doubt in Nazi Germany.

The International Military Tribunal never directly addressed the issue of whether a plan or policy was an element of the international crimes being prosecuted, and the reason is obvious: the Nazi plan and policy to wage aggressive war and to exterminate the Jews of Europe underpinned the entire case. Why would the Tribunal ever have considered the issue, under the circumstances? For the same reasons, the *Eichmann* trial—another source upon which the *Kunarac* Appeals Chamber relied—seems flimsy authority indeed for the suggestion that there is no plan or policy element to crimes against humanity. The judgment of the Jerusalem District Court is constructed around evidence of the Nazi plan or policy and of the 'desk murderer' who implemented it. The Israeli judges concluded that Eichmann had known of the 'secret of the plan for extermination' since mid-1941. He was acquitted of genocide for acts committed prior to that date.[7]

Among the other authorities listed by the *Kunarac* Appeals Chamber to support its position that there is no plan or policy element is the Report of the Secretary-General to the Security Council on the draft Statute of the International Criminal Tribunal for the former Yugoslavia. The footnote in *Kunarac* cites paragraphs 47 and 48 of that Report as proof of the 'overwhelming support' of the contention that there is no state plan or policy requirement under customary international law. The text of the two paragraphs follows:

47. Crimes against humanity were first recognized in the Charter and Judgment of the Nürnberg Tribunal, as well as in Law No. 10 of the Control Council for Germany. Crimes against humanity are aimed at any civilian population and are

---

[7] *AG Israel* v *Eichmann* (1968) 36 ILR 5 (District Court, Jerusalem), para. 195.

prohibited regardless of whether they are committed in an armed conflict, international or internal in character.

48. Crimes against humanity refer to inhumane acts of a very serious nature,
such as wilful killing, torture or rape, committed as part of a widespread or systematic attack against any civilian population on national, political, ethnic, racial
or religious grounds. In the conflict in the territory of the former Yugoslavia,
such inhumane acts have taken the form of so-called 'ethnic cleansing' and widespread and systematic rape and other forms of sexual assault, including enforced
prostitution.[8]

Do these two relatively laconic paragraphs really provide 'overwhelming
support' for the *Kunarac* Appeals Chamber's position?

The footnote in *Kunarac* also refers to the 1954 draft Code of Offences
Against the Peace and Security of Mankind developed by the International
Law Commission as an authority supporting its view that there is no state
plan or policy element. The contrary would actually appear to be the case.
The 1954 draft of the Commission's definition of crimes against humanity
reads as follows: 'Inhuman acts such as murder, extermination, enslavement,
deportation or persecution, committed against any civilian population on
social, political, racial, religious or cultural grounds *by the authorities of a
state or by private individuals acting at the instigation or with the toleration of such
authorities.*'[9] Members of the Commission had been attempting to reformu-
late the Nuremberg definition of crimes against humanity so as to eliminate the requirement of a connection with armed conflict (on the difficulties
of drafting the definition of crimes against humanity, see Chapter 4, 'The
Genocide Mystique'). Early in the 1954 session, the Commission had voted
to eliminate the nexus with armed conflict, but put nothing in its place.[10] At
a following meeting, after a night or two of reflection, the members of the
Commission realized that without the contextual element of armed conflict
they had made it difficult to distinguish between crimes against humanity
and ordinary crimes. They decided to reconsider their earlier decision,[11]
and subsequently voted to revise the earlier text. According to the 1954
Report of the International Law Commission, 'in order not to characterize any inhuman act committed by a private individual as an international
crime, it was found necessary to provide that such an act constitutes an

[8] Report of the Secretary-General Pursuant to Paragraph 2 of Security Council Resolution 808
(1993), UN Doc. S/25704 (1993), paras 47–8. The footnotes, which merely provide the bibliographic
references, have been omitted.
[9] Draft Code of Offences Against the Peace and Security of Mankind, UN Doc. A/2693 (my
emphasis).
[10] UN Doc. A/CN.4/SR.267, para. 59.   [11] UN Doc. A/CN.4/SR.268, para. 11.

international crime only if committed by the private individual at the instigation or with the toleration of the authorities of a state'.[12]

The International Law Commission did not return to the draft code for nearly thirty years. In the 1980s it went through a decade of often extravagant attempts at progressive codification before, at one point, deciding to abandon the classification of crimes against humanity altogether.[13] Basically, the Commission reformulated crimes against humanity as an umbrella concept addressing gross or systematic violations of human rights. The issue of state policy was rarely discussed during this period, although to the extent that the Commission had focussed on human rights violations, it can be said that state involvement may have been viewed as a *sine qua non*. Most members of the Commission would probably have taken the view that human rights violations concerned the relationship between the individual, who warranted protection, and the state, which was responsible for violations.

When it produced the final version of the Code of Crimes Against the Peace and Security of Mankind, in 1996, the International Law Commission dramatically revised its earlier drafts, and declared that the purpose of the threshold in crimes against humanity is to exclude 'a random act' or 'an isolated inhumane act'.[14] Although the Commentary did not explicitly mention 'non-state actors' or provide any examples to assist in understanding its views, it said that '[t]he instigation or direction of a Government or any organization or group, which may or may not be affiliated with a Government, gives the act its great dimension and makes it a crime against humanity imputable to private persons or agents of a state'.[15] The Commission supported this proposition by citing the Nuremberg judgment, specifically the convictions of Streicher and von Schirach. The rationale seems to have been that they were acquitted of crimes against peace because they were not Nazi insiders. But even if Streicher and von Schirach were 'non-state actors', in that they were not part of Hitler's inner circle, their acts were not random or isolated precisely because they were part of the Nazi plan or policy to persecute minorities, as has already been noted earlier in this chapter.

In *Kunarac* et al. the Appeals Chamber of the International Criminal Tribunal set aside one of the most well-known of the post-Second World War decisions, the *Alstötter* et al. case, which involved Nazi judges and

---

[12] Report of the International Law Commission to the General Assembly, UN Doc. A/2693, p. 150.

[13] Report of the International Law Commission on the work of its forty-third session (29 April–19 July 1991), UN Doc. A/46/10, para. 176.

[14] Eg *Tadić* (IT-94-1-T), Opinion and Judgment, 7 May 1997, para. 648.

[15] Report of the International Law Commission on the work of its forty-eighth session, 6 May–26 July 1996, UN Doc. A/51/10, art. 18, para. 5.

jurists, on the grounds that it 'has been shown not to constitute an author-itative statement of customary international law'. The authority for this proposition was an Australian judgment from the early 1990s. The Appeals Chamber admitted, in the footnote, that *Alstötter* 'has often been quoted in support of the plan or policy requirement'. The decision in *Alstötter* held that crimes against humanity required 'proof of conscious participation in systematic government organized or approved procedures amounting to atrocities and offenses'.[16] Moreover, 'governmental participation is a material element of the crime against humanity. Only when official organs of sovereignty participated in atrocities and persecutions did those crimes assume international proportions.'[17]

Like other authorities in the famous *Kunarac* footnote, the reference to the Australian judgment that discounts the validity of *Alstötter* crumbles upon closer scrutiny. The judgment of the Australian court does not in fact analyse the *Alstötter* decision at all. It dismisses it with the phrase: 'The opinion of this Tribunal has not been accepted as an authoritative statement of customary international law.'[18] This bald statement is then followed by a citation from a celebrated article by Egon Schwelb. But Schwelb's article has nothing to do with the state policy issue. It certainly does not consider *Alstötter*, which seems to be the implication of the refer-ence in the Australian judgment. There is a simple explanation for this. The Schwelb article appears to have been completed in late 1946, and is published in the British Yearbook of International Law for that year. The judgment in *Alstötter* was issued in December 1947. The devastating dis-missal of *Alstötter* in *Kunarac* by the Appeals Chamber of the International Criminal Tribunal for the former Yugoslavia, which is founded on a single ruling by one judge of the Australian High Court, in one of that tribunal's rare forays into public international law, turns out to be a chimera.

The Appeals Chamber later returned to the *Alstötter* decision, this time citing it as authority in the *Brđanin* case, perhaps having forgotten its earl-ier statement in *Kunarac* about not being an authoritative statement of cus-tomary international law. In *Brđanin*, the *Alstötter* case proved very helpful as judges struggled with adapting the theory of joint criminal enterprise liability, which had been first developed in early cases to deal with relatively isolated, low-level offenders like Tadić, to defendants at the leadership level. Amongst other responsibilities, Radoslav Brđanin had served as president of the 'Crisis Group' of the Autonomous Region of Krajina. Relying upon

---

[16] *United States of America* v *Alstötter* et al. ('The Justice Case') (1951) 3 TWC. 954 (United States Military Tribunal), at p. 982.

[17] Ibid., p. 984.

[18] *Polyukhovich* v *Commonwealth* [1991] HCA 32; (1991) 172 CLR 501, para. 62 (Brennan J.).

earlier pronouncements by the Appeals Chamber, the Trial Chamber had concluded that the joint criminal enterprise theory was inapplicable. It held that the primary perpetrator of the criminal act must be a member of the joint criminal enterprise.[19] The consequence was to confine the doctrine to small groups, and to exclude its relevance to large-scale criminal plans in which the primary perpetrator may even be ignorant of the overall intentions of the leaders and organizers.

The Appeals Chamber reversed the legal findings of the Trial Chamber, thereby holding that joint criminal enterprise was applicable not only to 'small cases' but to large-scale criminal enterprises involving primary perpetrators or offenders who are personally outside the common plan. Referring to *Alstötter*, the Appeals Chamber said it found strong support for the imposition of criminal liability upon an accused for participation in a common criminal purpose, 'where the conduct that comprises the criminal *actus reus* is perpetrated by persons who do not share the common purpose'. The Appeals Chamber cited one of the conclusions in the *Alstötter*: 'The material facts which must be proved in any case are (1) the fact of the great pattern or plan of racial persecution and extermination; and (2) specific conduct of the individual defendant in furtherance of the plan. This is but an application of general concepts of criminal law.'[20]

In its decision, the Appeals Chamber relied heavily on the analysis of Judge Iain Bonomy, who had considered *Alstötter* in some detail in his separate opinion in a preliminary ruling in the *Milutinović* case the previous year. Judge Bonomy wrote:

The Military Tribunal appears to have imposed criminal responsibility on both accused for their participation in the common criminal plan although they did not perpetrate the *actus reus* of the crimes of which they were convicted; the *actus reus* was instead perpetrated by executioners simply carrying out the orders of the court. Nowhere did the Tribunal discuss the mental state of the executioners who carried out the death sentences imposed as a result of the actions of Lautz, Rothaug, and their fellow participants in the common plan, or whether such persons even had knowledge that the death sentences formed part of a plan to pervert the law for the purpose of exterminating Jews and other 'undesirables'.[21]

Another post-Second World War decision referred to by the *Brđanin* Appeals Chamber, and discussed by Judge Bonomy in his separate opinion, involved the SS Race and Resettlement Main Office, and is known as the

---

[19] *Brđanin* (IT-99-36-T), Judgment, 1 September 2004, paras 355–6.

[20] *United States of America* v *Alstötter* et al. ('The Justice Case') (1951) 3 TWC 954 (United States Military Tribunal), p. 1063, cited in *Brđanin* (IT-99-36-A), Judgment, 3 April 2007, para. 397.

[21] *Milutinović* et al. (Case No. IT-05-87-PT), Separate Opinion of Judge Iain Bonomy, 22 March 2006, para. 20.

RuSHA case. The RuSHA leaders were charged with participating in a 'systematic programme of genocide'.[22] Judge Bonomy noted:

The Military Tribunal found that the Prosecution had established that there existed among Hitler, Himmler—the leader of the SS—and other Nazi officials a 'two-fold objective of weakening and eventually destroying other nations while at the same time strengthening Germany, territorially and biologically, at the expense of conquered nations.' It found additionally that the leadership of RuSHA—and particularly the accused Hofmann and Hildebrandt—adhered to and enthusiastically participated in the execution of this 'Germanization' plan.[23]

The Appeals Chamber of the Yugoslavia Tribunal concluded:

The Appeals Chamber notes that it is clear from the Military Tribunal's discussion of the various aspects of the Germanization plan that Hofmann and Hildebrandt, as the leaders of RuSHA, worked closely and interactively with Himmler, Kaltenbrunner, and other high SS officials in planning the details of how the plan was to be executed, especially with respect to the abortions and abduction programmes. On the basis of their active participation in this plan and their knowledge of the activities carried out pursuant to it, both accused were held responsible for the conduct of the RuSHA agents who carried out the crimes, without any discussion of whether the principal perpetrators had knowledge that their actions formed part of the Germanization plan, or of whether an agreement existed between the accused and these agents.[24]

The *Brđanin* Appeals Chamber also observed that much of the early case law of the Tribunal dealt with small-scale joint criminal enterprises, and was not therefore good authority when broader schemes were concerned.

The Appeals Chamber has never denied the relevance of a plan or policy in the commission of genocide and crimes against humanity. For example, in *Krstić*, it said that 'presence of such a plan or policy may be important evidence that the attack against a civilian population was widespread or systematic'.[25] But it has not wavered from its view that state policy is not an element of these crimes.

Eliminating the state plan or policy element from crimes against humanity has the potential to make the concept applicable to a wide range of criminal acts that go beyond those that are merely random or isolated. Instead of insisting upon a state plan or policy, the contextual element for crimes against humanity comes to depend solely on their 'widespread or systematic' nature. Crimes against humanity become applicable to serial killers,

---

[22] *United States of America* v *Greifelt* et al. ('RuSHA case') (1948) 4 TWC 1, at p. 609 (TWC).

[23] *Milutinović* et al. (IT-05-87-PT), Separate Opinion of Judge Iain Bonomy, 22 March 2006, para. 22.

[24] *Brđanin* (IT-99-36-A), Judgment, 3 April 2007, para. 403.

[25] *Krstić* (IT-98-33-A), Judgment, 19 April 2004, para. 225 (internal citations omitted).

mafias, motorcycle gangs, and small terrorist bands. This was certainly not what was intended by the United Nations War Crimes Commission, the London Conference, and the International Military Tribunal, when the category of crimes against humanity first received legal definition at the conclusion of the Second World War. Nor does it make good sense from the standpoint of the policy of international judicial institutions.

DIFFERENT LAW AT THE INTERNATIONAL CRIMINAL COURT

There is an important and rather glaring oversight in the Appeals Chamber's analysis in the famous footnote in *Kunarac*. No mention is made of article 7(2)(a) of the Rome Statute. By 2002, when *Kunarac* was issued, article 7 of the Rome Statute had become the gold standard in terms of definitions of crimes against humanity, having been accepted essentially by consensus at the Rome Conference. None of the states that abstained or voted against the Rome Statute appears to have done so because of disagreement with the text of article 7. Its detailed provisions develop the varied and laconic texts in the statutes that preceded it, making the Rome Statute definition very authoritative. The Rome Statute says that crimes against humanity must be committed in the course of an 'attack directed against any civilian population' that is 'pursuant to or in furtherance of a state or organizational policy to commit such attack'. If a student had been asked to write an essay or exam question on whether or not crimes against humanity contain a plan or policy element, and the student failed to discuss article 7(2) of the Rome Statute, as did the judges of the Appeals Chamber in *Kunarac*, points would surely be deducted.

With respect to the crime of genocide, at the International Criminal Court judges interpret exactly the same text as they do at the International Criminal Tribunal for the former Yugoslavia. But there are two differences of significance by comparison with the Statute of the International Criminal Tribunal for the former Yugoslavia. First, article 22 of the Rome Statute adopts a rule of restrictive interpretation in the case of definitions of crimes. It is a principle that is very well known and well accepted in domestic legal systems. But while formally imposed upon the judges of the International Criminal Court by their own Statute, the same rule of strict construction has had little resonance at the International Criminal Tribunal for the former Yugoslavia, where judges interpret their Statute in a rather broad and purposive manner.

The interpretation of the definition of genocide at the International Criminal Court must take into account the Elements of Crimes. The

Elements is a subsidiary document adopted by the Assembly of States Parties and declared to be part of the law applicable by the Tribunal. In fact, according to article 21(1) of the Rome Statute it is one of the three main sources of law, together with the Statute itself and the Rules of Procedure and Evidence. If there is incompatibility, the Statute prevails over the Rules and the Elements. The weight to be attached to the Elements of Crimes is a subject of controversy that has confronted judges at both the International Criminal Court and the International Criminal Tribunal for the former Yugoslavia.

The Elements of Crimes declare that genocidal conduct must have taken place 'in the context of a manifest pattern of similar conduct directed against that group or was conduct that could itself effect such destruction'. This is probably enough to eliminate the theory in *Jelisić* by which a lone maniac, acting alone, could perpetrate the crime of crimes. The Elements were discussed and negotiated in 1999 and 2000. The 'manifest pattern' language and the requirement that the conduct actually be capable of effecting genocide did not appear in the early drafts. It only emerged in March 2000, in the final stages of the drafting of the Elements, and—not a coincidence, certainly—after the Trial Chamber had issued its judgment in *Jelisić* in December 1999. It seems quite apparent: the limitation on the scope of genocide that appears in the Elements of Crimes was a reaction to *Jelisić*.

In 2001 the judges of the Appeals Chamber confirmed the lone *génocidaire* hypothesis developed by the Trial Chamber in *Jelisić*. They were obviously not swayed by the text of the Elements of Crimes, which had been adopted in the interim. They were not, of course, bound by the Elements of Crimes, which were meant to apply to the Rome Statute of the International Criminal Court and not the Statute of the International Criminal Tribunal for the former Yugoslavia. Nevertheless, they might have taken the Elements of Crimes and their requirement of a contextual element for the crime of genocide as an authoritative message from states about the interpretation of the definition of the crime. After all, the genocide text in the Rome Statute and the Statute of the Yugoslavia Tribunal is essentially the same, given that the two provisions have a common ancestor: article 2 of the 1948 Genocide Convention.

Judges of the Appeals Chamber of the International Criminal Tribunal for the former Yugoslavia may explain this by saying that the Rome Statute, and the Elements of Crimes, are not in fact authoritative. They insist that they are applying 'customary international law', unconstrained by the negotiated text of the Rome Statute and the Elements. The definition of genocide in the Rome Statute, to the extent that it is completed by the Elements of Crimes, has been disregarded as 'inapposite'. The Elements are 'not binding rules, but only auxiliary means of interpretation' and they do not 'reflect customary international law', the Tribunal's judges have said. This is somewhat cavalier disregard for the weight of the opinion of states that are, after all, the creators of international law. The 'manifest pattern' language of the Elements of Crimes is a form of subsequent agreement about the scope of the crime of genocide that at least ought to be considered seriously by international judges.

This is as much a quarrel about interpretations as it is about customary international law. Neither the Yugoslavia Tribunal nor the International Criminal Court has the jurisdiction to prosecute crimes under customary international law. At the International Criminal Tribunal for the former Yugoslavia, there is an interpretative presumption that the definitions of crimes in the Statute be consistent with customary international law as it stood in May 1993, when the Statute was adopted, or possibly at the beginning of 1991, which is the beginning of its temporal jurisdiction. Judges at the Yugoslavia Tribunal consider customary international law when they interpret the definitions, but they cannot go beyond the terms of their own Statute. Often they suggest they are applying customary international law. But in reality, they are using customary law to interpret the scope of provisions in the Statute.

The debate about the role of state policy in the scope of genocide and crimes against humanity has manifested itself in early decisions of the International Criminal Court. The Court has yet to render a final verdict, so its rulings on the definitions of crimes must be taken as still somewhat tentative. Nevertheless, judges at the International Criminal Court must interpret definitions of the crimes in a variety of contexts that arise prior to a final judgment on guilt or innocence. For example, they may consider the scope of crimes at the most preliminary stage, when they authorize the Prosecutor to proceed with an investigation, or in the issuance of an arrest warrant, or at the pre-trial confirmation hearing.

A Pre-Trial Chamber debated whether or not the crime of genocide requires a 'contextual element' when it authorized the issuance of an arrest warrant against President Omar El-Bashir, in March 2009. The Chamber noted that there was no express requirement of a contextual element in the definition of genocide, and it acknowledged the position taken by judges at the ad hoc tribunals, where the existence of any such contextual element, such as a policy or plan, has been rejected. It noted the reference in the Elements of Crimes to a 'manifest pattern of similar conduct directed against that group or...conduct that could itself effect such destruction'. The judges said they felt bound to apply the Elements of Crimes in the absence of 'irreconcilable contradiction' with the Statute. They might have gone even further, holding that the contextual requirement in the Elements was nothing more than an attempt at codification of a notion that is implied in the definition of genocide. They did say that it was consistent with the definition and, moreover, compelled by the rule that the definitions of crimes be strictly construed and the benefit of any doubt granted to the accused. The dissenting member of the three-member panel, Judge Anita Ušacka, noted that there was general agreement that the alleged conduct of the accused met the 'widespread or systematic attack' threshold for crimes against humanity. Consequently, she said, there was no need to decide whether the contextual element was indeed consistent with the definition of genocide in article 6 of the Statute.

After the *Bashir* arrest warrant decision, judges of a Pre-Trial Chamber turned their minds to the contextual element of crimes against humanity. The issue concerned the Statute itself rather than the legal significance of the Elements of Crimes. The disagreement was not about the existence of a contextual element but about its scope. As has already been explained, judges at the ad hoc tribunals have concluded that crimes against humanity must take place as part of a 'widespread or systematic attack on a civilian population', but they have rejected the idea that this be necessarily associated with the policy of a state. The Rome Statute definition of crimes against humanity is more elaborate than its predecessors, including the explicit requirement that the widespread or systematic attack be 'pursuant to or in furtherance of a state or organizational policy to commit such attack'.

In late 2009 the Prosecutor applied for authorization to begin an investigation into post-electoral violence in Kenya. Article 15 of the Rome Statute allows the Prosecutor to investigate situations on his own initiative, and without political determination by the Security Council or a State Party, but only with the blessing of a Pre-Trial Chamber. The Prosecutor's application was built around the claim that crimes against humanity had been perpetrated in Kenya by various groups and factions in the aftermath of national elections that took place on 27 December 2007. The Prosecutor referred to the possibility that four categories of crime against humanity had been committed: murder, rape, and other forms of sexual violence, deportation or forcible transfer of population, and the residual rubric, 'other inhumane acts'. Speaking to the state or organizational policy issue, the Prosecutor said that the alleged crimes were conducted primarily by members of organized groups associated with the main political parties.[26]

---

[26] *Situation in the Republic of Kenya* (ICC–01/09), Request for authorization of an investigation pursuant to Article 15, 26 November 2009, para. 80.

The majority of the Pre-Trial Chamber was satisfied with the Prosecutor's submission. It agreed to authorize the investigation to proceed. It said it was 'mindful of the jurisprudential evolution and the eventual abandonment of the policy requirement before the ad hoc tribunals'. Then it turned to the decisions of the ad hoc tribunals prior to the ruling in *Kunarac* for guidance in application of the 'state or organizational policy' contextual element. The majority said the term 'state' was self-explanatory, noting that a state policy to commit an attack 'does not necessarily need to have been conceived "at the highest level of the state machinery"',[27] giving as examples policies of regional or local governments. As for 'organizational policy', the majority adopted a results-based approach not unlike that required for genocide in the Elements of Crimes. It said that the organization in question should be capable of actually perpetrating the atrocities in question, but it specifically dismissed the suggestion that the organization be 'state-like'.

Judge Hans-Peter Kaul disagreed, taking the view that while the 'organization' in question need not have all of the constitutive elements of statehood, it must have characteristics of a state or quasi-state abilities. He said that 'non-state actors which do not reach the level described above are not able to carry out a policy of this nature, such as groups of organized crime, a mob, groups of (armed) civilians or criminal gangs'. Judge Kaul situated this analysis within the overall rationale for the international prosecution of crimes against humanity, which he said was to address state-sponsored atrocity. He referred to the origins of the concept at the London Conference, in 1945, saying that these historical factors were decisive in interpreting the scope of crimes against humanity today. He wrote:

If leaders of a state who normally have the duty to uphold the rule of law and to respect human rights engage in a policy of violent attacks against a civilian population, it is the community of states which must intervene and prevent, control and repress this threat to the peace, security and well-being of the world.[28]

This observation is just as appropriate with respect to genocide as with crimes against humanity.

SPECIFIC INTENT AND STATE RESPONSIBILITY

Good evidence as to why a state plan or policy is so important to any determination of the crime of genocide appears in the report of the

---

[27] *Situation in the Republic of Kenya* (ICC-01/09), Decision Pursuant to Article 15 of the Rome Statute on the Authorization of an Investigation into the Situation in the Republic of Kenya, 31 March 2010, paras 86, 89, citing *Blaškić* (IT-95-14-T), Judgment, 3 March 2000, para. 205.

[28] *Situation in the Republic of Kenya* (ICC-01/09), Dissenting Opinion of Judge Hans-Peter Kaul, 31 March 2010, paras 52, 63.

Commission of Inquiry on Darfur, set up in late 2004 at the behest of the Security Council and chaired by the distinguished international legal scholar Antonio Cassese. Answering the Security Council's question as to 'whether or not acts of genocide have occurred', the Commission said 'that the Government of Sudan has not pursued a policy of genocide'. The Commission did not challenge the case law of the Appeals Chamber of the International Criminal Tribunal for the former Yugoslavia, and did not exclude the possibility that an individual acting alone might have committed genocidal acts. The chairman of the Commission, Antonio Cassese, more than once expressed the view that there is no plan or policy requirement for genocide and crimes against humanity. Yet in practice, when the Commission was asked by the Security Council whether acts of genocide were committed in Darfur, it looked for evidence of a plan or policy attributable to the Sudanese state. A similar phenomenon appears in the February 2007 judgment of the International Court of Justice on the claim filed by Bosnia and Herzegovina against Serbia and Montenegro pursuant to article IX of the Convention on the Prevention and Punishment of the Crime of Genocide. The Court discussed whether or not the policy of Serbia and its Bosnian allies was one of ethnic cleansing or of genocide.

Both the Darfur Commission and the International Court of Justice were looking at genocide through a lens that included state responsibility as well as individual criminal liability. If the Darfur Commission and the International Court of Justice had actually accepted the theory by which genocide does not require a state plan or policy, they would have looked for evidence that a single individual had killed a member of a targeted group with the intent to destroy it in whole or in part. Then they would have considered whether such acts were attributable to the state in question. But the Darfur Commission interpreted the request of the Security Council that it 'determine also whether or not acts of genocide have occurred' to mean whether or not Sudan had a plan or policy to commit such acts. The International Court of Justice reasoned along the same lines.

Judgments of the international criminal tribunals are replete with declarations that the defining element of genocide is 'specific intent' or 'special intent' or, for continental jurists, its *dolus specialis.* The Darfur Commission described it as 'an aggravated criminal intention or *dolus specialis*: it implies that the perpetrator consciously desired the prohibited acts he committed to result in the destruction, in whole or in part, of the group as such, and knew that his acts would destroy in whole or in part, the group as such'. The definition of genocide does not actually refer to 'specific intent', but it speaks of an 'intent to destroy' the protected group. The concept of specific intent is borrowed from criminal law at the national level, where it describes the mental element of specific offenders. If the theory of a lone *génocidaire* is accepted, then the specific intent at the individual level becomes the object of the inquiry into the mental element of the perpetrator. If the vision of genocide involves crimes that can only be committed by a state-like body or entity, pursuant to a policy or plan, then the focus is not on the intent of the perpetrator but rather the knowledge of the policy or plan.

The Darfur Commission associated the notion of policy with that of specific intent: 'Generally speaking the policy of attacking, killing and forcibly displacing members of some tribes does not evince a specific intent to annihilate, in whole or in part, a group distinguished on racial, ethnic, national or religious grounds,' it concluded.[29] The International Court of Justice said that genocidal acts must be committed 'with the necessary specific intent (*dolus specialis*), that is to say with a view to the destruction of the group, as distinct from its removal from the region'. The Court concluded 'that it has been conclusively established that the massive killings of members of the protected group were committed with the specific intent (*dolus specialis*) on the part of the perpetrators to destroy, in whole or in part, the group as such'.[30] Note that the Court referred to 'the perpetrators' in a collective sense. In paragraph 292 of the judgment, there is a particularly interesting discussion of specific intent in the context of the Srebrenica massacre:

The issue of intent has been illuminated by the *Krstić* Trial Chamber. In its findings, it was convinced of the existence of intent by the evidence placed before it. Under the heading 'A Plan to Execute the Bosnian Muslim Men of Srebrenica', the Chamber 'finds that, following the takeover of Srebrenica in July 1995, the Bosnian Serbs devised and implemented a plan to execute as many as possible of the military aged Bosnian Muslim men present in the enclave' (IT-98-33-T, Judgment, 2 August 2001, para. 87).

As can be seen, in effect the Court analysed the issue of 'specific intent' in terms of the existence of a plan. But in criminal law this is not such a straightforward matter. Several individuals may participate in a common plan, but this does not necessarily mean that they all share the same specific intent.

In the *Bosnia* case, the applicant was responsible for some of the muddying of the distinction between specific intent and state plan or policy. The Court noted

---

[29] Report of the International Commission of Inquiry on violations of international humanitarian law and human rights law in Darfur, UN Doc. S/2005/60, paras 491, 4.

[30] *Application of the Convention on the Prevention and Punishment of the Crime of Genocide (Bosnia and Herzegovina v Serbia and Montenegro)* [2007] ICJ Reports 43, paras 190, 277.

that this argument of the Applicant moves from the intent of the individual per-petrators of the alleged acts of genocide complained of, to the intent of higher authority, whether within the VRS or the Republika Srpska, or at the level of the Government of the Respondent itself. In the absence of an official statement of aims reflecting such an intent, the Applicant contends that the specific intent (*dolus specialis*) of those directing the course of events is clear from the consistency of practices, particularly in the camps, showing that the pattern was of acts com-mitted 'within an organized institutional framework.'

Bosnia was arguing that the specific intent to commit genocide could be revealed by a pattern of acts perpetrated 'within an organized institu-tional framework'. The Court considered evidence of official statements by Bosnian Serb officials, but observed that '[t]he Applicant's argument does not come to terms with the fact that an essential motive of much of the Bosnian Serb leadership to create a larger Serb state, by a war of conquest if necessary did not necessarily require the destruction of the Bosnian Muslims and other communities, but their expulsion'. Here the Court added yet another ingredient to the discussion, the question of 'motive'. But again, in reality 'policy' is the better term to describe what was being con-sidered. Conflating specific intent and plan or policy once again, the Court concluded: 'The *dolus specialis*, the specific intent to destroy the group in whole or in part, has to be convincingly shown by reference to particu-lar circumstances, unless a general plan to that end can be convincingly demonstrated to exist.' Moreover, 'the Applicant has not established the existence of that intent on the part of the Respondent, either on the basis of a concerted plan, or on the basis that the events reviewed above reveal a consistent pattern of conduct which could only point to the existence of such intent'.[31]

Actually, neither the Darfur Commission nor the International Court of Justice was actually looking for the specific intent of individual offend-ers. Rather, they were looking for the 'specific intent' of a state, like Sudan, or a state-like entity, like the 'Bosnian Serbs'. But states do not have spe-cific intent, or for that matter intent *tout court*. Individuals have intent. States have policies. The term 'specific intent' has been used to describe the inquiry into the volitional dimension of genocide when actually the issue is state policy.

Under the umbrella of a state policy that is not genocidal, there may well be individuals who harbour genocidal ambitions. They may or may not be deemed to commit genocide, depending upon the position that is taken with respect to the role of state policy as an element of the crime. It seems

---

[31] Ibid., paras 371–6.

plausible, indeed likely, that in a campaign involving persecution of ethnic or racial groups carried out at the instigation of a state on a large scale there will be individual perpetrators who are so driven by racist hatred that they will seek the physical extermination of the victimized group. In other words, acts whose purpose—from the standpoint of the underlying policy—is not genocidal may be attributable to groups of individuals some of whom have a genocidal mentality. But obviously when asked whether 'acts of genocide have been committed', bodies like the Darfur Commission and the International Court of Justice do not pursue their search for these marginal individuals. Rather, they look to the policy.

An important legal difficulty here concerns the relationship between state responsibility and individual criminal liability. The Darfur Commission and the International Court of Justice appear to address this through the fiction that a state can have a specific intent. This logic should be reversed. In determining state responsibility for genocide, instead of a mechanistic and unsatisfying attempt to impose concepts devised within a context of individual criminality, like specific intent, it would be better to take the state policy as the starting point and attempt to relate this to individual guilt. Following such an approach, the first issue to be resolved in determining if genocide is being committed is whether there exists a state policy. If the answer is affirmative, then the inquiry shifts to the individual, with the central question being not the individual's intent but rather the individual's knowledge of the policy. Individual intent arises in any event, because the specific acts of genocide, such as killing, have their own mental element. But as far as the plan or policy is concerned, knowledge is the key to international criminality for genocide (and crimes against humanity).

One important difficulty that this approach helps to resolve is the potential for different results in terms of state responsibility and individual criminal liability. But it also assists in addressing another problem that has perplexed judges at the international tribunals, that of complicity in genocide. They have addressed complicity by convicting those who assist in perpetrating the crime to the extent that the accused knows the intent of the perpetrator. Again, it is not really very realistic to expect an individual to know the intent of another, especially when it is specific intent that is being considered. Even courts will only deduce the intent from the behaviour of the perpetrator. The inquiry seems so much more logical and efficient when the question posed is whether the accomplice had knowledge of the policy. General Krstić was convicted of complicity because the Appeals Chamber believed that he knew of the policy being pursued by General Mladić, not because it believed he had read Mladić's mind and knew of his 'specific intent'.

The state policy issue remains one of the unresolved issues in the interpretation of both genocide and crimes against humanity. The ad hoc tribunals have made their position clear, declaring this to be excluded as an element of the crimes in question. To be entirely accurate, state policy has never really been an issue at either the International Criminal Tribunal for Rwanda, where the prosecutions have been confined to genocide charges associated with a brutal regime, or the Special Court for Sierra Leone, where the targets of prosecution were always senior leaders in the apparatus of the state or state-like rebel groups. Only at the Yugoslavia Tribunal, which spent its early years dealing with marginal thugs and deranged hooligans, has the matter been of any consequence.

The role of contextual elements pointing to state policy is made more explicit in the law applicable at the International Criminal Court. There is a debate about the authority of the Rome Statute regime outside prosecutions at the Court itself. For example, were Ireland to prosecute an individual for the crime of genocide, should its courts require evidence of a 'manifest pattern' in accordance with the Elements of Crimes, or should they disregard this as an idiosyncratic norm of no relevance to general international law? Judges at the Yugoslavia Tribunal would say it should not be applied. Some judges at the International Criminal Court might say it is irrelevant and not even binding on them, given alleged inconsistency with the definition of genocide in the Statute itself. Others would take the view that the contextual requirement in the Elements is merely a clarification of a factor that was always implicit in the definition of genocide.

The latter position is the most compelling. Judge Kaul's historical perspective on crimes against humanity sets out the logic of linking prosecution of such offences to the acts of a state or of a state-like body. It makes sense to extend the same reasoning to the crime of genocide. Admittedly, for both categories some effort of interpretation is required. The words in the statutory definitions can bear a range of constructions. A purposive or teleological approach strengthens the argument favouring state policy as an element of both crimes. Those who take the contrary position will press the case for enlarging international criminal justice to cover a broad range of so-called terrorist organizations and rebel bands.

Returning to the origins of the concept, at Nuremberg, it seems clear that the rationale for recognition of crimes against humanity was to punish crimes that were either authorized by Nazi law or tolerated by the authorities. Is that not why article VI(c) of the Charter of the International Military Tribunal concludes with the words 'whether or not in violation of the domestic law of the court where perpetrated'? Over the decades, one important justification for prosecuting crimes against humanity as such has been the fact that these atrocities generally escape prosecution in the state that normally exercises jurisdiction, under the territorial or active personality principles, because of the state's own involvement or acquiescence. International atrocity crimes, and crimes against humanity in particular, were created so that such acts could be punished *elsewhere*, and therefore so that impunity could be addressed effectively. This issue is discussed in greater detail in Chapter 1, '"Unimaginable Atrocities": Identifying International Crimes'.

We do not, by and large, have the same problem of impunity with respect to 'non-state actors'. Most states are both willing and able to prosecute the terrorist groups, rebels, mafias, motorcycle gangs, and serial killers who operate within their own borders. At best, international law is mainly of assistance here in the area of mutual legal assistance. For example, there is little real utility in defining 'terrorism' as an international crime, because as a general rule the states where the crimes are actually committed are willing and able to prosecute. Usually they have problems apprehending the offenders, but this issue is addressed through international cooperation rather than by defining the acts as international crimes so that they may be subject to universal jurisdiction or by establishing international tribunals for their prosecution. Neither international tribunals nor universal jurisdiction is necessary in order to deal adequately with terrorist crimes. In February 2011 the Special Tribunal for Lebanon ventured a definition of terrorism as an international crime but not for the purpose of international prosecution. Rather, it only sought to use the definition so as to expand the interpretation of a domestic legal provision in a prosecution undertaken with the concurrence of the concerned state.

Possibly the most compelling argument for stressing the plan or policy requirement is its capacity to better articulate the relationship between state responsibility and individual criminal liability. The Nuremberg judgment was correct to insist that crimes are committed by individuals, and not by abstract entities. But individual crimes committed in isolation from 'abstract entities' are of little or no interest at the international level. Indeed, the existence of a state plan or policy may be the best criterion in distinguishing between individual crimes that belong to national justice systems, and international crimes with their special rules and principles concerning jurisdiction, immunities, statutory limitations, and defences.

Concerns that requiring a state plan or policy will leave an impunity gap are misplaced. Most so-called non-state actors find themselves more than adequately challenged by various national justice systems. The needs in prosecution are not a broadening of the definitions of international crimes, but rather a strengthening of international judicial cooperation mechanisms so as to facilitate bringing offenders to book for 'ordinary' crimes. Mainly it is when perpetrators commit heinous acts precisely because they are acting on behalf of a state, and in pursuit of its policies, that we require international justice to step in. Insisting that the plan or policy is an element of the crime clarifies the reality of this special form of criminality, and facilitates its distinction.

Finally, this debate also bears upon criminal justice policy at the international level. It seems unlikely that international tribunals will be used in the future in the way that they were in the early days of International Criminal Tribunal for the former Yugoslavia. Isolated individuals pursuing personal criminal agendas should be brought to book somewhere, but the International Criminal Court or an international ad hoc tribunal is not the right place for this. These institutions should confine their activity to the 'big fish'. Definitions of crimes are a bit like a fishing net. If the mesh is fine, the fisher will end up with a boatful of sardines, anchovies, plastic bottles, and other detritus as well as the occasional shark. If the mesh is large, the small stuff will pass through the net and only the shark will get caught. To the extent that they exist to give jurisdiction to international tribunals and to third states acting under the principle of universal jurisdiction, the definitions of genocide and crimes against humanity work better if they resemble fishing nets for sharks, not sardines. The state policy requirement helps to accomplish this.

6

HISTORY, INTERNATIONAL JUSTICE, AND THE RIGHT TO TRUTH

German hotel guest: 'Will you stop talking about the war!'
Basil Fawlty (John Cleese): 'You started it!'
Guest: 'No we didn't!'
Fawlty: 'Yes you did, you invaded Poland!'

Concluding scene in 'The Germans', Fawlty Towers,
BBC Television Series, 1975

A few weeks after the Nazis attacked Poland, in September 1939, the Soviet Union occupied the eastern part of the country. Soon Moscow had absorbed these Polish territories into Belorussia and the Ukraine, effectively wiping Poland off the map. Thousands of Polish military leaders, professionals, and intellectuals were taken prisoner by the Soviets. On 5 March 1940 the head of the secret police, Lavrentiy Beria, informed Stalin that the prisoners were 'hardened, irremediable enemies of Soviet power' for whom the 'supreme punishment, shooting' should be imposed. With Politburo approval, the prisoners were murdered in the Katyń forest, which is located a few kilometres from Smolensk within the borders of Russia itself. The victims were buried in mass graves over which young trees were planted, to disguise the crime.

Three years later, with parts of western Russia still under Nazi occupation, the graves were discovered. The Germans organized an international commission of forensic experts. With the exception of a Swiss professor from the University of Geneva, François Naville, most of its members were associated with Nazi institutions and lacked any credibility. The International Committee of the Red Cross refused to participate in the exercise. Naville himself travelled to Smolensk to see the graves of the 10,000 or so victims, apparently overflying Warsaw, where he saw an entire neighbourhood in flames. Naville later reported that he inquired about what was going on, to be told that something had happened in the ghetto.[1] In fact, this was the destruction of half a million Jews resident in the cities. Perhaps this was a case of Professor Naville missing the forest in Warsaw for the trees in Katyń. When the commission concluded that the Soviets were responsible, Nazi propagandist Goebbels was ecstatic. He welcomed the opportunity this provided to divide the allied powers in the post-Stalingrad phase of the war.

After the Soviets drove the Germans from Russian territory, they set up their own commission of inquiry. It concluded that the Nazis, and not Soviet intelligence, were responsible for the mass murder at Katyń.

At Nuremberg, the Soviet prosecutors insisted upon charging the German defendants with responsibility for the Katyń forest massacre, as it came to be called. The British and American prosecutors were opposed, but it is not clear whether this was because they suspected the Russians were themselves responsible. They may simply have considered that this would be difficult to prove without lengthy testimony, given the conflicting versions, and that there were many other much clearer examples of Nazi barbarism, on a more awesome scale than Katyń. The Soviet prosecutors, who probably accepted in good faith their regime's official and dishonest version, did not themselves seem particularly enthusiastic about proving the crime. They confined their evidence to the perfunctory submission of the report of the Soviet commission of inquiry.

This was the opening that the Nazi defendants were waiting for. 'I did not think they would be so shameless as to mention Poland,' the most prominent defendant, Hermann Göring, is alleged to have said. Another of the accused, Baldur von Schirach, apparently remarked: 'When they mentioned Poland, I thought I'd die.' Göring's lawyer, Otto Stahmer, indicated his intention to produce evidence in reply. The judges allowed the accused Germans to call three witnesses in defence; the Soviet prosecutor was permitted three witnesses in rebuttal. The result, on any fair reading of the transcript, was inconclusive. If anything, contemporary observers felt that the Soviets had made a strong showing and that the Germans had not had much success with their witnesses in making the case for Soviet responsibility. The Soviet prosecutor probably helped the Germans by producing evidence of the Nazi commission of inquiry, which had not previously been submitted. Katyń was not mentioned in the final judgment. Even the Soviet judge, Nikitchenko,

---

[1] Kazimierz Karbowksi and Elisabeth Curti-Karbowksi, 'Le rôle du professeur François Naville dans l'enquête sur le massacre de Katyn', in Delphine Debons, Antoine Fleyr, and Jena-François Pitteloud (eds), *Katyn and Switzerland, Forensic Investigators and Investigations in Humanitarian Crises, 1920–2007*, Geneva: Georg, 2009, pp. 25–35, at p. 28.

avoided the subject in his dissenting opinion. The silence spoke volumes. Nikitchenko is usually dismissed as the least impartial of the judges, but on Katyń he glistens with rectitude.

The Katyń forest massacre is often invoked, along with the fire bombing of German cities and the nuclear destruction of Hiroshima and Nagasaki, in the 'victors' justice' critique of Nuremberg, a matter discussed elsewhere in this volume (see Chapter 3, 'Victors' Justice? Selecting Targets for Prosecution'). The Soviets could not, of course, have been convicted of the crime by the International Military Tribunal. Its jurisdiction *ratione personae* was confined to the 'major war criminals of the European axis'. It would have been improper for the judges to have implied that the Soviets were responsible, even if the evidence before them had been reasonably conclusive, which it was not. While the claim that the Soviets were to blame was certainly plausible, the charge that this was a German crime could hardly be dismissed as preposterous, given the magnitude of Nazi atrocities and the manipulation of the crime for propaganda purposes by Goebbels and others.

When the Soviets first led the evidence of Katyń, in February 1946, the British ambassador to Tehran, Sir Reader Bullard, telegraphed his own view to the Foreign Office. The Soviets were responsible, he wrote. The Acting Counsellor of the British Mission in Moscow sympathized with Bullard's view that the Soviets had not proven Nazi responsibility for the crime, but seemed to think that the case for Soviet liability was also not clearly established. He warned that 'whatever the facts...the effect on Anglo-Soviet relations of any apparent tendency on our part to accept the German case about Katyń would be calamitous'.[2] In London J. Galsworthy of the Foreign Office's Northern Department noted that Bullard's 'doubts may be well founded—and shared by many others—but there could be no question of our "blowing" the Russian case either in public or in private and, in many ways, it might be as well that Katyń should be disposed of once and for all—onto the Germans'. This bureaucrat in the Foreign Office, with studied indifference to the truth, seemed to welcome the possibility that 'justice' would provide a politically convenient albeit dishonest answer to the issue of responsibility.

It took half a century for the fog of war in which the Katyń forest had been shrouded to dissipate entirely. A commission of inquiry established by the United States House of Representatives in the early 1950s did a thorough job of investigating the massacre, concluding that it was indeed the Soviets who were responsible. But despite the quality of its work, the

---

[2] Cited in 'The Katyń Massacre and Reactions in the Foreign Office, Memorandum by the Historical Adviser', 10 April 1973, para. 39.

findings could not escape the complaint that this was part of the anti-communist witch-hunt, directed not only at the Soviet leadership but at left-wing sympathizers in the Department of State and in the prosecution team at Nuremberg. Only in 1990, probably enticed by an opportunity to undermine Mikhail Gorbachev rather than a principled commitment to the search for historical truth, Boris Yeltsin revealed publicly what had been well known to generations of senior Soviet leaders.

The consequences of the Soviet admission have yet to be fully resolved. Two decades later, the Russians are still resisting the efforts of the victims, and of the Polish nation more generally, to ensure justice and accountability. In July 2011 two applications to the European Court of Human Rights filed against Russia by descendants of the Katyń victims charging inadequate investigation into the events were declared admissible. This does not yet mean the Court has made a firm finding against Russia. One of the difficult issues concerns the retroactivity of the European Convention on Human Rights. The applicants insist they are not litigating the events of 1940, but rather the failure of Russia in recent years to carry out a proper inquiry.

There is a widespread impression that the Nuremberg trial is in some way tainted by its handling of the Katyń forest massacre. Yet in their wisdom the four judges did nothing to distort the truth of history; quite the contrary. They were of course limited by their jurisdiction and therefore unable to inquire fully into the responsibility for the atrocity. But they did not, as the cynical British diplomat cited above might have hoped, demean the credibility of the judgment by endorsing a lie or simply obscuring the truth in the interests of political convenience. It is more compelling to view the treatment of Katyń at Nuremberg as a confirmation both of the integrity of the proceedings and of the power of criminal justice to reach accurate conclusions about historical fact. The Nuremberg judgment could not, in a few hundred pages, adequately describe the entire history of Nazi atrocity, nor could it in any meaningful way address the features of the conflict that were outside its jurisdiction, like Katyń. But it did not distort the historical record. It stands as an important benchmark, an anchor for an accurate vision of the Nazi regime with detail and nuance to be drawn from other sources. Perhaps for this reason the Nuremberg judgment is so reviled by Holocaust deniers and negationists, who sometimes point to the treatment of Katyń as evidence to support their attacks.

ESTABLISHING A RECORD OF PAST EVENTS

In 2004 the United Nations Secretary-General presented a report to the Security Council entitled 'The Rule of Law and Transitional Justice in

Conflict and Post-conflict Societies'. The document considered the range of initiatives undertaken at the international level over the previous decade or so, including the ad hoc criminal tribunals. The Secretary-General noted that these institutions sought to advance a number of objectives,

among which are bringing to justice those responsible for serious violations of human rights and humanitarian law, putting an end to such violations and preventing their recurrence, securing justice and dignity for victims, *establishing a record of past events*, promoting national reconciliation, re-establishing the rule of law and contributing to the restoration of peace.

He added that criminal trials 'can also help societies to emerge from periods of conflict by establishing detailed and well-substantiated records of particular incidents and events'.[3]

The role of criminal tribunals as arbiters of historical truth has been contested since the first serious efforts of international justice, at Nuremberg and Tokyo. Referring to a national trial, but one subject to provisions of international law and widely regarded as part of the corpus of international criminal law, Hannah Arendt, in *Eichmann in Jerusalem*, wrote:

The purpose of the trial is to render justice and nothing else; even the noblest of ulterior purposes—'the making of a record of the Hitler regime which would withstand the test of history', as Robert G. Storey, executive trial counsel at Nuremberg formulated the supposed higher aims of the Nuremberg Trials—can only detract from the law's main business: to weigh the charges brought against the accused, to render judgment, and to mete out due punishment.[4]

Storey's remarks, cited by Arendt, cannot be found in the published proceedings of the trial and the source of her quotation is not evident. Ironically, the closest resemblance in the transcripts of the International Military Tribunal is a comment by Otto Freiherr von Londinghausen, who was defence counsel to Konstantin Freiherr von Neurath:

In this age it may be said that one cannot imagine any avowed dictator or omnipotent despot who can rule without or against the will, or at least the tacit approval of the nation, at least its majority. And so—it is necessary to make this known to the world—invisible behind the defendants, there sits also in the prisoners' dock our poor beaten and tortured German people, because it placed upon a pedestal and selected as leader a man who led it to its doom. From this follows of necessity the inescapable demand that, contrary to the concept of a conspiracy applied in regard to ordinary criminals, application of the concept of conspiracy

---

[3] The rule of law and transitional justice in conflict and post-conflict societies, UN Doc. S/2004/616, paras 38, 39 (my emphasis).

[4] Hannah Arendt, *Eichmann in Jerusalem: A Report on the Banality of Evil*, New York: Viking, 1964, p. 253.

applied in international law must first proceed to investigate and examine how it happened—how it could happen that an intellectual, high ranking people, a people who gave so much to the world in terms of cultural and spiritual gifts as the German people did—that it could hail a man such as Hitler, follow him into the bloodiest of all wars, giving him the best it had. Not until you, Your Honours, have taken this into consideration and examined this question, will you be able to establish a just verdict in regard to the individual defendants themselves, with due consideration for their dissimilarity—a judgment which will stand the test of history.[5]

Von Neurath was judged to be a relatively less egregious figure by comparison with his co-accused, and he was one of the minority of Nuremberg defendants to be condemned to a fixed term of imprisonment rather than to life imprisonment or death. His counsel never received an answer from the Tribunal. The question was left to genuine historians.

The modern international criminal tribunals, for the former Yugoslavia, Rwanda, and Sierra Leone, were established to address major conflicts in different parts of the world. Each has now generated an enormous volume of case law. The tribunals have held many dozens of major trials. In most of these, there have been important debates about the historical dimensions of the situations being considered. These have gone much beyond the specifics of the charges against any particular individual accused. In a general sense, the pattern of prosecutions has confirmed perceptions of the conflicts that are widely shared by contemporary historians. In some respects, however, they disappoint. For example, although observers of the conflicts in the Balkans have noted the prevalence of rape, and its use as a weapon of war, there have been relatively few prosecutions for sexual violence, and those that have taken place do not reveal the sort of plan or pattern described in the literature. The standard explanation for this is that victims of rape and similar crimes are very reluctant to testify, making prosecution problematic.

Expert testimony from historians has often been adduced in these trials, generally in order to provide some background for the charges or, from the defence standpoint, to generate perspective and sometimes offer evidence in mitigation. But in the *Milošević* trial, when the Prosecutor put someone identified as an historian on the witness list, presiding Judge May said that

according to your list, you're going to call somebody who is simply identified as a historian who will apparently deal with the historical context of relations between Serbs and Albanians in Kosovo. Now, again, let me put you on notice that we shall

---

[5] (1948) 19 IMT 221.

look very carefully at this sort of evidence. While it's right that historians have been called before this Tribunal, there must be a limit to the amount of evidence which we can obtain or have put before us, particularly in the light of history. The amount of historical evidence we will want to hear is very limited.[6]

Many other defendants had already stood trial at the Tribunal prior to Slobodan Milošević, however, and Judge May was probably satisfied that most of the historical context had already been elucidated in earlier judgments.

In a presentation to the United Nations General Assembly in the early years of the International Criminal Tribunal for the former Yugoslavia, its first president, Antonio Cassese, said the institution was creating 'an historical record of what occurred during the conflict thereby preventing historical "revisionism"'.[7] The Tribunal's 1998 Annual Report said that ensuring 'that history listens' was 'a most important function of the Tribunal'. The Tribunal strove 'to establish as judicial fact the full details of the madness that transpired in the former Yugoslavia'. The Report said that in the future, 'no one will be able to deny the depths to which their brother and sister human beings sank. And by recording the capacity for the evil in all of us, it is hoped to recognise warning signs in the future and to act with sufficient speed and determination to prevent such bloodshed.'[8]

Similar pronouncements appear, but only relatively occasionally, in judgments: 'It is one of the purposes of the International Tribunal to establish a historical record of the event [sic] in the former Yugoslavia. It is also a purpose of the International Tribunal, and a duty owed by the prosecution to the International Tribunal, to look for the "truth" of those events.'[9] In one case, a Trial Chamber said that the ethnic cleansing of the village of Ahmici had 'gone down in history' as one of the most vicious illustrations of inhumanity. 'Today, the name of that small village must be added to the long list of previously unknown hamlets and towns that recall abhorrent misdeeds and make us all shudder with horror and shame: Dachau, Oradour sur Glâne, Katijn, Marzabotto, Soweto, My Lai, Sabra and Shatila, and so many others,' said the judgment. The Trial Chamber cautioned, however, that its

primary task...was not to construct a historical record of modern human horrors in Bosnia and Herzegovina. The principal duty of the Trial Chamber was

---

[6] *Milošević* (IT-02-54-T), Transcript, 9 January 2002, pp. 242–3.

[7] UN Doc. A/52/PV.44, p. 2.

[8] Fifth Annual Report of the International Tribunal for the Prosecution of Persons Responsible for Serious Violations of International Humanitarian Law Committed in the Territory of the former Yugoslavia sine 1991, UN Doc. A/53/219-S/1998/737, para. 296.

[9] *Halilović* (IT-01-48-T), Motion for Judicial Notice, 1 March 2005, para. 9 (references omitted).

simply to decide whether the six defendants standing trial were guilty of partaking in this persecutory violence or whether they were instead extraneous to it and hence, not guilty.[10]

Later, another Trial Chamber said it preferred to avoid 'expressing rhetorical indignation that these events should ever have occurred at all'. It said it would leave it 'to historians and social psychologists to plumb the depths of this episode of the Balkan conflict and to probe for deep-seated causes. The task at hand is a more modest one: to find, from the evidence presented during the trial, what happened' during the brief period relevant to the indictment.[11] In a strategy paper, the Prosecutor of the International Criminal Court explained that his 'mandate does not include production of comprehensive historical records for a given conflict', although he acknowledged that in selecting specific violations for prosecution there was an effort 'to provide a sample that is reflective of the gravest incidents and the main types of victimization'.[12]

A BY-PRODUCT, NOT AN OBJECTIVE

Sometimes, historical truth has been presented as a by-product of the international criminal proceedings rather than as an objective. In *Milutinović* a Trial Chamber said that it had 'one core task: to determine whether the Prosecution had proved the guilt of any of the Accused on any of the charges'. Nevertheless, '[c]oincidentally, the narrative of this Judgment includes information which may help to provide a fuller understanding of events in 1998 and 1999 in Kosovo. This Judgment is, however, simply one element in an array of material from which historians will derive a complete historical account.'[13] In a decision of the International Criminal Tribunal for Rwanda, judges noted that defence and prosecution evidence was not necessarily contradictory and that 'when viewed in combination as a whole' it provided 'a broader historical record of the killings at Kabuye hill'.[14]

Sometimes, judges have refused to address issues that are of undoubted historical importance but essentially irrelevant for the purposes of a determination of criminal liability. This may be because they are without jurisdiction, as was the case at Nuremberg with Allied atrocities, like the fire bombing of German cities. Defendants have frequently challenged

[10] *Kupreškić* et al. (IT-95-16-T), Judgment, 14 January 2000, paras 755, 756.
[11] *Krstić* (IT-98-33-T), Judgment, 2 August 2001, para. 2.
[12] Prosecutorial Strategy 2009–2012, 1 February 2010, para. 20.
[13] *Milutinović* et al. (IT-05-87-T), Judgment, 26 February 2009, para. 4.
[14] *Kalimanzira* (ICTR-05-88-T), Judgment, 22 June 2009, para. 386.

prosecutions that deal with crimes committed by one side but not the other. This is sometimes called a *tu quoque* defence ('the other side did the same thing...'), and it has been given short shrift by judges. For example, the International Criminal Tribunal for Rwanda has ignored the issue of responsibility for the shooting down of the presidential airplane, an event that sparked the killings in April 1994.[15] Even if it could be proven that the Rwandese Patriotic Front forces were responsible for the assassination, as some have argued, this could in no way provide a defence to persons charged with subsequent acts of genocide.[16]

Certain commentators have assessed with favour the function of tribunals as writers of history. For example, Professor Richard Wilson has stated that '[j]udgments handed down by the International Criminal Tribunal for the Former Yugoslavia (ICTY or Tribunal) challenge the long-held assumption in socio-legal scholarship that courts are inappropriate venues to construct wide-ranging historical explanations of past conflicts'.[17] But a former judge of the Yugoslavia Tribunal, Patricia Wald of the United States, said that

dozens of pages in [International Criminal Tribunal for the former Yugoslavia] judgments focus on the causes and precursors of the 1991 outbreak of hostilities. However, commentators, citizens, and officers of the implicated countries increasingly suggest that the adversarial trial process and the findings of judges may not produce the best approximations of history. Moreover, the 'adjudication' by [International Criminal Tribunal for the former Yugoslavia] of who started, prolonged, or ended the war and why in the context of criminal proceedings without the states themselves having input is basically unfair, or at least does not contribute to future reconciliation.[18]

At various times, prosecutors, defence counsel, and judges have all insisted that this is not a burden that should be placed upon the shoulders of judicial institutions. It has the potential to distort both prosecution and defence, they have asserted. On other occasions, however, these actors in the process have acknowledged that their role as historians is inescapable.

One of the earliest trials at the International Criminal Tribunal for the former Yugoslavia involved brutality in the Čelebići concentration camp

---

[15] See: *Nahimana* et al. (ICTR-99-52-A), Decision on Appellant Jean-Bosco Barayagwiza's Motion for Leave to Present Additional Evidence Pursuant to Rule 115, 5 May 2006, para. 20; *Nahimana* et al. (ICTR-99-52-A), Judgment, 28 November 2007, paras 249–50.

[16] *Bagosora* et al. (ICTR-98-41-T), Decision on Request for Subpoenas of United Nations Officials, 6 October 2006, paras 12–18

[17] Richard Ashby Wilson, 'Judging History: The Historical Record of the International Criminal Tribunal for the Former Yugoslavia' (2005) 27 *Human Rights Quarterly* 908, at p. 908.

[18] Patricia Wald, 'The International Criminal Tribunal for the Former Yugoslavia Comes of Age: Some Observations on Day-to-Day Dilemmas of an International Court' (2001) 5 *Washington University Journal of Law & Policy* 87, pp. 116–17.

in central Bosnia, located on the road between Sarajevo and Mostar aside the Neretva river. It was quite typical of the first cases in that it focussed on low-level perpetrators. This did not lend itself to discussions about the broad features of the conflict and its background. A trial like Nuremberg, which is directed at the masterminds and leaders, is a better platform for historical analysis than one involving minor figures, remote from the centres of power. According to the judgment in the *Čelebići* case:

[t]he Indictment at issue in the present case is solely concerned with events in the municipality (*opstina*) of Konjic, in central Bosnia and Herzegovina, during a period of months in 1992. The Trial Chamber does not consider it necessary to enter into a lengthy discussion of the political and historical background to these events, nor a general analysis of the conflict which blighted the whole of the former Yugoslavia around that time. The function of the Trial Chamber is to do justice in the case at hand and while this naturally involves presenting its findings in context, we will limit this background section to those facts which are necessary to situate the evaluation of the present case.[19]

Often, judges have insisted that the portions of their judgments concerning history be viewed as background information rather than as proven facts. What they have labelled 'historical context' amounts to 'essentially a brief explanation of events in deliberately neutral language aimed at allowing the Trial Chamber to form some idea of the historical backdrop'.[20]

STRAYING FROM THE MAIN ISSUE AND LENGTHENING THE TRIAL

Debates about the history-recording function of international prosecutions have arisen in the context of determining the scope of a given trial. In order to shorten the length of proceedings, judges have often requested that the content of indictments be limited. In reply, prosecutors have maintained that broad indictments are necessary for the purpose of establishing the historical record. For example, a Trial Chamber of the Yugoslavia Tribunal wrote that

[a]s a final argument, the Prosecution submits that reducing the scope of the Indictment would risk the creation of an inaccurate historical record. It argues that '[t]he loss of the Slobodan Milosevic Judgment left an inevitable void in terms of the historical record of the scope of the atrocities committed by Milosevic and his co-perpetrators' and that 'the Tribunal is now faced with the opportunity [...]

---

[19] *Delalić* et al. (IT-96-21-T), Judgment, 16 November 1998, para. 88.
[20] *Kayishema* et al. (ICTR-95-1-T), Judgment and Sentence, 21 May 1999, paras 32–3; *Bizimungu* et al. (ICTR-99-50-T), Decision on Prosecutor's Motion for Judicial Notice, paras 14–15.

to create a permanent historical record of these atrocities and to bring justice to the victims of these heinous crimes'. In this regard, it also submits that a further reduction of the Indictment 'would result in a historically and factually inaccurate record, and a loss of possibly the last opportunity the Tribunal has to achieve one of its core goals [...]—to bring effective redress to the victims of international humanitarian law violations'. However, the Tribunal was established to administer justice, and not to create a historical record. The Trial Chamber will therefore not consider this argument as relevant.[21]

The reference to the Milošević trial is apt but perhaps mistaken. The former Serbian President died of natural causes after proceedings had been underway for several years. Arguably, had the charges against him been more focussed, and the different aspects of the conflicts in the former Yugoslavia addressed through distinct trials, at least one set of proceedings might have been completed. Indeed, when he passed away suddenly in his cell in Scheveningen, a headline in *The Guardian* stated: 'Slobodan Milosevic Dies Alone with History Still Demanding Justice.'

In *Milošević* the Prosecutor had sought the joinder of the different indictments, invoking an argument related to the role of the Tribunal as historian. According to one commentator, the thrust of Prosecutor Carla Del Ponte's approach was that 'the separation of the charges against Milošević into two distinct trials would work to establish two distinct historical narratives, constituting the conflicts in Croatia and Bosnia and Herzegovina as one event, and the conflict in Kosovo as an entirely distinct historical event'. Del Ponte insisted that the two conflicts were linked, and that 'the constitution of two separate narratives actually causes prejudice to victims...provid[ing] an alternative to the discriminatory historical narratives which form the legitimating basis for the violence perpetrated upon them'.[22]

Milošević contested the proposal to join the indictments in a single trial, arguing it was a gambit by the Prosecutor in order to push back the Kosovo charges. He said: 'It is a consequence of the 11th of September. They wish to place in the background the charges for Kosovo because those charges of Kosovo inevitably open up the issue of the cooperation of Clinton's administration with the terrorists in Kosovo, including the bin Laden organization.'[23] Milošević contended that a single trial would aim

---

[21] *Stanisić* et al. (IT-03-69-PT) Decision Pursuant to Rule 73*bis* (D), 4 February 2008, para. 21.

[22] James Cockayne, 'Commentary', in André Klip and Göran Sluiter (eds), *Annotated Leading Cases of International Criminal Tribunals, The International Criminal Tribunal for the Former Yugoslavia 2001–2002*, vol. 8, Antwerp/Oxford: Intersentia, 2005, pp. 175–83, at p. 179.

[23] *Milošević* (IT-02-54-T), Transcript, 11 December 2001, p. 134.

at 'creating an historical fallacy that will be [used] to accuse those who defended Yugoslavia of breaking it up'.[24]

The judges decided to join the indictments so as to hold one long trial, covering the distinct conflicts in Croatia, Bosnia and Herzegovina, and Kosovo, rather than two shorter ones. James Cockayne has noted that

the decision crucially affected the construction of the historical narrative through the Milosevic trial. The Appeals Chamber's decision required the Trial Chamber to hear the Kosovo Indictment first. In effect, this makes the players in the drama act out Act III before Acts I and II. Inevitably, the Prosecution has had to engage in a number of re-writes of the script along the way, to help the trial's audience contextualise the drama it sees played out in the Churchillplein courtrooms.

As he explained, decisions by prosecutors and judges about 'the process of determining individual legal liability [are], in the context of trying the architects of mass violence, inevitably bound up with a larger project of constructing an alternative public historical narrative'.[25]

GUILTY PLEA PROCEEDINGS

These issues have also been considered in the context of guilty plea proceedings, of which there have been several, especially at the Yugoslavia Tribunal. With a guilty plea, a defendant acknowledges culpability and proposes not to contest the charges laid by the Prosecutor in exchange for a reduction in the list of crimes for which a conviction will be registered and a position shared with the Prosecutor on the appropriate sentencing range. An agreed statement of facts is filed with the Court. This is said to be beneficial to victims, because they are saved the trauma of testifying; critics argue that such proceedings deprive victims of their voices. Guilty pleas save precious resources, expedite proceedings, and avoid the risk of full acquittals. Guilty pleas are taken as mitigating circumstances because they 'may contribute to the process of national reconciliation'.[26]

Concerns have been expressed that guilty plea proceedings may distort the historical record that some contend the tribunals are expected to construct.[27] Judges have noted that a plea agreement may impede the fulfilment of their mandate, 'which is to bring the truth to light and justice to the people of the former Yugoslavia. Neither the public, nor the judges themselves come closer to know the truth beyond what is accepted in

---

[24] Ibid., Transcript, 30 January 2002, p. 337.   [25] James Cockayne, 'Commentary', p. 181.

[26] *Seregundo* (ICTR-2005-84-I), Judgment and Sentence, 12 June 2006, para. 57.

[27] Nancy Amoury Combs, *Guilty Pleas in International Criminal Law, Constructing a Restorative Justice Approach*, Stanford: Stanford University Press, 2007, at pp. 67, 207.

the plea agreement.'[28] As a result, they have warned, there might be 'an unfortunate gap in the public and historical record of the concrete case'.[29] Accordingly,

[a] public trial, with the presentation of testimonial and documentary evidence by both parties, creates a more complete and detailed historical record than a guilty plea, which may only establish the bare factual allegations in an indictment or may be supplemented by a statement of facts and acceptance of responsibility by the accused.[30]

Nevertheless,

when coupled with an accused's substantial co-operation with the prosecution, an agreement grants more insights into previously undiscovered areas. However, while treating plea agreements with appropriate caution, it should be recalled that this Tribunal is not the final arbiter of historical facts. That is for historians. For the judiciary focusing on core issues of a criminal case before this International Tribunal, it is important that justice be done and be seen to be done.[31]

It has been said that before accepting a plea agreement, the court 'may seek to ensure that the totality of the accused's criminal conduct is reflected and that an accurate historical record exists'.[32]

Sometimes, trial chambers have underscored the limited extent of their assessments of the factual background, pointing out that for the purposes of 'history' their account is inadequate. Momčilo Krajišnik was a Bosnian Serb leader who was closely associated with Radovan Karadzić. Convicting Krajišnik of crimes against humanity and war crimes, a Trial Chamber concluded that there had been 3,000 Muslim and Croat victims during the indictment period, a figure that would be generally perceived as a grotesque understatement. The judgment explained '[t]o avoid any misunderstanding' that its conclusion was 'not a historical finding, but a legal one'. It said it could only base its conclusions on the evidence received, and that it could not 'exclude for the possibility that more Muslims and Croats were killed in these municipalities during the relevant time period'.[33] Indeed.

One of the major decisions of the International Criminal Tribunal for Rwanda, concerning military leaders, resulted in dismissal of charges of conspiracy to commit genocide although the accused were convicted of

---

[28] *Dragan Nikolić* (IT-94-2-S), Sentencing Judgment, 18 December 2003, para. 122 (references omitted). Also: *Deronjić* (IT-02-61-S), Sentencing Judgment, 4 March 2004, para. 135.

[29] Ibid.

[30] *Momir Nikolić* (IT-02-60/1-S), Sentencing Judgment, 2 December 2003, para. 61.

[31] *Dragan Nikolić* (IT-94-2-S), Sentencing Judgment, 18 December 2003, para. 122 (references omitted).

[32] *Momir Nikolić* (IT-02-60/1-S), Sentencing Judgment, 2 December 2003, para. 52.

[33] *Krajisnik* (IT-00-39-T), Judgment, September 2006, para. 71.

other crimes. The judges explained that they were not asked to determine 'whether there was a plan or conspiracy to commit genocide in Rwanda' but rather 'whether the Prosecution has proven beyond reasonable doubt based on the evidence in this case that the four Accused committed the crime of conspiracy'.[34] The acquittal on the conspiracy charges ignited a chorus from genocide deniers. They said the judgment proved they were right all along. Bagosora's rather partisan defence counsel, Peter Erlinder, wrote that:

after seven years of receiving the best evidence the [Rwandese Patriotic Front] could muster, three judges of the UN tribunal for Rwanda unanimously concluded that the story of the Rwanda genocide told by the victors...of a 'long-planned conspiracy to commit a genocide of Tutsi civilians' by top military officers was *not supported by the evidence*.[35]

Professor Charles Jalloh has properly described this as mischaracterization, noting that the Trial Chamber was well aware of 'the weightiness of its finding in the specific case before it but also for Rwanda's contested history'. He has pointed to portions of the decision where the judges said they 'cannot exclude that there were in fact plans *prior to 6 April* [*1994*] to commit genocide in Rwanda', and that 'there are certain indications in the evidence of a prior plan or conspiracy to perpetrate a genocide as well as other politically motivated killings in Rwanda, which could have been triggered upon the resumption of hostilities between the government and the RPF or following some other significant event'.[36]

THE RIGHT TO TRUTH

Rulings of the International Criminal Tribunal for Rwanda describe the 1994 genocide as a proven fact that is no longer subject to dispute. Relying on precedent from the Nuremberg Tribunal, modern international criminal tribunals take judicial notice of 'facts that are not subject to reasonable dispute including, common or universally known facts, such as general facts of history'. According to one Trial Chamber, these must be facts 'so notorious, or clearly established or susceptible to determination by reference to readily obtainable and authoritative sources that evidence of their existence

---

[34] *Bagosora* et al. (ICTR-98-41-T), Judgment and Sentence, 18 December 2008, para. 2092.

[35] Peter Erlinder, *Rwanda: Flawed Elections and the Politics of 'Genocide Denial'*, JURIST—Forum, 28 August 2010 <http://jurist.org/forum/2010/08/rwanda-flawed-elections-and-the-politics-of-genocide-denial.php> (emphasis in the original).

[36] Charles Jalloh, *(Re)Writing History After Rwanda's Genocide: A Response to Peter Erlinder*, JURIST—Forum, 31 August 2010 <http://jurist.org/forum/2010/08/rewriting-history-after-rwandas-genocide-a-response-to-peter-erlinder.php> (emphasis in the original).

is unnecessary'.[37] Judicial notice can only be taken of 'facts not subject to reasonable dispute'.[38] The mission of the tribunals as historians has been invoked as one of the justifications for judicial notice. To attain this objective, it is said to be desirable that they arrive at relatively similar conclusions.[39] In *Karemera* et al. the Appeals Chamber of the International Criminal Tribunal for Rwanda described the Rwandan genocide as 'a part of world history':

> The Appeals Chamber agrees with the Prosecution: the fact that genocide occurred in Rwanda in 1994 should have been recognized by the Trial Chamber as a fact of common knowledge. Genocide consists of certain acts, including killing, undertaken with the intent to destroy, in whole or in part, a national, ethnical, racial or religious group, as such. There is no reasonable basis for anyone to dispute that, during 1994, there was a campaign of mass killing intended to destroy, in whole or at least in very large part, Rwanda's Tutsi population, which (as judicially noticed by the Trial Chamber) was a protected group. That campaign was, to a terrible degree, successful; although exact numbers may never be known, the great majority of Tutsis were murdered, and many others were raped or otherwise harmed. These basic facts were broadly known even at the time of the Tribunal's establishment; indeed, reports indicating that genocide occurred in Rwanda were a key impetus for its establishment, as reflected in the Security Council resolution establishing it and even the name of the Tribunal. During its early history, it was valuable for the purpose of the historical record for Trial Chambers to gather evidence documenting the overall course of the genocide and to enter findings of fact on the basis of that evidence. Trial and Appeal Judgements thereby produced (while varying as to the responsibility of particular accused) have unanimously and decisively confirmed the occurrence of genocide in Rwanda, which has also been documented by countless books, scholarly articles, media reports, U.N. reports and resolutions, national court decisions, and government and NGO reports. At this stage, the Tribunal need not demand further documentation. The fact of the Rwandan genocide is a part of world history, a fact as certain as any other, a classic instance of a 'fact of common knowledge'.[40]

Although the International Criminal Tribunal for the former Yugoslavia and the Special Court for Sierra Leone have also determined the existence of 'historical facts of common knowledge',[41] there are no comparable

---

[37] *Semanza* (ICTR-97-20), Decision on the Prosecutor's Motion for Judicial Notice and Presumptions of Fact Pursuant to Rules 94 and 54, 3 November 2000, para. 25.

[38] *Simić* et al. (IT-95-9-PT), Decision on Pre-trial Motion by the Prosecution Requesting the Trial Chamber to take Judicial Notice of the International Character of the Conflict in Bosnia-Herzegovina, 25 March 1999.

[39] *Norman* et al. (SCSL-04-14-AR73), Fofana—Decision on Appeal Against 'Decision on Prosecution's Motion for Judicial Notice and Admission of Evidence', 16 May 2005, para. 21.

[40] *Karemera* et al. (ICTR-98-44-AR73(C)), Decision on Prosecutor's Interlocutory Appeal of Decision on Judicial Notice, 16 June 2006.

[41] *Strugar* (IT-01-42-T), Judgment, 31 January 2005, para. 13.

defining events like the Rwandan genocide that have been adjudicated in this manner.

Unlike the International Criminal Court, where the Prosecutor has enormous leeway in the choice of 'situations' for prosecution, the exercise of discretion at the ad hoc tribunals for the former Yugoslavia, Rwanda, and Sierra Leone is limited to the selection of specific offenders within relatively narrow temporal and territorial jurisdictional parameters. But even these determinations can have an enormous impact on the narrative that emerges from the work of the institutions. For example, although the International Criminal Tribunal for the former Yugoslavia has jurisdiction over the NATO bombing campaign in early 1999, the Prosecutor chose not to pursue charges of war crimes directed against military leaders of the United States and some countries in Western Europe. Carla Del Ponte assigned a rather traditional military lawyer with a NATO background to direct an inquiry. He concluded that there was no basis for a prosecution. She followed the advice. Reporting to the Security Council, she said: 'Although some mistakes were made by NATO, I am very satisfied that there was no deliberate targeting of civilians or of unlawful military targets by NATO during the bombing campaign.'[42] But in her memoirs, published a few years after she had left office, Del Ponte said she 'never closed the book' on NATO bombing. When General Wesley Clark testified during the Milošević trial, the accused cross-examined him about the NATO campaign. He was promptly halted by Presiding Judge Richard May. 'I was disappointed,' wrote Del Ponte. 'It was the only moment during the entire trial that I found myself pulling for Milošević.' She described how she then asked a court-appointed defence adviser to tell Milošević that she would like to discuss the subject with him. Milošević declined to meet with her.[43]

So-called 'truth commissions' are often established in transitional justice contexts as a complement to traditional prosecutions or as a substitute for them. There was no truth commission at Nuremberg or Tokyo. Rwanda resisted truth commission proposals, and instead developed its own indigenous and innovative form of local justice involving a strong truth-telling dimension, known as *gacaca*. However, it seems likely that in the future, truth commissions will be an ineluctable component of international justice projects. They will work alongside criminal prosecutions, at both national and international levels. In his 2004 report on the rule of law the United Nations Secretary-General acknowledged that 'other transitional justice mechanisms', such as truth and reconciliation commissions,

---

[42] UN Doc. S/PV.4150, p. 3.

[43] Carla Del Ponte, *Madame Prosecutor, Confrontations with Humanity's Worst Criminal and the Culture of Impunity*, New York: Other Press, 2009, pp. 62–3.

may address 'the inherent limitations of criminal justice processes—to do the things that courts do not do or do not do well—in particular ... to meet the need for a full, comprehensive historical record of what happened during the period of conflict and why'.[44] At the very least, they may be better equipped to explore aspects of the truth that elude the courts.

The post-conflict justice initiatives in Sierra Leone offered the first occasion for an international criminal tribunal and an internationally supported truth commission to operate in parallel. Although there were occasional moments of tension, the relationship between the two bodies was relatively benign. They worked in separate spheres, divided by a virtual firewall that helped to avoid conflicts over access to witnesses and information. The two institutions were considered to be broadly complementary, each having its own field of action and specific mandate. There were some initial suggestions that the Truth and Reconciliation Commission might provide the historical background for the prosecutions before the Special Court for Sierra Leone.[45] The Court would simply incorporate the Commission's findings on issues of truth and historical fact that fell within its own sphere of expertise.

However, the two institutions did not come to a common understanding of the history of the conflict. The Court tended to emphasize external causes, such as political manipulation by foreign political leaders and the international diamond trade, while the Commission's conclusions focussed on internal factors, such as despotic rule over several decades by a corrupt oligarchy. It is not apparent that the perspectives of the Truth and Reconciliation Commission and the Special Court can be explained by differences in their mandates or their structures. Rather, this is probably attributable to the assessments of the individuals who were involved and the scope of the materials before each of the bodies. Perhaps such diversity is inevitable when different researchers or organizations seek to understand historical truth. They do not always reach the same conclusions. They will not disagree about certain 'established' facts of the sort of which a Court might take judicial notice, for example that genocide was committed in Rwanda or in Nazi-occupied Europe. However, that does not ensure that there will be unanimity of views about the causes of the conflicts, the role of specific individuals, and the relative weight of the complex factors that contribute to the making of historic events. Michael Ignatieff has said

---

[44] 'The Rule of Law and Transitional Justice in Conflict and Post-conflict Societies', UN Doc. S/2004/616, para. 47.

[45] *Norman* (SCSL-2003-08-PT), Decision on Appeal by the Truth and Reconciliation Commission for Sierra Leone ('TRC' or 'The Commission') and Chief Samuel Hinga Norman JP Against the Decision of His Lordship Mr Justice Bankole Thompson Delivered on 30 October 2003 to Deny the TRC's Request to Hold a Hearing with Chief Samuel Hinga Norman JP, 28 November 2003.

that it is asking too much of truth commissions to expect them to develop an entire version of the history of a conflict. It is enough that they put certain lies out of commission. The same might be said of courts.

The diversity in perspectives should be a generally healthy phenomenon. Courts may tend to develop frozen narratives, deprived of flexibility by the tendency to follow earlier decisions, especially if these emanate from 'higher' or more authoritative tribunals. A version of historical fact that emerges in decisions of the International Court of Justice or the Appeals Chamber of the International Criminal Tribunal for the former Yugoslavia will not readily be re-examined by other courts. Judicial decisions can very desirably draw a line in the sand, putting certain notorious facts beyond question. But they can also discourage the constant reconsideration and re-evaluation of the past that is so familiar to the work of professional historians. Moreover, they often develop a version that is flat and lacking in nuance. The work of parallel bodies such as truth commissions may provide opportunities to enrich and reassess the historical narrative. This helps to present history in three dimensions, not two.

Modern authorities on transitional justice often speak of different types of truth. The South African Truth and Reconciliation Commission identified four categories. The first was objective or factual or forensic truth; the second was personal or narrative truth; the third was social or 'dialogical truth'; and the fourth, healing and restorative truth.[46] Courts are probably superior at searching for the factual or forensic truth, to the extent that this falls within the scope of their inquiries. But other forms of truth are more likely to emerge in the rather more informal setting of a truth and reconciliation commission.

There is a growing body of authority within human rights law for the existence of a 'right to truth'. The United Nations Human Rights Council, and the Commission on Human Rights before it, have adopted a number of resolutions on the right to truth. Although they tend to focus on the personal or narrative truth rather than the social or dialogical truth, in that they are addressed specifically to issues of disappearances and the obligation to search for persons who are missing in armed conflict, they are also concerned with the broader historical narrative. For example, a resolution adopted by the Human Rights Council in 2009 declares: *'Recognizing the importance of preserving historic memory related to gross human rights violations and serious violations of international humanitarian law*

---

[46] See vol. I of the Report of the Commission, at pp. 111–14. This is discussed in detail in the memoir of the vice-chairman of the Commission: Alex Boraine, *A Country Unmasked*, Oxford: Oxford University Press, 2000, pp. 288–91.

through the conservation of archives and other documents related to those violations'.[47]

There is also a general formulation by Diane Orentlicher in the principles on impunity proposed to the Commission on Human Rights in 2005. Principle No. 2 states:

Every people has the inalienable right to know the truth about past events concerning the perpetration of heinous crimes and about the circumstances and reasons that led, through massive or systematic violations, to the perpetration of those crimes. Full and effective exercise of the right to the truth provides a vital safeguard against the recurrence of violations.[48]

The reference to 'people' rather than 'person' indicates that this is more of a collective right, and that the truth concerned may be social as well as personal. Principle No. 3, entitled 'the duty to preserve memory', is even more to the point:

A people's knowledge of the history of its oppression is part of its heritage and, as such, must be ensured by appropriate measures in fulfilment of the state's duty to preserve archives and other evidence concerning violations of human rights and humanitarian law and to facilitate knowledge of those violations. Such measures shall be aimed at preserving the collective memory from extinction and, in particular, at guarding against the development of revisionist and negationist arguments.[49]

The Inter-American Court of Human Rights has also recognized a right to truth, grounding it in the freedom to receive and impart information.[50]

International justice is a potent mechanism for the promotion of the rights and freedoms that involve truth and information, subject to the reservations that have already been expressed. The facts established in the Nuremberg trials provide an enormous repository of knowledge about the aggressive war and the atrocities committed in its wake. This benefits enormously the few victims who still survive while at the same time both stabilizing and enriching our contemporary understanding of the past. Much the same can be said of more recent ventures dealing with the former Yugoslavia, Rwanda, and Sierra Leone. There are, to be sure, many shortcomings. International justice has blind spots that result from its jurisdictional framework. These may sometimes be inadvertent, but they can also result from deliberate attempts to obscure part of the truth. Complementing international criminal justice are truth commissions and

---

[47] Right to Truth, UN Doc. A/HRC/RES/12/12, preamble.
[48] Updated Set of principles for the protection and promotion of human rights through action to combat impunity, UN Doc. E/CN.4/2005/102/Add.1, p. 7.
[49] Ibid.   [50] *Lund* et al. v *Brazil*, 24 November 2010.

similar bodies that are capable of filling some of the gaps left by trials. It is important to foreclose the questioning of established historical facts when this pursues sinister agendas. At the same time, neither trials nor truth commissions should be allowed to stifle a constant reconsideration and reassessment of the past, something that is the essential contribution of professional historians.

7

NO PEACE WITHOUT JUSTICE? THE AMNESTY QUANDARY

Fiat justitia ne pereat mundus ('let justice be done lest the world should perish')

Georg Friedrich Hegel, *The Philosophy of Right*, 1821

'There can be no lasting peace without justice... [P]eace and justice are thus complementary requirements,' affirms the Kampala Declaration, adopted at the Review Conference of the International Criminal Court on 9 June 2010. One of the stocktaking sessions held at the Conference was entitled 'peace and justice'. During the discussion, a panellist said: 'Amnesties for crimes under the Statute were now definitively off the table.' In his summary of the debate, moderator Ken Roth, who is the head of the NGO Human Rights Watch, said that 'amnesty was no longer an option for the most serious crimes under the Rome Statute'. It is a proposition that this chapter contests.

The Rome Statute of the International Criminal Court, adopted in July 1998, is actually silent on the subject of amnesty, as are the constitutive instruments of the other modern-day international criminal tribunals, with one exception. The Statute of the Special Court for Sierra Leone declares: 'An amnesty granted to any person falling within the jurisdiction of the Special Court in respect of the crimes referred to in articles 2 to 4 of the present Statute shall not be a bar to prosecution.' This text, which entered into force in January 2002, is specifically targeted at the Lomé Agreement of July 1999. The Agreement brought an end to a decade-long civil war that had devastated one of the world's poorest countries. A clause in the Lomé Agreement promises 'free pardon and reprieve to all combatants and collaborators in respect of anything done by them in pursuit of their objectives, up to the time of the signing of the present Agreement'.

There is also an historic example. Control Council Law No. 10, which was the legal basis for postwar trials inside Germany, stated that no 'immunity, pardon or amnesty granted under the Nazi regime' could be admitted as a bar to trial or punishment. It seems that in Japan, following the Second World War, an Imperial Rescript granting an amnesty by general pardon for war crimes committed by members of the Japanese Armed Forces during the Second World War was issued on 3 November 1946. It had no effect upon war crimes trials conducted by the victorious allies, including the International Military Tribunal for the Far East.

In his report on the establishment of the Special Court for Sierra Leone, the United Nations Secretary-General explained that

[w]hile recognizing that amnesty is an accepted legal concept and a gesture of peace and reconciliation at the end of a civil war or an internal armed conflict, the United Nations has consistently maintained the position that amnesty cannot be granted in respect of international crimes, such as genocide, crimes against humanity or other serious violations of international humanitarian law.

The Secretary-General recalled that his Special Representative had objected to the amnesty clause contained in article IX of the Lomé Peace Agreement, noting in addition its 'illegality under international law'.[1] Contrast the account with a report published in 2009 by the United Nations High Commissioner for Human Rights:

The lawfulness of amnesty for war crimes, genocide and crimes against humanity was first questioned in relation to the 1999 Lomé Peace Agreement between the Government of Sierra Leone and the Revolutionary United Front, which contained a broad amnesty. Upon witnessing the Agreement, the Special Representative of the Secretary-General in Sierra Leone appended a disclaimer to his signature, reading 'The United Nations does not recognize amnesty for genocide, crimes against humanity, war crimes, and other serious violations of international humanitarian law.'[2]

The High Commissioner's version is closer to reality. Far from 'consistently maintaining' such an approach to amnesty, in reality the United Nations was charting a new course. The United Nations had not, in fact, objected to an amnesty clause contained in an earlier peace agreement reached with respect to the Sierra Leone conflict, on 30 November 1996. In his objection to the Lomé Agreement in 1999, the Special Representative did not employ the term 'illegality', contrary to the subsequent description by the Secretary-General cited above. There was also something

---

[1] Report of the Secretary-General on the Establishment of a Special Court for Sierra Leone, UN Doc. S/2000/915, paras 22–4.

[2] Analytical study on human rights and transitional justice, UN Doc. A/HRC/12/18, para. 53.

disingenuous about the declaration, because in objecting to the amnesty clause in the Lomé Agreement the Secretary-General was not in fact calling for the peace talks to be aborted and for the parties to return to war until a new agreement could be reached *without* an amnesty clause. Rather, the Secretary-General praised the fact that the parties had agreed to lay down their arms and join in a power-sharing government. He welcomed the end of the conflict. In any case, his concurrence was hardly required for the parties to stop fighting.

The amnesty condition may well have been a *sine qua non* for acceptance by the parties to the Lomé Agreement. Its removal might have prompted a return to warfare and atrocity. Sometimes, warring groups may only be prepared to lay down their arms in return for a guarantee they will not be prosecuted. What do we do then? At Lomé, was it in fact the 'lawfulness' of amnesty that was being questioned? Did the Special Representative of the Secretary-General object to the Sierra Leone amnesty because it was contrary to international law, or because it was inconsistent with a new policy direction of the United Nations Secretariat? Similarly, when panellists at the Kampala Review Conference said amnesty was 'off the table', did they mean that it was prohibited by law or simply undesirable and unadvisable?

The issue of amnesty was not ignored by the 1998 Rome Conference when the Statute of the International Criminal Court was adopted, or in previous negotiations concerning the establishment of the institution. In fact, it had been raised regularly in the course of the debates, especially by delegates from South Africa. They were concerned that the Statute might directly or indirectly encroach upon the amnesty granted as part of the transitional process from apartheid to pluralist democracy. From their standpoint, the issue did not need to be resolved definitively once it was agreed that the Court would only operate prospectively, that is, with regard to acts and events subsequent to its entry into force. Nevertheless, the South Africans were proud of the approach to post-conflict justice that they had adopted. The South African Truth and Reconciliation Commission constituted an innovative mechanism of transitional justice and accountability that enjoyed broad support within the country's civil society as well as much admiration elsewhere in the world. It was not without its critics as well. But it would have been impossible for the drafters of the Rome Statute to reach agreement on how the future Court would deal with initiatives like those of South Africa. Views on the appropriateness of truth-seeking followed by amnesty as a way of dealing with atrocities, in certain circumstances, were simply too divergent. Nobody had managed to devise a legal norm that might respect the kind of amnesty that Nelson Mandela had granted de Klerk and his henchmen, yet exclude the self-proclaimed amnesty qua retirement present like that of Chilean dictator Augusto Pinochet.

Many delegates to the Rome Conference seemed to believe that an amnesty like that of South Africa would be effective to block prosecution by the Court. They probably thought that such a measure would be respected by the Prosecutor in deciding whether to proceed with situations and cases, given his or her discretion not to proceed when this would be contrary to the 'interests of justice' (pursuant to article 53 of the Statute). Should that fail, some believed the judges themselves might intervene in an appropriate case and declare inadmissible any case that was 'not of sufficient gravity to justify further action by the Court' in accordance with article 17 of the Statute. But others argued that with the adoption of the Rome Statute, we had entered a new international legal regime that made a South African transition, premised as it was on a pledge not to prosecute in exchange for peaceful surrender of power, no longer possible.

Their voices seemed to prevail at Kampala. Perhaps they had gained momentum in the decade since the Rome Conference. To date, the hypothesis has not been tested in judicial proceedings. No defendant before the International Criminal Court has raised amnesty as an objection to the admissibility of a case, or as a defence. The Prosecutor has indicated that the 'interests of justice' provision is to be used sparingly. He has said that decisions not to prosecute a case because it might disrupt the pursuit of peace do not belong with his Office. Rather, he considers that they are properly the domain of political bodies, especially the United Nations Security Council.

Amnesty is defined by the *Oxford English Dictionary* as 'an act of forgetfulness, an intentional overlooking, a general pardon, esp. for a political offence'. The word is used in many languages. It originates in the Greek language as ἀμνηστία, where it means 'oblivion' or 'forgetfulness'. Sometimes de facto amnesties result from a political decision not to prosecute crimes committed during a conflict rather than from a formal agreement or declaration. They may also be the consequence of an offer of asylum which has, as its corollary, the removal of a threat of criminal prosecution. The exile of Napoleon to Elba and later to St Helena furnishes an historic example. A modern one would be Nigeria's promise of refuge to Charles Taylor as part of the deal brokered by its president to end the civil war in Liberia. In July 2011 the United Kingdom and France contemplated sheltering Libyan dictator Muammar Gaddafi from prosecution by the International Criminal Court if he would consent to leave power.

Amnesty has long figured in peace agreements, including the mother of all international treaties, the 1648 Peace of Westphalia. At the dawn of international criminal justice, the Treaty of Lausanne of 1923 contained a 'Declaration of Amnesty' for all offences committed between 1 August 1914 and 20 November 1922. It replaced the Treaty of Sèvres of 1920, which was never accepted by Turkey, and which authorized prosecution by the victorious allies not only of 'violations of the laws and customs of war', but also for the 'massacres committed during the continuance of the state of war on territory which formed part of the Turkish Empire on 1 August 1914', a reference to the Armenian genocide.

IS AMNESTY PROHIBITED BY INTERNATIONAL LAW?

The Appeals Chamber of the Special Court for Sierra Leone considered whether the prohibition of amnesty in its Statute was actually a rule of international law of more general application. It took the view that amnesty was 'not only incompatible with, but is in breach of an obligation of a state towards the international community as a whole'.[3] There have been similar pronouncements from the Inter-American Court of Human Rights, where the obligation is presented as a right of victims rather than a duty to the international community. If indeed the prohibition of amnesty is an affirmative rule of international law, where did it come from and what are its exact parameters?

In terms of the principle of amnesties, there are only two references in major multilateral treaties. Actually, both of them are favourable to the concept. Article 6(4) of the International Covenant on Civil and Political Rights, which is one of the principal United Nations human rights treaties, declares: 'Anyone sentenced to death shall have the right to seek pardon or commutation of the sentence. Amnesty, pardon or commutation of the sentence of death may be granted in all cases.' The context suggests that it applies to specific cases of imposition of capital punishment, rather than to situations of post-conflict justice. Much more relevant is the Protocol Additional to the 1949 Geneva Conventions and Relating to The Protection of Victims of Non-International Armed Conflicts. Known as Protocol II, it was adopted in 1977 to govern civil wars, filling a gap left by the almost exclusive focus of the law of armed conflict on international wars. According to article 6(5) of Protocol II, '[a]t the end of hostilities, the authorities in power shall endeavour to grant the broadest possible amnesty to persons who have participated in the armed conflict, or those

---

[3] *Kallon* (SCSL-04-15AR72(E)) and *Kamara* (SCSL-04-16-AR72(E)), Decision on Challenge to Jurisdiction: Lomé Accord Amnesty, 13 March 2004, para. 73. See also: *Kondewa* (SCSL-2004-14-AR72(E)), Separate Opinion of Justice Robertson, 25 May 2004.

deprived of their liberty for reasons related to the armed conflict, whether they are interned or detained'.

Thus, from the standpoint of treaties, which are after all the clearest formulation of legal obligations that states are prepared to assume, it is not only the legality of amnesty but its wisdom, and not the contrary, that emerges. Human societies have been negotiating peace agreements since the beginning of recorded time. Amnesties have often been part of such transitional justice mechanisms, which existed, after all, long before the modern term 'transitional justice' had been invented. The relevant treaty provisions probably reflect the inherited wisdom derived from these peace processes.

Article 6(5) of Protocol II is a bone that sticks in the throats of those who insist upon the illegality of amnesty. It has been argued that article 6(5) was never intended to authorize or encourage amnesty for serious viola-tions of international humanitarian law, such as war crimes, crimes against humanity, and genocide. Much of the literature on this point harks back to a reference in an article by Douglass Cassel citing a letter from a lawyer in the International Committee of the Red Cross, Toni Pfanner, who claimed that the purpose of the drafters of article 6(5) was not to provide impunity for war crimes.[4] It is of course not unknown for participants in the drafting of an international treaty to suggest subsequently that it be interpreted in a certain way because 'that is what we meant' at the time. The problem is that such agreements are often reached precisely because the negotiators intend somewhat different results, yet are able to agree upon language that may bridge a gap between different possible interpretations. In any case, Pfanner did not participate in the negotiations of Protocol II in the 1970s and his belief is at the best premised on hearsay from those who did.

In assessing what the drafters of the Protocol intended in article 6(5), it is probably better to look at the documents themselves. They are not hard to locate. The International Committee of the Red Cross has itself published a collection of some seventeen volumes consisting of documents on the drafting of the Protocols. Evidence in these materials that the drafters of article 6(5) of Protocol II meant to exclude serious violations of international humanitarian law is actually very slender. The record shows that when article 6(5) of Protocol II was adopted, the representative of the Soviet Union declared that in his country's opinion, the provision could not be interpreted as applying to war criminals and those who had committed crimes against humanity. This appears to be the only mention of the issue

---

[4] Douglass Cassel, 'Lessons from the Americas: Guidelines for International Response to Amnesties for Atrocities' (1997) 59 *Law & Contemporary Problems* 197, at p. 218.

in the record of the Diplomatic Conference of 1974–7 at which the Protocol was adopted. More than three decades have passed, and it is now perhaps more difficult to recall the international context of the time. Suffice it to say that an isolated statement from the Soviet Union at a diplomatic conference in the mid-1970s is probably better interpreted as evidence of an absence of agreement, rather than as proof of consensus or acquiescence. One statement of this nature is flimsy authority as a basis for interpretation of a treaty provision.

Moreover, we know that the drafters of Protocol II quite intentionally excluded the concept of war crimes in non-international armed conflict altogether. Early drafts of the Protocol spoke of war crimes known as 'grave breaches', parallel to a concept applicable in international armed conflict. But these references were dropped in the final text, failing agreement on the relevance of the entire notion of war crimes to civil wars. Why would the drafters of Protocol II have excluded the concept of war crimes in non-international armed conflict, but at the same time intended to refer implicitly to a non-existent notion in the amnesty provision? This rejection of the very concept of war crimes during non-international armed conflict persisted until the mid-1990s, and continued to be questioned by large states as recently as the 1998 Diplomatic Conference at which the Rome Statute was adopted.

In 2004 the International Committee of the Red Cross published a study of the customary law applicable to armed conflict. The four Geneva Conventions of 1949 have been ratified by virtually every country in the world, and it is often said that their provisions now amount to a codification of customary norms. The same cannot so readily be said of the two Protocols of 1977, where the ratification pattern is not as unanimous. An important objective of the customary law study was to fill the gaps in treaty ratification, building the case that norms in the 1977 Protocols are also customary in nature. Amongst other things, the authors of the customary law study turned their sights on article 6(5) of Protocol II, which they reformulated slightly by the addition of a final phrase to the text, excluding 'persons suspected of, or accused of or sentenced for war crimes'.[5] The authors of the Red Cross study on customary law, Jean-Marie Henckaerts and Louise Doswald-Beck, explained that the intent of the drafters of the Protocol was to exclude war crimes from such an amnesty. They asserted that 'state practice establishes this rule as a norm of customary

---

[5] Jean-Marie Henckaerts and Louise Doswald-Beck, *Customary International Humanitarian Law*, Cambridge: Cambridge University Press, 2005, p. 611.

international law applicable in non-international armed conflicts'. This is a dubious proposition.

In the commentary on the rewritten 2004 version of article 6(5), several amnesties that specifically excluded war crimes from their scope are cited to support the claim about state practice. But surely this is not the way to establish a consistent rule that might then be deemed to be customary in nature. One does not prove a norm that is generally accepted by demonstrating that some people appear to abide by it. Should not the analysis begin by asking whether there are examples of amnesties that include war crimes and other atrocities? The study acknowledges a judgment of the South African Constitutional Court that interpreted article 6(5) of Protocol II and upheld a broad amnesty. It attempts to distinguish this by adding that the amnesty 'required full disclosure of all the relevant facts' in exchange, nourishing the argument that South Africa did not have a 'blanket amnesty'. It selectively omits discussing the other South African amnesty, resulting from a gentleman's agreement between Mandela and de Klerk, later confirmed in the postamble of the interim constitution, not to prosecute those responsible for the crime against humanity of apartheid.

The Red Cross study also considers the Sierra Leone amnesty, noting that the Security Council confirmed it could not apply to war crimes. That too is an overstatement. The Security Council Resolution in question involved the establishment of the Special Court for Sierra Leone, which in effect repealed an amnesty accorded to a handful of senior perpetrators, making 'those who bear the greatest responsibility' punishable before the international tribunal. In reality, it also implicitly confirmed the ongoing validity of the amnesty accorded to all of the participants in the conflict with the exception of the dozen or so who were subject to the Special Court. There is another relevant Security Council resolution concerning Sierra Leone that the customary law study did not mention. Several weeks after the Lomé Peace Agreement was reached the Security Council convened to assess progress in resolving the conflict. It adopted a resolution that alluded to the Secretary-General's statement on the amnesty provision. The oblique reference was an obvious compromise, reflecting the varied opinions within the Council about the legality and the wisdom of the amnesty. For example, speaking in the debate, the British representative said that the 'blanket amnesty' had 'rightly caused concern. But this was one of many hard choices that the Government and the people of Sierra Leone had to make in the interests of securing a workable agreement.' The United States said it was 'committed to the pursuit of accountability' but that '[a]t the same time, we recognize the need to allow the Lomé Agreement to bear fruit'. Argentina declared its disapproval of the amnesty, but said 'we understand that very delicate decisions can be taken only by the parties involved, which assume the historical responsibility inherent in that decision'. Gabon expressed satisfaction with the amnesty. Gambia said that it understood the circumstances under which the amnesty was granted; it mentioned the disclaimer by the Special Representative, saying it shared the views expressed. The Netherlands was the only other state to refer to the Special Representative's reservation, strongly condemning the amnesty. Slovenia said the Lomé Agreement 'highlighted the difficult choices that often confront the peacemakers'. Others, including Canada and France, said nothing about the amnesty.[6]

Surely it would have been more prudent for the International Committee of the Red Cross to acknowledge that there is actually quite inconsistent practice in this area, and that for this reason realistically one cannot conclude that there is a prohibition under customary international law. A review of the more detailed sources provided in volume III of the customary law study confirms the widespread practice of amnesty and the fact that while in some cases war crimes are excluded, this cannot be said to be a general rule.

In the introduction the customary study says that if it is to constitute a basis for a customary norm, state practice must be 'virtually uniform'. A fairer assessment of law and practice appears in the reasons of Lord Lloyd of the United Kingdom House of Lords in the Pinochet case, in 1998:

Further light is shed on state practice by the widespread adoption of amnesties for those who have committed crimes against humanity including torture. Chile was not the first in the field. There was an amnesty at the end of the Franco–Algerian War in 1962. In 1971 India and Bangladesh agreed not to pursue charges of genocide against Pakistan troops accused of killing about one million East Pakistanis. General amnesties have also become common in recent years, especially in South America, covering members of former regimes accused of torture and other atrocities. Some of these have had the blessing of the United Nations, as a means of restoring peace and democratic government... It has not been argued that these amnesties are as such contrary to international law by reason of the failure to prosecute the individual perpetrators.[7]

There is no doubt that the Red Cross would prefer that article 6(5) be amended so as to exclude amnesty for war crimes. But to claim this is a binding customary norm established by 'virtually uniform' state practice is surely an exaggeration. Louise Mallinder, in her very thorough recent

---

[6] UN Doc. S/PV.4035, p. 5.
[7] R v Bow Street Metropolitan Stipendiary Magistrate, Ex Parte Pinochet [1998] 4 All ER 897 (HL), at 929 h–i.

study based on a database of more than 500 situations, concludes that the practice of amnesty has actually increased in popularity in recent years.[8]

Perhaps it bears repeating: there is no treaty text in public international law instruments explicitly prohibiting amnesty and there is no consistent practice of states allowing the conclusion that this is a norm of customary international law. The argument that amnesty is prohibited by international law relies upon implication. With respect to certain treaties, such as the Convention Against Torture and the Genocide Convention, as well as the 1949 Geneva Conventions, it is said that the duty to prosecute specific crimes precludes the possibility of amnesty. But treaties are also to be interpreted in light of the subsequent practice of parties to the treaty. For the same reasons that generate doubts about the consistent practice necessary to conclude that a customary norm exists, the argument that the obligation to prosecute set out in certain treaties is unconditional and without any exception cannot be sustained. Even when states assume their duties to ensure that such atrocity crimes are prosecuted, they often pursue the matter rather like the United Nations did with respect to Sierra Leone. There may be some symbolic trials, but there is no attempt at full-blown and exhaustive implementation.

In 2006 four senior Rwandan officials against whom credible allegations of genocide had been made were located in the United Kingdom. The government cooperated with the Rwandan Government in developing an extradition request. When British courts denied the application, in mid-2009, because they considered the Rwandan justice system to be inadequate, the four were released and returned to rather banal lives somewhere on the sceptered isle. They now remain at large without any prospect they will be brought to justice. Britain does not have legislation enabling it to exercise universal jurisdiction over the crime of genocide. Presumably, if it believed that it was required by international law to prosecute genocide suspects found on its territory, it would have enacted appropriate laws. The United Kingdom acceded to the Genocide Convention on 30 January 1970, so it has had more than forty years to reflect upon the shortcomings in its legal framework.

Similar examples can be found in many other countries around the world. They suggest the frailty of a theory by which an international legal prohibition on amnesty can be implied from 'duty to prosecute' norms in various treaties, or under customary law. In effect, when a state declines to prosecute certain crimes, possibly for policy reasons, or because its legislation

---

[8] Louise Mallinder, *Amnesty, Human Rights and Political Transitions, Bridging the Peace and Justice Divide*, Oxford and Portland: Hart Publishing, 2008.

is not adequate, it is in practice ensuring impunity to the perpetrator. A distinction should be drawn for prosecutions of crimes committed on a state's territory, where the impetus for prosecution and the legal imperative are obviously much stronger than for offences with no traditional jurisdictional link. The British may be prepared to let suspected Rwandan murderers live in their midst, but they would obviously never tolerate such a situation if the crimes had been perpetrated within their own borders or by their own nationals but outside their borders. Here, the case is framed by human rights norms which posit a duty to prosecute all serious crimes against the person. No distinction is made between international crimes, such as genocide and crimes against humanity, and ordinary, garden-variety murders and rapes. It is posed not as a duty to the international community—the situation for international crimes—but rather as a right of the victim.

VICTIMS AND THE RIGHT TO JUSTICE

In the absence of any clear treaty provision declaring amnesty to be contrary to international law, and indeed given an important suggestion to the contrary in Protocol II to the Geneva Conventions, efforts to provide a legal basis for an anti-amnesty norm have focussed on the rights of victims, in particular the rights to reparation and to a remedy. It is contended that victims have a right to see justice done, and that the rights of the victims are violated by amnesty. According to the 'Basic Principles and Guidelines on the Right to a Remedy and Reparation for Victims of Gross Violations of International Human Rights Law and Serious Violations of International Humanitarian Law', adopted by the United Nations Commission on Human Rights in 2005:

[i]n cases of gross violations of international human rights law and serious violations of international humanitarian law constituting crimes under international law, states have the duty to investigate and, if there is sufficient evidence, the duty to submit to prosecution the person allegedly responsible for the violations and, if found guilty, the duty to punish her or him.[9]

This can support an argument for the prohibition of amnesty. Note, however, that the Resolution does not clarify whether this applies to crimes committed outside the territory as well as those over which the state in question would normally exercise jurisdiction.

There is much authority in the case law of the European Court of Human Rights, the United Nations Human Rights Committee, and the Inter-American Court of Human Rights for the proposition that

---

[9] UN Doc. E/CN.4/RES/2005/35, para. 4.

fundamental rights are breached where a state fails to investigate, prosecute, and punish. In one case, the European Court of Human Rights held
that Bulgaria had breached the European Convention because it did not
adequately investigate a complaint of so-called 'date rape'.[10] Another recent
decision involves a violent attack on Jehovah's Witnesses during a religious
meeting. A Chamber of the Court wrote:

Article 3 of the [European] Convention [on Human Rights] gives rise to a positive obligation to conduct an official investigation. Such a positive obligation
cannot be considered in principle to be limited solely to cases of ill-treatment
by state agents. Thus, the authorities have an obligation to take action as soon
as an official complaint has been lodged. Even in the absence of an express complaint, an investigation should be undertaken if there are other sufficiently clear
indications that torture or ill-treatment might have occurred. A requirement
of promptness and reasonable expedition is implicit in this context. A prompt
response by the authorities in investigating allegations of ill-treatment may generally be regarded as essential in maintaining public confidence in their maintenance of the rule of law and in preventing any appearance of collusion in or
tolerance of unlawful acts. Tolerance by the authorities towards such acts cannot
but undermine public confidence in the principle of lawfulness and the state's
maintenance of the rule of law.[11]

Sometimes, this is spoken of as the procedural obligation associated with
the protection of the right to life and the prohibition of torture and inhuman
or degrading treatment.

The Inter-American Court of Human Rights has addressed this issue
somewhat differently, in the specific context of amnesty laws. According to
the Inter-American Court, 'states cannot neglect their duty to investigate,
identify, and punish those persons responsible for crimes against humanity by enforcing amnesty laws or other similar domestic provisions'.[12]
The Court

considers that all amnesty provisions, provisions on prescription and the establishment of measures designed to eliminate responsibility are inadmissible,
because they are intended to prevent the investigation and punishment of those
responsible for serious human rights violations such as torture, extrajudicial,
summary or arbitrary execution and forced disappearance, all of them prohibited because they violate non-derogable rights recognized by international
human rights law.[13]

---

[10] *MC* v *Bulgaria* (Application No. 39272/98), ECHR 2003-XII, para. 149.
[11] *Case of 97 Members of the Glldani Congregation of Jehovah's Witnesses and 4 Others* v *Georgia*
(Application No. 71156/01), Judgment, 3 May 2007, para. 97 (references omitted).
[12] *Almonacid-Arellano* et al. v *Chile*, No. 45 (2006), para. 114.
[13] *Barrios Altos* v *Peru*, 14 March 2001, para. 41.

The Inter-American Court appears to predicate the obligation on violations of 'non-derogable rights'. These are obligations that cannot be suspended, even in time of war or national emergency. The formulation is imprecise because non-derogable rights include freedom of religion and the prohibition of imprisonment for debt. What the Court probably meant was that there is a hierarchy of rights, with some being so essential to the protection of human dignity that they cannot ever be subject to amnesty. At a minimum, these would be the right to life and the prohibition of torture and cruel, inhuman, and degrading treatment or punishment.

These pronouncements from the human rights bodies apply to all serious crimes involving violence against the person, and not only to war crimes, crimes against humanity, and genocide. There seems to be no logical basis in international human rights law for making any distinction between the rights of the victim of an ordinary murder or rape and the rights of the victim of a murder qua crime against humanity or genocide. From the standpoint of the individual victim, how could the legal qualification of such a crime have any significance? Should one victim be denied justice, as a matter of principle, because the perpetrator did not have the elevated degree of criminal intent necessary for a finding of crimes against humanity or genocide? To the extent that the duty to prosecute, which is based upon the rights of victims to justice and redress, finds its roots in international human rights law, then amnesties ought to be prohibited altogether, and not only for the core international crimes listed in the Rome Statute. But there is no real suggestion in the case law or academic commentary, and certainly no support in state practice, for the position that amnesties for all serious crimes against the person be prohibited completely and without exception.

The contention that human rights law prohibits amnesties because this violates the rights of victims to redress, truth, and accountability obviously flies in the face of article 6(5) of Protocol II, which encourages amnesty at the end of a civil war. Even the restrictive gloss placed upon it by the International Committee of the Red Cross and certain academic commentators, discussed and criticized above, is to no avail when the rather absolute formulations adopted by human rights bodies are applied.

There is a way out of this quandary. The encouragement of amnesty in Protocol II and its condemnation by the human rights courts can actually be reconciled. Human rights norms are rarely viewed as absolutes. It may be—there is some authority here—that the prohibition of torture and of enforced disappearance brook no exception, but such norms are the exception that proves the rule. Therefore, it may be helpful to consider whether the general 'procedural obligation' imposed by human rights law by which violations of the right to life must be investigated is absolute or whether it is subject to limitations.

Any specific human rights norm must normally be balanced against other norms, so that the protection of human rights is viewed as a coherent, indivisible ensemble and not a hierarchical system where one right invariably trumps another. An example of a fundamental right that might enter into the calculus is the right to peace, discussed in greater detail in the final chapter in this volume (see Chapter 8, 'Crimes Against Peace'). If amnesty is the price to be paid for an end to armed conflict, and the death and destruction that it brings to ordinary people, shouldn't this be a relevant factor that may outweigh or limit, in specific circumstances, the rights of victims of specific crimes associated with that same conflict to have their tormentors brought to book? Moreover, some attention must surely be paid to the cost of justice. States have limited resources. These must be apportioned in such a manner as to ensure that all fundamental rights, including the economic and social rights to education, housing and medical care, are fulfilled. Do the investments required to ensure justice necessarily override those that would otherwise be devoted to schools and hospitals? In reality, we always make such calculations. When the United Nations insisted on quashing the amnesty in Sierra Leone, it limited its ardour to a tribunal of modest expectations, likely to judge about a dozen people. If justice for all was really such an imperative, would it not have devoted its entire budget to the Special Court for Sierra Leone? But what then would have happened to the humanitarian assistance programmes of the United Nations Development Programme or the World Food Programme or the many peace support operations throughout the world helping to stave off armed conflict?

Article 29(2) of the Universal Declaration of Human Rights affirms that

[i]n the exercise of his rights and freedoms, everyone shall be subject only to such limitations as are determined by law solely for the purpose of securing due recognition and respect for the rights and freedoms of others and of meeting the just requirements of morality, public order and the general welfare in a democratic society.

Thus, in the application of the fundamental rights of defendants to a fair trial, international criminal tribunals have held that the right to defend oneself in person, and the right to be present at trial, are not absolute. Both of these rights are set out in article 14(3) of the International Covenant on Civil and Political Rights in an apparently unqualified manner. If these rights are subject to reasonable limitations, why then are the rights to reparation and remedy also not subject to limitation? The right of victims to justice and to a remedy for a serious violation of human rights, which is the foundation of the condemnation of amnesties by the human rights tribunals, may be limited or tempered by other rights and priorities. In this way, amnesty cannot be totally prohibited, even if there may be a rebuttable presumption of its unacceptability.

This more nuanced approach to amnesty was adopted by the Sierra Leone Truth and Reconciliation Commission. In its final report, the Commission concluded:

Accordingly, those who argue that peace cannot be bartered in exchange for justice, under any circumstances, must be prepared to justify the likely prolongation of an armed conflict. Amnesties may be undesirable in many cases. Indeed there are examples of abusive amnesties proclaimed by dictators in the dying days of tyrannical regimes. The Commission also recognizes the principle that it is generally desirable to prosecute perpetrators of serious human rights abuses, particularly when they rise to the level of gravity of crimes against humanity. However amnesties should not be excluded entirely from the mechanisms available to those attempting to negotiate a cessation of hostilities after periods of brutal armed conflict. Disallowing amnesty in all cases is to deny the reality of violent conflict and the urgent need to bring such strife and suffering to an end.

The Commission is unable to declare that it considers amnesty too high a price to pay for the delivery of peace to Sierra Leone, under the circumstances that prevailed in July 1999. It is true that the Lomé Agreement did not immediately return the country to peacetime. Yet it provided the framework for a process that pacified the combatants and, five years later, has returned Sierra Leoneans to a context in which they need not fear daily violence and atrocity.[14]

The Commission's view is probably a minority voice in the current debate, at least in international law circles. But at the very least, it usefully recalls that there is no unanimity on these issues.

Between the two extremes on this subject lie several approaches whereby amnesty is partially prohibited and partially tolerated or even encouraged. The most common of these intermediate views posits the prohibition of certain types of amnesty. For example, it is often stated that absolute or 'blanket amnesties' are prohibited, whereas amnesties associated with some degree of accountability—as in South Africa or Sierra Leone—may pass muster. Of course, in an emotional sense most people warm to the generous and charitable amnesty granted by a victim like Nelson Mandela and recoil at the self-indulgent amnesty proclaimed by a tyrant like Augusto Pinochet. Yet it is daunting to try to formulate distinctions in a legal norm

---

[14] *Witness to Truth: Report of the Sierra Leone Truth and Reconciliation Commission*, Vol. 3B, Freetown, 2004, ch. 6, paras 11–12 (the author of this volume was one of the members of the Commission).

that separate these two phenomena. Moreover, it is difficult to construct a rationale for a theory of good versus bad amnesties. If victims have a right to justice, why should this depend upon whether or not the amnesty is 'blanket' or not, or is proclaimed by the perpetrator rather than the victim? As suggested above, it may be correct to balance the rights of victims against other rights, but it seems difficult to understand why the absolute nature of an amnesty should be a relevant factor. Indeed, once the balancing approach is accepted, it may prove necessary, in certain circumstances, to support a full and unequivocal amnesty in order to obtain cessation of a conflict.

It might be safer to say that although state practice is evolving, and that amnesties in peace agreements are increasingly viewed with disfavour, a prohibitive legal rule has not crystallized. Some international lawyers tend to exaggerate the reality of both the law and the practice out of concern that if the door to amnesty is left even slightly ajar, unprincipled politicians will pry it wide open. It is better to tell peace negotiators that amnesty is simply not an option, they reason, rather than let them retain it in their toolbox as a mechanism to end conflict in appropriate situations, however exceptional these may be. But misunderstanding of the law prompted by misrepresentation of its scope will discourage peacemakers from resorting to amnesty in appropriate cases, making it harder for them to complete their task. To the extent that conflict is prolonged, human suffering, hardship, and violations of rights will result from rigid application of the so-called prohibition on amnesty. This is not desirable.

THE APPROACH OF THE INTERNATIONAL
CRIMINAL COURT

The Special Court for Sierra Leone applied article 10 of its Statute, and refused to consider the amnesty of the Lomé Agreement when it was invoked by defendants. Nothing in the Statute of the Special Court for Sierra Leone authorized the judges to do otherwise. They could not ignore article 10. It was clearly the will of those who established the Special Court, including the United Nations Security Council, that the amnesty in the Lomé Agreement be disregarded with respect to the limited prosecutions undertaken. The same cannot be said of the International Criminal Court, however. No provision in the Rome Statute is comparable to article 10 of the Statute of the Special Court for Sierra Leone. As mentioned earlier in this chapter, during the drafting of the Rome Statute, the very issue of how the Court would deal with future amnesties was frequently considered, often at the behest of the South African delegates. Because of the impossibility of reaching consensus on this matter, any definitive conclusion was avoided.

Two provisions of the Rome Statute reflect the ambivalence of the drafters, articles 17 and 53. Article 17 of the Rome Statute is the principal provision concerning the admissibility of cases. Article 17 sets out the rule of 'complementarity' by which the Court is only allowed to proceed with a trial if the national courts that would ordinarily exercise jurisdiction have failed to investigate or prosecute. It also says that judges may rule a case inadmissible if it 'is not of sufficient gravity to justify further action by the Court'. Some writers have speculated that article 17 might be applied by judges of the Court in a spirit of deference towards alternative mechanisms of accountability and more specifically truth and reconciliation commissions. It can be argued that 'investigation' is a concept that is broad enough to encompass the work of a truth commission. But article 17 marries 'investigation' to 'prosecution', and therefore it seems difficult to square the work of a truth commission with the first three paragraphs of article 17(1). Nevertheless, a truth commission process addresses impunity and provides a degree of accountability for atrocities, with the consequence that the objective gravity of the acts in question declines in overall importance, above all in relation to other possible crimes within the jurisdiction of the Court. Perhaps that might push a situation beyond the 'sufficient gravity' standard.

Article 53 is the other relevant provision of the Rome Statute. It authorizes the Prosecutor to decline to investigate or prosecute when this does not serve 'the interests of justice'. There have been suggestions that this 'interests of justice' criterion would enable a Prosecutor to refuse to proceed where a truth commission process with an acceptable level of legitimacy in civil society is underway. Given the malleability of the 'interests of justice concept', much will depend upon the personal vision of the Prosecutor. In 2007 the first Prosecutor, Luis Moreno-Ocampo, issued a policy paper outlining his interpretation of the 'interests of justice' concept as set out in article 53. He described the issue as 'one of the most complex aspects' of the Rome Statute. 'It is the point where many of the philosophical and operational challenges in the pursuit of international criminal justice coincide (albeit implicitly), but there is no clear guidance on what the content of the idea is,' he explained. The Prosecutor noted that although the phrase 'interests of justice' appears in several places in the Rome Statute and Rules of Procedure and Evidence, it is never defined, nor does the drafting history provide any assistance in construction of the provision.

According to the Prosecutor, the exercise of discretion not to proceed with a case on the grounds that it would be contrary to the 'interests of justice' is 'exceptional in nature', and 'there is a presumption in favour of investigation or prosecution'. The Prosecutor observed that '[m]any developments in the last ten or fifteen years point to a consistent trend imposing a duty on states to prosecute crimes of international concern committed within their jurisdiction'. Here he cited, in a footnote, a press release issued by the United Nations Security Council on 22 June 2006 that spoke directly to the amnesty issue:

Touching on another issue highlighted in today's debate, Nicolas Michel, Under-Secretary-General for Legal Affairs and United Nations Legal Counsel, said that ending impunity for perpetrators of crimes against humanity was one of the principal evolutions in the culture of the world community and international law over the past 15 years. 'Justice should never be sacrificed by granting amnesty in ending conflicts', he said, adding that justice and peace should be considered as complementary demands and that the international community should 'consider ways of dovetailing one with the other'. The trend was confirmed in the statement of the President of the Security Council where he stated that, 'The Council intends to continue forcefully to fight impunity with appropriate means and draws attention to the full range of justice and reconciliation mechanisms to be considered, including national, international and "mixed" criminal courts and tribunals, and as truth and reconciliation commissions'.

Although the Prosecutor did not explore this, there are obvious distinctions in the press release between the views of the United Nations Legal Counsel and those of the President of the Security Council. The former essentially condemns the phenomenon of amnesty as a mechanism of conflict resolution, whereas the latter seems open to 'the full range of justice and reconciliation mechanisms', including truth and reconciliation commissions. If anything, they ought to have implied uncertainty about the issue rather than confirm a 'consistent trend'.

The claim by the Prosecutor that there is 'presumption in favour of investigation or prosecution' is hard to reconcile with the productivity of the Court. Three incomplete trials in eight years does not look like a presumption favouring investigation and prosecution. For every one of the handful of suspects who has been targeted for investigation, there are tens of thousands of individuals within the jurisdiction of the Court for whom the Prosecutor has decided to take a pass. Some presumption!

Be that as it may, the Prosecutor proceeded to develop an interpretation of 'interests of justice' that suggests little or no sympathy for alternative accountability mechanisms, such as truth commissions, as a justification for a decision not to proceed in a particular case. The Prosecutor pointed to paragraph 6 of the preamble of the Rome Statute, which recalls that 'it is the duty of every state to exercise its criminal jurisdiction over those responsible for international crimes'. He added that criteria for application of the 'interests of justice' concept set out in article 53 'will naturally be guided by the objects and purposes of the Statute—namely the prevention of serious crimes of concern to the international community through ending impunity'. Finally, the Prosecutor insisted that 'there is a difference between the concepts of the interests of justice and the interests of peace and that the latter falls within the mandate of institutions other than the Office of the Prosecutor'. The implied reference here is to the United Nations Security Council, which is authorized by article 16 of the Rome Statute to defer prosecutions before the Court. But while it may be true that the Security Council is mandated to attend to 'the interests of peace', it too has viewed this as comprising the 'interests of justice', as can be seen by its establishment of the ad hoc international criminal tribunals.

From the standpoint of statutory construction, separating the 'interests of justice' from the 'interests of peace' may be reading too much into the text of article 53. As the Prosecutor's position paper concedes, there is really nothing in the drafting history of the Rome Statute to assist in the interpretation of the phrase. It is not at all obvious that the drafters intended any such distinction between the 'interests of justice' and the 'interests of peace'. There is ample authority within the Statute itself that the drafters prized the achievement and maintenance of peace, as the Prosecutor noted in his policy paper. The term 'interests of justice' is commonly used in legal drafting where it has proven impossible to provide any precise language in a situation where discretion and common sense must be exercised. An equally valid interpretation of the 'interests of justice' in article 53 would be that the Prosecutor is to consider a range of factors, including the risk that proceeding with arrest and trial might complicate rather than assist initiatives at peacemaking. A different Prosecutor might well read article 53 differently.

In the Policy Paper, the Prosecutor noted that the Rome Statute creates 'a new legal framework' that 'necessarily impacts on conflict management efforts'. He said: 'The issue is no longer about whether we agree or disagree with the pursuit of justice in moral or practical terms: it is the law. Any political or security initiative must be compatible with the new legal framework insofar as it involves parties bound by the Rome Statute.' The proposition that the law has changed because of the Rome Statute implies that previous experiments with transitional justice, such as the South African experience, might no longer be acceptable, as some commentators have proposed. It also suggests that the Court will frown on amnesties rather than consider whether they have made constructive contributions to peace processes.

This may well be a step too far. The South African apartheid system has been at the core of international human rights activity since the 1960s. It is the paradigmatic human rights violation of the past half-century. No other single issue—the Chilean junta and the Occupied Palestinian Territories are close competitors—did as much to galvanize the human rights machinery of the United Nations. The South African experiment presents an extremely attractive model of peaceful transition from an oppressive, racist regime to a pluralist modern democracy. At its helm was the moral compass of the modern world, Nelson Mandela. South Africa's approach is sometimes misunderstood. Although the Truth and Reconciliation Commission had the authority to grant amnesty in specific cases, there was a more global amnesty granted at the political level by which the overarching international offence of the previous regime, namely the crime against humanity of apartheid, went unpunished.

According to the report of the South African Truth and Reconciliation Commission:

[t]he definition of apartheid as a crime against humanity has given rise to a concern that persons who are seen to have been responsible for apartheid policies and practices might become liable to international prosecutions. The Commission believes that international recognition should be given to the fact that the Promotion of Unity and Reconciliation Act, and the processes of this Commission itself, have sought to deal appropriately with the matter of responsibility for such policies.[15]

It would appear that the international community has responded favourably to this appeal from the Truth and Reconciliation Commission. It has almost certainly done so not out of a sense of legal obligation but rather because of its willingness to accept the South African model. Otherwise, we would expect to find resolutions of the United Nations General Assembly calling for the creation of an international tribunal to deal with impunity for apartheid, similar to those for Cambodia under the Khmer Rouge, for example, or initiatives directed at the exercise of universal jurisdiction over the leaders of the apartheid regime, as in the case of the Argentine dictatorship or the Guatemalan civil war.

Why are there no credible initiatives to unleash the Security Council, or universal jurisdiction investigations and indictments by hyperactive national prosecutors, or calls for prosecution from the major international non-governmental organizations, to deal with what has amounted to virtual impunity for South African apartheid? This is explained by near-universal respect, indeed admiration, for the approach taken in the South

---

[15] *Truth and Reconciliation Commission Report*, vol. 5, 1998, p. 349.

African transition. In other words, the Prosecutor of the International Criminal Court may have overstated the case when he declared that 'developments in the last ten or fifteen years point to a consistent trend imposing a duty on states to prosecute crimes of international concern committed within their jurisdiction'. Of course, there is no shortage of uncompromising statements from United Nations special rapporteurs and similar experts about the predominance of justice over peace. But the discourse seems contradicted by the practice of states and by international civil society in the case of South Africa. Where there is a credible transition process, without criminal prosecution and associated with de facto or *de jure* amnesty, as in South Africa, this is met not with disdain but with general approval. The South African experience stands as a valuable and effective model, and it may prove helpful to other societies confronted with similar problems. To exclude it from the palette of the peacemaker would be a great shame.

SHOULD AMNESTIES BE 'OFF THE TABLE'?

It is certainly an exaggeration to say that amnesty is forbidden by international law. But it cannot be gainsaid that there is growing support for a prohibition, as the panel discussion at the Kampala Review Conference, discussed at the beginning of this chapter, reflects. It seems unlikely that this could be crystallized in a treaty or convention. But a definitive statement by an authoritative body like the International Court of Justice is certainly a plausible development at some point in the future. For many, this would be a positive outcome. Some of those who defend the illegality thesis confuse the reality of the law as it now stands with what they would like it to be. But is it, in fact, desirable that law evolve in this direction?

There is a sense in which the Prosecutor of the International Criminal Court is entirely accurate when he states that 'a new legal framework' is established by the Rome Statute. Previously, states were unfettered in their ability to agree to amnesty as a component of a peace agreement with rebel groups or, for that matter, with other states with whom they were at war. Amnesty is an emanation of the national legal order. It cannot, of course, bind other legal systems. As has been explained, South Africa's amnesty applies only within its own borders. Other states are free to disregard it. They may contemplate prosecution on the basis of universal jurisdiction. Despite this, none of them have done so in the South African case, disproving the claim of an emerging prohibitive norm concerning amnesties or of an obligation to prosecute. International or intergovernmental judicial institutions may also proceed with prosecution, regardless of the decisions of national lawmakers. The establishment of the Special Court for Sierra Leone is an example.

With the advent of the International Criminal Court, however, it can no longer be said that states are able to ensure the effectiveness of an amnesty within their own legal orders when they make peace agreements. States that are members of the Court are subject to its intervention when they prove themselves to be 'unwilling or unable' to prosecute serious international crimes. Concretely, this means that negotiators of a peace agreement may undertake pledges not to prosecute at the national level, but they cannot guarantee that their wishes will be shown any consideration by the Prosecutor of the International Criminal Court or by its judges. Moreover, they will be required by the Rome Statute to cooperate with the Court should it choose to proceed. The Court had barely opened its doors when this very difficulty arose in the context of the civil war in Northern Uganda.

Uganda's government had been unable to achieve military victory in a conflict that had lasted nearly two decades. Prompted by the international Prosecutor, the President of Uganda, Yoveri Museveni, referred the situation concerning the Lord's Resistance Army in Northern Uganda to the fledgling International Criminal Court. The letter of referral made reference to the 'situation concerning the Lord's Resistance Army in northern and western Uganda'. The press release issued by the Office of the Prosecutor at the time spoke of 'locating and arresting the [Lord's Resistance Army] leadership'.

In mid-2005 five arrest warrants were issued by a Pre-Trial Chamber of the Court against leaders of the rebel group. This appears to have had a decisive effect, in that it prompted the rebels to sue for peace. The fighting stopped, and peace talks commenced. It is widely acknowledged that the threat of prosecution by the International Criminal Court helped to bring the Lord's Resistance Army to the negotiating table. On a visit to the Court, the Ugandan Minister for Security, Amama Mbabazi, noted that the issuance of warrants had contributed to driving the Lord's Resistance Army leaders to discuss a settlement. In September 2006 Jan Egelund, the United Nations Under-Secretary-General for Humanitarian Affairs and Emergency Relief, made similar observations in a briefing to the Security Council. Speaking to the Assembly of States Parties in November 2006, Prosecutor Moreno-Ocampo said:

The Court's intervention has galvanized the activities of the states concerned... Thanks to the unity of purpose of these states, the LRA has been forced to flee its safe haven in southern Sudan and has moved its headquarters to the DRC border. As a consequence, crimes allegedly committed by the LRA in Northern

Uganda have drastically decreased. People are leaving the camps for displaced persons and the night commuter shelters which protected tens of thousands of children are now in the process of closing. The loss of their safe haven led the LRA commanders to engage in negotiations, resulting in a cessation of hostilities agreement in August 2006.[16]

So far so good. Issuance of the arrest warrants had contributed to conflict resolution in northern Uganda. New and welcome efforts to mediate an end to the civil war gained momentum. The Court was demonstrating its effectiveness.

The situation was somewhat reminiscent of the one faced by Richard Goldstone, Prosecutor of the International Criminal Tribunal for the former Yugoslavia, in July 1995. While the war in Bosnia and Herzegovina was still raging, he obtained indictments against Serb leaders Radovan Karadžić and Ratko Mladić. Judge Goldstone was later admonished by United Nations Secretary-General Boutros Boutros-Ghali for failing to consult at a political level. Goldstone replied that as a prosecutor it was not his job to take political factors into account. Nevertheless, the charges helped to isolate Karadžić and Mladić, and may well have contributed to the successful outcome of peace negotiations at Dayton later that same year.

Predictably, one of the demands of the Lord's Resistance Army leaders was that the International Criminal Court arrest warrants not be pursued. They had been brought to the table by the threat of criminal prosecution and this was obviously high on their list of matters to be resolved as part of a negotiated settlement. Jan Egelund reported to the Security Council that in meetings with internally displaced persons, civil society, and the parties themselves, the 'International Criminal Court indictments were the number one subject of discussion... All expressed a strong concern that if the indictments were not lifted, they could threaten the progress in these most promising talks ever for northern Uganda.' President Museveni was himself more than happy to do this, and promised as much to the Lord's Resistance Army. But he could not himself withdraw the international arrest warrants which were valid within Uganda as a result of the country's ratification of the Rome Statute. For the first time in human history, a sovereign government could not pledge an amnesty in exchange for peace within an internal armed conflict. This was prevented by the international obligations that Uganda had itself accepted.

Museveni turned to The Hague in the hopes it would cooperate and lift the charges which had by then become an obstacle to a negotiated peace.

---

[16] 'Opening Remarks, Luis Moreno Ocampo, Fifth Session of the Assembly of States Parties', 23 November 2006.

Possibly he referred to the potential application of articles 17 and 53, discussed earlier in this chapter. But the Prosecutor refused. His inflexible position is easy to understand in light of the 'interests of justice' paper that he issued subsequently. In the end, at least in part because Museveni could not remove the threat of prosecution by the International Criminal Court, the peace deal broke down. The Lord's Resistance Army leaders did not show up at the meeting where they were to sign the agreement. They retreated into the bush, to fight another day, and to take new victims. After the negotiations faltered, there were more rapes, more killings, and more abductions.

The threat of prosecution by the International Criminal Court had initially helped bring peace. Supporters of the Court were very pleased to accept credit for this. But peace had a price that the Court was not willing to pay. As a result, instead of assisting in a permanent peace, it may have contributed to a revival of conflict. If international justice is brought to bear on situations like that of northern Uganda because it can help promote peace, perhaps it should be prepared to stand down when criminal prosecution becomes an obstacle to peace. To the extent that the leaders of the Lord's Resistance Army came to the negotiating table *because* of the threat of prosecution, the withdrawal of the charges would seem to have been necessary in order to complete the process.

Otherwise, the threat of criminal prosecution only does half the job, and the boast that the Court has helped to promote peace is ultimately a specious one. On this point, however, there is great resistance, not from the Ugandan authorities but rather from the Prosecutor himself and the various players in the international criminal justice community who surround him. They argue that to attempt to withdraw the charges would betray the search for justice and discredit the Court.

This position seems too extreme. Those who argue that prosecution should not be sacrificed in a peace bargain should be prepared to answer for the alternative, which can never be ruled out, namely a return to conflict *because* of the inability of negotiators to be able to promise the rebel leaders that if they lay down their arms they will not be prosecuted. Are those who argue that the arrest warrants cannot be dropped as a matter of principle truly prepared for a resumption of hostilities, with all of the terrible human suffering that this may involve?

The tension between amnesty and international prosecution also manifested itself in the removal of Charles Taylor from power in Liberia. In August 2003 Taylor agreed to leave office in exchange for a promise of asylum in nearby Nigeria. The deal brought an end to a lengthy conflict. Not only were lives spared as a result, Liberia was launched on an impressive process of reform and democratization, recognized in 2011 when its president received the Nobel Peace Prize. Those with an intransigent attachment to justice were shocked, given that Taylor had been indicted for war crimes and crimes against humanity by the Special Court for Sierra Leone only months earlier. But even they cannot dispute the impressive deliverables that resulted from the departure of Taylor. Without the promise of asylum and, in effect, immunity from prosecution, Taylor probably would have prolonged the conflict. Indeed, he might still be in power.

Later, intense international pressure led Nigeria to revoke the protection of Taylor, and facilitate his transfer to The Hague for trial before the Special Court for Sierra Leone. This may have been an error, not because Taylor does not deserve to be tried for the crimes with which he has been charged, but because the withdrawal of his effective amnesty smells of a double-cross, and makes it less likely that the same technique of conflict resolution can be employed again. Unconditional opponents of amnesty welcome such developments, of course. Yet a useful implement has been removed from the toolbox of the African peacemaker. More innocent people will die on the continent as a result.

For example, one of the more intractable situations in contemporary Africa is posed by Mugabe's Zimbabwe. A Taylor-like solution, whereby the country's ageing despot might be convinced to leave power in return for a promise he would escape prosecution, is an attractive option and deserves consideration. But Mugabe is an observant man, and he has already noted publicly how the pledge to Taylor was ultimately rescinded. What was a useful option in 2003, when it was taken up by Taylor, has become a trap that Mugabe will probably avoid at all costs.

Aside from the claims that such amnesties are not permitted under international law—a matter discussed earlier in this chapter—it is also argued that they are unwise, and that they resolve nothing. A failure to punish perpetrators of serious crimes means uncertain and unstable peace, and strengthens the likelihood of a return to conflict, it is said. This is slightly different from the argument that amnesty is unacceptable because it violates the rights of individual victims. Rather, amnesty is challenged precisely because it does not contribute to lasting peace. The argument is utilitarian, not retributive. Presumably, those who subscribe to this view are not opposed to amnesty as a matter of principle, but rather because it fails to deliver its alleged benefits.

The contention that amnesty does not promote lasting peace is an interesting hypothesis, but it is unproven, and there is much empirical evidence to the contrary. It may well be the case that in some circumstances, a situation of impunity has contributed to continuing instability or at least accompanied it. In the Balkans, for example, it was fashionable to explain the wars of the 1990s as the consequence of unsettled scores dating back to the Second World War and even earlier, to distant centuries. Perhaps that explanation has some validity. However, there are other conflicts that ended with impunity, where peace seems permanent enough. Spain is the usual example here—a country that suffered through a fierce civil war followed by more than three decades of brutal dictatorship. Its transition, in the 1970s, was premised upon an amnesty. There are unsatisfied victims, or their descendants, to be sure, and some rumblings from the judiciary and civil society, but this alone does not mean that a generalized social peace has not been achieved.

Much has been written about Sierra Leone in this chapter and elsewhere in this volume. The Sierra Leone amnesty is a case in point. The Lomé Agreement launched a peace process that has been essentially free of conflict. It might be argued that the Special Court has abolished the amnesty, but in practice the effect of the Court has only been confined to a small number of offenders. The rest of the perpetrators, and they number in the tens of thousands, have escaped justice. The amnesty of these hideous souls may have been a high price to pay, but it did end the fighting. In early 1999, when negotiations began, it was far from apparent that the war could have been brought to an end without an amnesty (as the Sierra Leone Truth and Reconciliation Commission noted). President Kabbah and his allies were simply unable to defeat the Revolutionary United Front on the battlefield. But in the post-Lomé environment they managed to outmanoeuvre their opponents, achieving politically the victory that had earlier eluded them militarily. History will no doubt record its appreciation of the fact that the gratuitous declaration about amnesty by the Special Representative of the Secretary-General at the Lomé negotiations, on 7 July 1999, did not scupper the deal. More than a decade after the Lomé amnesty, Sierra Leone remains at peace. The vast majority of perpetrators continue to live their lives inside the country without realistic fear of prosecution.

The point here is not that amnesty is desirable, or that it should be encouraged. Preferably, there will be some measure of justice and accountability, particularly for the most serious perpetrators. Their condemnation, whether by criminal trial or some less drastic alternative like a truth commission, offers real benefits that not only respond to the rights of victims but may also, in many circumstances, help to secure peaceful transition. Absolute formulations here are always dangerous. Both peace and justice are to be sought. But sometimes, peace will only be attainable if justice is sacrificed. Moreover, too much justice may imperil peace. Rigid, inflexible approaches to these issues, characterized by the exaggerated claim that amnesty is prohibited by international law, or that impunity inexorably leads to further conflict, are counterproductive.

8

CRIMES AGAINST PEACE

The fourth is freedom from fear—which, translated into world terms, means a world-wide reduction of armaments to such a point and in such a thorough fashion that no nation will be in a position to commit an act of physical aggression against any neighbour—anywhere in the world.

Franklin D. Roosevelt, 'Four Freedoms Speech' to Congress, 6 January 1941

'If we can root out of men's thinking the idea that all wars are legal, and if we can substitute the conviction that aggressive war is criminal, at last we will have mobilized the forces of law on the side of peace,' wrote Justice Robert Jackson in the *New York Times Magazine* on 9 September 1945. Jackson, who was a member of the United States Supreme Court, had been sent to Europe by President Harry Truman earlier in the year. After negotiating the Charter of the International Military Tribunal at the London Conference, Jackson took on the job of American Prosecutor (there were four, one for each of the powers) in the great trial at Nuremberg. '[I]if we give to all men in positions of power over the lives of people and the policy of nations an object-lesson that the making of aggressive war is the way to the prisoner's dock, we may somewhat change the psychology of statesmanship', he continued. 'Too long, and in too many parts of the world, it has been a crime to advocate peace in the midst of war. It is time that it became a crime to make war when the world so needs peace.' It was a phenomenal innovation. Jackson noted that laymen would be shocked to learn that 'the international law of the nineteenth and early twentieth centuries did not regard a war—even one of flagrant aggression—as a crime. All wars were "legal," and no one could be made to answer at law for causing them.'

A start had been made in 1919, with the aborted threat in article 227 of the Treaty of Versailles to hold the German emperor responsible for 'a supreme offence against international morality and the sanctity of treaties'. At Nuremberg and Tokyo the making of aggressive war was prosecuted under the heading: 'crimes against peace'. The Charter of the International Military Tribunal defined this as '[p]lanning, preparation, initiation or waging of a war of aggression or a war in violation of international treaties, agreements or assurances', including '[p]articipation in a common plan or conspiracy for the accomplishment' of such acts. In the final judgment, this was described as the 'supreme international crime differing only from other war crimes in that it contains within itself the accumulated evil of the whole'.[1]

But the crime of aggression proved to be an immense stumbling block in the development of international criminal law. The United Nations General Assembly, mainly through its subordinate body, the International Law Commission, attempted to consolidate the accomplishments of Nuremberg and set the stage for a permanent court. The project was suspended in 1954 so that aggression could be defined. This took twenty years. General Assembly Resolution 3314(XXX), entitled 'Definition of Aggression', was adopted in 1974. Two decades later, when the first of the modern generation of international criminal tribunals was established by the United Nations Security Council, for the former Yugoslavia, the crime of aggression was nowhere to be found. Its absence was intriguing. After all, the basic premise of the Security Council in establishing the Tribunal, and indeed the reasoning that gives it the authority to do so, was that there was a threat to the peace, breach of the peace, or act of aggression, to reprise the terms of article 39 of the Charter of the United Nations. Moreover, there were frequent charges that aggression had been committed, specifically against Bosnia and Herzegovina. In drafting the Statute of the International Criminal Tribunal for the former Yugoslavia, the Secretary-General had quite explicitly taken the Nuremberg codification as a model. He borrowed Nuremberg's language with respect to war crimes and crimes against humanity, but ignored the issue of crimes against peace and gave no explanation for this in his report. Essentially the same scenario recurred the following year in the creation of the International Criminal Tribunal for Rwanda.

Nevertheless, crimes against peace had not entirely disappeared from the radar screen of international criminal law. In its 1994 draft statute of the future International Criminal Court, the International Law Commission proposed a list of core crimes that essentially replicated that of Nuremberg and included 'the crime of aggression', but it noted that '[t]he position of

---

[1] *France* et al. v *Göring* et al. (1948) 22 IMT 411, at p. 427.

aggression as a crime is different, not least because of the special responsibilities of the Security Council under Chapter VII of the Charter of the United Nations, but the Commission felt that it too should be included, subject to certain safeguards'. No longer was it being described as the 'supreme international crime'. Rather, its place within the international enumeration of atrocity crimes had become somewhat uncertain.

PUTTING AGGRESSION IN THE ROME STATUTE

The climax was the Rome Conference, in June and July 1998, at which the Statute of the International Criminal Court was adopted. With about ten days remaining, the chair of the negotiating process proposed dropping aggression from the list of crimes altogether, given the slow progress in reaching agreement on how it should be incorporated within the Statute. This met with angry responses from many delegations. Some of them recalled the language in the Nuremberg judgment about the 'supreme international crime' and the historic importance of the crime of aggression. Ultimately, article 5(1) of the Rome Statute listed aggression as a crime within the jurisdiction of the Court, along with genocide, crimes against humanity, and war crimes, but added, in article 5(2):

The Court shall exercise jurisdiction over the crime of aggression once a provision is adopted in accordance with articles 121 and 123 defining the crime and setting out the conditions under which the Court shall exercise jurisdiction with respect to this crime. Such a provision shall be consistent with the relevant provisions of the Charter of the United Nations.

The somewhat cryptic language of article 5(2) indicated that the real obstacle was not with the definition of aggression so much as with the conditions for exercise of jurisdiction. Article 39 of the Charter of the United Nations says '[t]he Security Council shall determine the existence of any threat to the peace, breach of the peace, or act of aggression'. The five permanent members believed this meant the Security Council had a monopoly on such determinations. The head of the United Kingdom delegation, Franklyn Berman, said this quite clearly in the final plenary of the Rome Conference. The permanent members were only prepared to agree with incorporating aggression into the Rome Statute if the Council's approval of prosecutions was a prerequisite. This had not been a problem at Nuremberg.

The vast majority of states at the Rome Conference were unwilling to let the Court's Statute be used to reaffirm, reinforce, or strengthen the interpretation of the Charter of the United Nations favoured by the permanent five. For many, the goal was the opposite: use the Rome Statute to do indirectly what they had been unable to do directly, and trim the prerogatives of the Security Council. The debate about incorporating the crime of aggression in the Rome Statute concealed a much larger argument about the post-Second World War world order and the architecture of the United Nations.

Over the decade or so that followed the 1998 Diplomatic Conference, a determined group of states and individuals pursued the incorporation of the crime of aggression in the Rome Statute. Organized through much of this period in the 'Special Working Group on the Crime of Aggression', they explored various formulae and approaches. Eventually, the Special Working Group reached broad agreement on a definition of aggression but no clarity whatsoever on the conditions for the exercise of jurisdiction. In the course of its work, the negotiators discovered that the dysfunctional amendment provisions of the Statute presented an additional problem. To the surprise of most and the joy of many, their work culminated in the crafting of a set of amendments to the Rome Statute that was adopted at the Kampala Review Conference, in early June 2010. By general agreement, the Conference accepted provisions that define the crime of aggression and that establish the conditions for exercise of jurisdiction. In a radical development, they contemplate prosecution for aggression by the Court without any prior authorization from the Security Council.

The president of the Review Conference had put the package before delegates just before midnight on the final day of the meeting. All that was required to defeat the proposal was for one delegation to call for a vote, given the near certainty that there were not enough voting delegations left in the room to comply with the two-thirds requirement set out in the Statute. But neither of the two permanent members of the Security Council who were also States Parties to the Rome Statute, France and the United Kingdom, raised their flags to ask for a vote. They had repeatedly insisted that any amendment allowing the Court to proceed without a Security Council blessing would be unthinkable. Now, *in extremis*, they meekly allowed the provision to be adopted without protest. Had the inflexible pronouncements been nothing but a bluff from London and Paris? Or were the tectonic plates of world politics shifting, pulverizing prerogatives of the permanent members of the Security Council that had existed since 1945?

The 2010 amendments to the Rome Statute provide a definition of the crime of aggression inspired by General Assembly Resolution 3314(XXX). The list of 'acts of aggression' in that resolution is nevertheless conditioned on contextual factors, principally the requirement in the amendments to the Rome Statute that such an act, 'by its character, gravity and scale, constitutes a manifest violation of the Charter of the United

Nations'. An 'understanding' agreed to at the Kampala Conference specifies that

aggression is the most serious and dangerous form of the illegal use of force; and that a determination whether an act of aggression has been committed requires consideration of all the circumstances of each particular case, including the gravity of the acts concerned and their consequences, in accordance with the Charter of the United Nations.

The Conference rejected an American proposal for an additional understanding intended to prevent any use of force motivated by humanitarian purposes from being labelled aggression. In effect, the Conference was saying that self-appointed proponents of humanitarian intervention (or the 'responsibility to protect') risk prosecution if they proceed without Security Council authorization.

Pursuant to the amendments, the Security Council retains the initiative in determining whether the Court should prosecute the crime of aggression. The Court must wait for six months before proceeding if it does not receive a green light from the Security Council. The Security Council also retains the right to block a prosecution, but only temporarily, by adopting resolutions on an annual basis. The jurisdictional scope of the aggression amendments is narrower than is the general rule for crimes under the Rome Statute. Only a State Party (or rather, the leaders of that state) can be subject to prosecution for aggression committed against another State Party. By contrast, leaders and other nationals of a non-party state may be prosecuted under the Statute for genocide, crimes against humanity, and war crimes where the acts are perpetrated on the territory of a State Party. A broader scope of jurisdiction would have been desirable, allowing the Court to address aggression committed against a State Party by a non-party state. But consensus was probably impossible on this more radical vision. Sometimes the best can be the enemy of the good. And perhaps the unique jurisdictional regime for aggression may provide an incentive to non-party states to join the Court. It is the only way they can give the Court the authority to prosecute aggression of which they may be the victim if it is perpetrated by a State Party.

The most enigmatic dimension of the 2010 amendments concerns the formula for amendment and entry into force. Article 121 of the Rome Statute offers two options, depending upon the nature of the amendment. Each of these has its own problems and shortcomings. In the end, the Kampala Conference appears to have adopted a third approach to amendment, which may or may not be judged compatible with article 121. There is no problem, of course, with a Review Conference deciding to create a new amending formula, but it seems that it is locked in by the existing one. It can only amend the amending formula by respecting the provision that already exists. With a bit of imagination and creativity, the new amendment may sit rather approximately within article 121. Only time will tell whether it can resist judicial scrutiny.

The 2010 amendments require ratification by thirty States Parties, and cannot enter into force in any case prior to 2017, at which time, an additional two-thirds vote of States Parties is required. These conditions should not present much difficulty. Once fulfilled, they give the Court jurisdiction with respect to the crime of aggression over all States Parties that have ratified the amendment, at a minimum, and probably over all States Parties generally, depending upon how one interprets the amendment. A State Party unhappy with the amendments may make a declaration withdrawing from the jurisdiction over aggression. Though a simple matter procedurally, this is likely to be politically unpalatable for most states and few such declarations are to be expected. The price to be paid vis-à-vis public opinion for an admission that a state fears prosecution for the crime of aggression will probably be judged to be too high.

It may be decades before there are any prosecutions for the crime of aggression. Few events that have taken place since 1945 actually respond to the definition, and there is no reason to think that this situation will change in the future. That observation is merely a tribute to the effectiveness of the Charter of the United Nations and the collective security regime that it establishes. The jurisdictional scheme of the aggression provisions of the Rome Statute may complicate matters still further, because several of the 'usual suspects' will remain outside the system. Eventually, the Rome Statute will achieve universal ratification. But even if the amendments adopted in 2010 are not applied by the Court, they still perform a vital declaratory function that may, in some situations, act as a deterrent. Perhaps prosecutors and judges will return to the insights of their predecessors at Nuremberg who saw wars of aggression as the 'supreme international crime'. If so, this may influence decisions about the priorities of international justice and its relationship with the constant quest for lasting peace.

INDIFFERENCE FROM THE BIG NGOS

The major international human rights NGOs, generally highly devoted to the creation and work of the International Criminal Court, were surprisingly indifferent to the issue of the crime of aggression. Although present at the Kampala Conference, they concentrated their attention on the 'stock-taking' sessions, a series of panel discussions held during the first days of the meeting on thematic issues such as complementarity and cooperation. This was an environment where NGOs felt right at home and where they could thrive. There were persuasive speeches and eloquent declarations about fighting impunity. States were hectored about living up to their responsibilities. Policy papers were distributed. But when the foreplay was over and the Conference shifted its attention to the main act, which was the crime of aggression, most of the NGOs retreated. Many of them simply returned to their homes in Europe or America. Most of those that stayed behind were out of sorts, probably frustrated by their self-imposed irrelevance to the profound developments that were underway.

How did they explain their positions? Amnesty International said it had not

taken a stance on the definition of the crime of aggression because its mandate—to campaign for every person to enjoy all of the human rights (civil and political and economic, social and cultural rights) enshrined in the Universal Declaration of Human Rights and other international human rights standards—does not extend to the lawfulness of the use of force.[2]

Human Rights Watch took a more pragmatic, policy-oriented view:

Human Rights Watch's institutional mandate includes a position of strict neutrality on issues of *jus ad bellum*, because we find it the best way to focus on the conduct of war, or *jus in bello*, and thereby to promote our primary goal of encouraging all parties to a conflict to respect international humanitarian law. Consistent with this approach, we take no position on the substance of a definition of the crime of aggression.

In a footnote to its explanation, Human Rights Watch added: 'The only exceptions that Human Rights Watch has made to this policy is to call for military intervention where massive loss of human life, on the order of genocide, can be halted through no other means, as was the case in Bosnia and Rwanda in the 1990s.'[3]

The footnote in the Human Rights Watch statement may provide a useful clue to understanding the reticence of the big NGOs in this area. A militaristic tendency has crept into human rights discourse in recent years, encouraged by talk of 'humanitarian intervention' and the 'responsibility to protect'. Of course, human rights law has never been pacifistic, in the sense of a principled and intransigent opposition to the use of force under all circumstances. The preamble of the Universal Declaration of Human

---

[2] Amnesty International, 'International Criminal Court, Concerns at the seventh session of the Assembly of States Parties', October 2008, Index: IOR 40/022/2008, p. 22.
[3] Human Rights Watch, 'Memorandum for the Sixth Session of the Assembly of States Parties of the International Criminal Court'.

Rights says that human rights must be protected by the rule of law so that 'man is not to be compelled to have recourse, as a last resort, to rebellion against tyranny and oppression'. But there has been a growing willingness to contemplate military interventions as the ultimate solution to serious human rights violations. In these discussions, it seems that an appeal to the Pentagon (or often an *ex post facto* rationalization), albeit framed in reluctant language, is rarely very distant.

Another influence may be the debates about the relationship between peace and justice in the context of prosecutorial strategy at the International Criminal Court (see Chapter 7, 'No Peace Without Justice? The Amnesty Quandary'). In situations where there is an arguable case that peace negotiations may be jeopardized by prosecution, such as northern Uganda and even Darfur, there has been political pressure on the Court to back off in the interests of promoting peace. Encouraged by human rights NGOs, the Prosecutor of the Court has taken the view that the quest for peace should not condition his decisions about selection of cases (see Chapter 3, ' "Victors' Justice". Selecting Targets for Prosecution'). In a policy paper issued in September 2007, the Prosecutor cited paragraph 3 of the preamble to the Rome Statute ('Recognizing that such grave crimes threaten the peace, security and well-being of the world'), noting that '[t]he ICC was created on the premise that justice is an essential component of a stable peace'. He wrote that 'there is a difference between the concepts of the interests of justice and the interests of peace and that the latter falls within the mandate of institutions other than the Office of the Prosecutor'. Furthermore, 'the broader matter of international peace and security is not the responsibility of the Prosecutor; it falls within the mandate of other institutions'.[4]

Yet there is also much to be said for the view that the rationale of the International Criminal Court is to promote peace, just as it was for the ad hoc tribunals. The latter were, after all, created by the United Nations Security Council in pursuit of its mandate to promote international peace and security, with Chapter VII of the Charter invoked in support. According to the first annual report of the International Criminal Tribunal for the former Yugoslavia:

it would be wrong to assume that the Tribunal is based on the old maxim *fiat justitia et pereat mundus* (let justice be done, even if the world were to perish). The Tribunal is, rather, based on the maxim propounded by Hegel in 1821: *fiat justitia ne pereat mundus* (let justice be done lest the world should perish). Indeed, the

---

[4] Office of the Prosecutor, Policy paper on the interests of justice, September 2007.

judicial process aims at averting the exacerbation and aggravation of conflict and tension, thereby contributing, albeit gradually, to a lasting peace.[5]

These words wisely suggest that the pursuit of peace lies at the heart of international justice. The idea dovetails neatly with the approach of the International Military Tribunal, whereby a war of aggression was the supreme international crime, an overarching paradigm within which the other atrocity crimes, crimes against humanity and war crimes, find their place.

In suggesting that it should confine its activity to the *jus in bello*, Human Rights Watch transplants to the field of human rights law a concept that is well accepted in the law of armed conflict. For a century and a half, the International Committee of the Red Cross has insisted that its work of civilizing the conduct of hostilities imposes a duty of neutrality. In order to intervene effectively on the battlefield, it cannot be seen to favour one side over the other. It is the very essence of the law of armed conflict that both parties to a conflict be held to the same normative standards. But why should this logic apply to human rights law, which is concerned primarily with the protection of individuals from violations attributable to a state? This is not a matter of choosing sides so much as one of determining that the use of force by a state, which inexorably results in human suffering of huge proportions, violates the human rights of the victims to the extent that such use of force is unlawful. The problem with the contrary view— the one proposed by Human Rights Watch—is that it accepts rather too easily the loss of human life and the destruction of property resulting from the use of force by an aggressor, which is written off as 'collateral damage'. The law of armed conflict tolerates 'incidental' loss of life and destruction of property as an inevitable accompaniment of war. When the war is itself unlawful, the law of human rights should not tolerate loss of life and destruction of property based upon the trite proposal that it is unconcerned about *jus ad bellum*.

PEACE AND THE UNIVERSAL DECLARATION OF HUMAN RIGHTS

Human Rights Watch and Amnesty International reach the same result, albeit by different routes. Amnesty International frames its indifference to the crime of aggression with reference to the Universal Declaration of Human Rights. Of course, the word 'aggression' is not to be found in

---

[5] First Annual Report of the International Criminal Tribunal for the former Yugoslavia, UN Doc. A/49/342-S/1994/1007, annex, para. 18.

the laconic text of the Universal Declaration of Human Rights. But there are several references to peace, some explicit and some implicit. It is certainly unfortunate that the Universal Declaration of Human Rights does not affirm a right to peace expressly. Perhaps that is because the drafters viewed human rights and the quest for peace as being inextricably linked, but considered human rights to be a condition for the attainment of peace rather than a right requiring precise enumeration and definition. The initial 48-article draft of the Declaration prepared by John Humphrey of the Secretariat began by noting that the preamble would refer to the four freedoms and was to start by stating the principle that 'that there can be no peace unless human rights and freedoms are respected'.[6]

The first sentence of the preamble to the Declaration reads: 'Whereas recognition of the inherent dignity and of the equal and inalienable rights of all members of the human family is the foundation of freedom, justice and peace in the world'. The immortal four freedoms of Franklin D. Roosevelt, which include 'freedom from fear', are cited, as Humphrey initially planned. The preamble also says that 'it is essential to promote the development of friendly relations between nations'. Article 26 declares that education is to 'further the activities of the United Nations for the maintenance of peace'. Probably most important is article 28: 'Everyone is entitled to a social and international order in which the rights and freedoms set forth in this Declaration can be fully realized.'

There is also a structural argument. The Universal Declaration of Human Rights is an emanation of the Charter of the United Nations. Originally, the Charter was to have included a 'bill of rights'. That would have left no doubt about the link between peace and human rights. To the disappointment of many states, delegates to the San Francisco Conference could not agree on how to incorporate a catalogue of fundamental rights in the Charter itself. They settled on general references to human rights in several provisions of the Charter, notably articles 1 and 55, as well as the preamble, leaving the work of codification to the Commission on Human Rights in accordance with article 68. That mandate was fulfilled on 10 December 1948 with the adoption of the Universal Declaration of Human Rights. To contend that the Universal Declaration is somehow neutral on the issue of aggressive war is to dissociate that document from the context of its adoption and its place within the postwar legal order, which is founded on the prohibition of recourse to force to settle international disputes.

There is much support for the concept of a 'peoples' right to peace'. For example, this is recognized by the African Charter of Human and Peoples'

[6] UN Doc. E/CN.4/AC.1/3, p. 2.

Rights, adopted in 1981 ('All peoples shall have the right to national and international peace and security'). In 1984 the United Nations General Assembly adopted a resolution entitled 'The Peoples' Right to Peace'. The text proclaimed that 'the peoples of our planet have a sacred right to peace' and that 'the preservation of the right of peoples to peace and the promotion of its implementation constitute a fundamental obligation of each state'.[7] In 2002 a resolution of the Commission on Human Rights affirmed 'the solemn proclamation that the peoples of our planet have a sacred right to peace'. The Commission stated 'that the preservation of the right of peoples to peace and the promotion of its implementation constitute a fundamental obligation of each state'.[8] The following year, a General Assembly resolution was entitled 'Promotion of the right of peoples to peace'.[9] In 2005 the Commission on Human Rights adopted a resolution entitled 'Promotion of peace as a vital requirement for the full enjoyment of all human rights by all'.[10] It was again echoed subsequently by a resolution in the General Assembly along the same lines.[11] All of these resolutions referred to the 1984 Declaration.

The Human Rights Council replaced the Commission in 2006. Shortly after its foundation, a resolution on 'Promotion of the right of peoples to peace' was adopted.[12] Like previous efforts, it failed to obtain consensus and a recorded vote was required. The European Union explained that it voted against the resolution, but noted the call for a seminar which could provide 'a more comprehensive and open debate' on the subject.[13] No seminar was convened, however, the ostensible reason being a lack of budget provisions for the event.[14] The following year, another resolution was adopted along similar lines.[15] Explaining the negative vote of the European Union members of the Council, the delegate from Germany said:

The European Union supports some of the principles set out in this draft resolution and recognizes the linkage between peace and enjoyment of human rights. However, the draft resolution omits to state that the absence of peace cannot justify failure to respect human rights. Besides, it deals almost exclusively with the relationship between states and not with the relationship between the state and its citizens, and the state's respect for human rights, which is the core mandate of

---

[7] UN Doc. A/RES/39/11, annex, paras 1–2.

[8] Promotion of the right of peoples to peace, UN Doc. E/CN.4/RES/2002/71.

[9] UN Doc. A/RES/57/216.   [10] UN Doc. E/CN.4/RES/2005/56.

[11] Promotion of peace as a vital requirement for the full enjoyment of all human rights by all, UN Doc. A/RES/60/163.   [12] UN Doc. A/HRC/RES/8/9.

[13] Explanation of vote by Slovenia (on behalf of EU) concerning UN Doc. A/HRC/8/L.13, 18 June 2008 <http://www.un.org/webcast/unhrc/archive.asp?go=080618>.

[14] Implementation of Human Rights Council resolution 8/9 on the promotion of the right of peoples to peace, Note by the Secretariat, UN Doc. A/HRC/11/38.

[15] Promotion of the right of peoples to peace, UN Doc. A/HRC/RES/11/4.

this council. We believe that most of the issues raised in this resolution are better dealt with in other fora which have the competence to do so and which are already dealing with these issues.[16]

This time the seminar took place in December 2009. The keynote address was delivered by Antônio Cançado Trindade, the distinguished Brazilian human rights scholar and judge at the International Court of Justice.

In its preamble the 2009 resolution takes note of the 1984 Declaration of the General Assembly as well as the United Nations Millennium Declaration and the Purposes and Principles enshrined in the Charter of the United Nations. It also speaks of the obligation to refrain from the threat or use of force in international relations, and the importance of friendly relations and cooperation among states, with a reference to the Declaration on Friendly Relations (General Assembly Resolution 2625). The concept of the peoples' right to self-determination, drawn from common article 1 of the human rights covenants, is also reaffirmed. The preamble of the Resolution '[r]ecogniz[es] that peace and security, development and human rights are mutually interlinked and reinforcing'. Echoing article 28 of the Universal Declaration of Human Rights, it also '[r]ecall[s] that everyone is entitled to a social and international order in which the rights and freedoms set forth in the Universal Declaration of Human Rights can be fully realized'.

In the operative paragraphs the 2009 resolution of the Human Rights Council affirms 'that the peoples of our planet have a sacred right to peace'. It stresses 'the importance of peace for the promotion and protection of all human rights for all'. The issue of the peoples' right to peace is linked to 'the deep fault line that divides human society between the rich and the poor and the ever-increasing gap between the developed world and the developing world'. It insists that 'the policies of states be directed towards the elimination of the threat of war, particularly nuclear war, the renunciation of the use or threat of use of force in international relations and the settlement of international disputes by peaceful means on the basis of the Charter of the United Nations'.

Other initiatives concerning the 'right to peace' have not explicitly taken their bearings from the 1984 General Assembly Declaration. In 1996 and 1997 the now-defunct Sub-Commission on the Promotion and Protection of Human Rights adopted resolutions that affirmed: '[i]nternational peace and security as an essential condition for the enjoyment of human rights,

---

[16] Explanation of vote by Germany (on behalf of EU) concerning UN Doc. A/HRC/11/L.11, 17 June 2009 <http://www.un.org/webcast/unhrc/archive.asp?go=090617>.

above all the right to life'.[17] During the 1980s and 1990s UNESCO held a number of meetings on the subject of solidarity rights and, specifically, the right to peace. In 1995 the General Conference of UNESCO adopted the 'Declaration of Principles of Tolerance', which states that humans 'have the right to live in peace and to be as they are'.[18] In 1998 Director-General Federico Mayor convened a meeting of representatives and experts to aid in drafting a declaration for the right to peace. While some state representatives voiced doubts about the content of the right during the 1998 conference, they all supported the right to peace as a moral principle. However, the resulting draft was edited to leave out any explicit reference to the right to peace, and remained rather ambiguous. For example, the General Conference spelled out its goal, 'to build the defences of peace in the minds of human beings in everyday life', rather than recognizing the right to peace.[19]

JUS AD BELLUM AND JUS IN BELLO

To explain its reticence on the incorporation of the crime of aggression in the Rome Statute of the International Criminal Court, Human Rights Watch invoked a Latin expression—*jus ad bellum, jus in bello*—that is more familiar to the field of international humanitarian law than to that of international human rights law. The legality of the resort to force (*jus ad bellum*) is distinguished from the lawfulness of the conduct in the conflict (*jus in bello*). Neutrality with respect to the responsibility of one or the other parties for the outbreak of war is one of the hallmarks of the law of armed conflict, for good reason. It is probably overstating things, however, to suggest that even international humanitarian law, which is a more modern term for the law of armed conflict, is purely and exclusively focussed on the *jus in bello*. The International Red Cross movement, which is in many respects the custodian of the law of armed conflict, has repeatedly underscored the importance of peace in the accomplishment of its work. Adopting principles to guide its work, in 1961, the International Federation of Red Cross and Red Crescent Societies said the movement was

born of a desire to bring assistance without discrimination to the wounded on the battlefield, [and] endeavours, in its international and national capacity, to prevent

---

[17] UN Doc. E/CN.4/Sub.2/RES/1996/16; UN Doc. E/CN.4/Sub.2/RES/1997/36.

[18] Janusz Symonides, 'New Human Rights Dimensions, Obstacles and Challenges: Introductory Remarks', in Janusz Symonides (ed), *Human Rights: New Dimensions and Challenges*, Paris: Unesco, 1998, pp. 1–25, at p. 8.

[19] Director-General of UNESCO, Report on the Result of the International Consultation of Governmental Experts on the Human Right to Peace, para. 13, delivered to Executive Board, UN Doc. 154 EX/40 (17 April 1998).

and alleviate human suffering wherever it may be found. Its purpose is to protect life and health and to ensure respect for the human being. It promotes mutual understanding, friendship, cooperation *and lasting peace amongst all peoples.*[20]

The great Jean Pictet wrote that the founders of the Red Cross, and in particular Henry Dunant,

> considered at the very beginning that the ultimate objective of the work they set in motion and the Convention they inspired was none other than that of universal peace. They understood the fact that the Red Cross, by pressing its ideal to its logical outcome, would be working for its own abolition, that a day would come when, men having finally accepted and put into effect its message of humanity by laying down and destroying their arms and thus making a future war impossible, the Red Cross would no longer have any reason for being.[21]

In 1977 the Twenty-third International Conference of the Red Cross adopted a mission statement affirming that 'the Red Cross, in respecting its principles and in developing its manifold activities, should play an essential part in disseminating to the population, and especially to youth, the spirit of mutual understanding and friendship among all peoples, and thus promoting lasting peace'. It seems that as the Red Cross movement sought greater rapprochement with the growing area of human rights, the view that this was related to the quest for peace was of considerable importance in the search for a common perspective.

There has been some infiltration of *jus ad bellum* into the law of armed conflict itself. For example, article 1 of Protocol Additional I to the Geneva Conventions admits a special regime applicable to 'armed conflicts which peoples are fighting against colonial domination and alien occupation and against racist regimes in the exercise of their right of self-determination'. The International Court of Justice has held that norms of humanitarian law relative to the prohibition of weapons that cause unnecessary suffering or superfluous harm, or are indiscriminate, do not apply strictly in the case of a country placed in an extreme situation of self-defence.[22]

But even if, as a general principle, international humanitarian law is confined essentially to the *jus in bello*, why should the same be the case for human rights law? In its early years, the United Nations stood rather aloof from the law of armed conflict, out of concern that regulating war

---

[20] *The Fundamental Principles of the Red Cross and Red Crescent*, Geneva: International Committee of the Red Cross, 1996 (my emphasis). I am indebted to Nancie Prud'homme, who thoroughly researched this issue in the preparation of her doctoral thesis, and from whose work this material is derived.

[21] Jean Pictet, 'The Fundamental Principles of the Red Cross: Commentary, 1979' <http://www.icrc.org/eng/resources/documents/misc/fundamental-principles-commentary-010179.htm>.

[22] *Legality of the Threat or Use of Nuclear Weapons (Advisory Opinion)* [1996] ICJ Reports 226, para. 97.

was somehow incompatible with the Charter.[23] The 1949 report of the International Law Commission states:

The Commission considered whether the laws of war should be selected as a topic for codification. It was suggested that, war having been outlawed, the regulation of its conduct had ceased to be relevant… The majority of the Commission declared itself opposed to the study of the problem at the present stage. It was considered that if the Commission, at the very beginning of its work, were to undertake this study, public opinion might interpret its action as showing lack of confidence in the efficiency of the means at the disposal of the United Nations for maintaining peace.[24]

Views evolved, however, and in 1968 the International Conference on Human Rights, held in Tehran, affirmed that basic humanitarian principles must apply even in time of armed conflict. Since the Tehran Conference, there has been a concerted effort to reconcile humanitarian law and human rights law, as if they are parts of the same system and can be joined together seamlessly. The most significant attempt to relate the two bodies of law comes from the International Court of Justice, which has said, with respect to the protection of the individual from arbitrary deprivation of the right to life set out in article 6(1) of the International Covenant on Civil and Political Rights, that in armed conflict this human rights norm is to be assessed in light of a specialized legal regime (the *lex specialis*), which is the law of armed conflict.

The Court observes that the protection of the International Covenant of Civil and Political Rights does not cease in times of war, except by operation of Article 4 of the Covenant whereby certain provisions may be derogated from in a time of national emergency. Respect for the right to life is not, however, such a provision. In principle, the right not arbitrarily to be deprived of one's life applies also in hostilities. The test of what is an arbitrary deprivation of life, however, then falls to be determined by the applicable *lex specialis*, namely, the law applicable in armed conflict which is designed to regulate the conduct of hostilities. Thus whether a particular loss of life, through the use of a certain weapon in warfare, is to be considered an arbitrary deprivation of life contrary to Article 6 of the Covenant, can only be decided by reference to the law applicable in armed conflict and not deduced from the terms of the Covenant itself.[25]

The Court developed its thinking on the subject of the relationship between international human rights law and international humanitarian

---

[23] See, eg, UN Doc. A/CN.4/SR.6, paras 45–67.

[24] Report to the General Assembly on the work of the first session, UN Doc. A/CN.4/13, para. 18.

[25] *Legality of the Threat or Use of Nuclear Weapons (Advisory Opinion)* [1996] ICJ Reports 226, para. 25.

law somewhat further in the advisory opinion on the separation wall in occupied Palestine:

More generally, the Court considers that the protection offered by human rights conventions does not cease in case of armed conflict, save through the effect of provisions for derogation of the kind to be found in Article 4 of the International Covenant on Civil and Political Rights. As regards the relationship between international humanitarian law and human rights law, there are thus three possible situations: some rights may be exclusively matters of international humanitarian law; others may be exclusively matters of human rights law; yet others may be matters of both these branches of international law. In order to answer the question put to it, the Court will have to take into consideration both these branches of international law, namely human rights law and, as *lex specialis*, international humanitarian law.[26]

According to Professor Hampson, the above citation makes it clear 'that *lex specialis* is not being used to displace [human rights law]. It is rather an indication that human rights bodies should interpret a human rights norm in the light of [the law of armed conflict/international humanitarian law].'[27] In the final analysis, however, the Court's formulation about the coexistence of humanitarian law and human rights law sounds a bit facile. The same observation about coexistence can be said of many bodies of law, both international and domestic, that may apply alongside the law of armed conflict during wartime.

BELT AND SUSPENDERS

The fundamental compatibility of international human rights law and international humanitarian law in most situations would seem to be beyond question. Because both bodies of law have as their essential purpose the protection of individuals from attacks on their dignity and other basic rights, as a practical matter it is unlikely that conflicts will often appear. The paradigm is not one of *lex specialis* and *lex generalis* but rather that of 'belt and suspenders'. Each body of law complements the other, each fills the gaps in the regime of the other. This is the approach taken by the Human Rights Committee in its General Comment 29.[28] The Human Rights Committee does not refer to *lex specialis*, nor does it contemplate the hypothesis that the provisions of the Covenant be in effect set aside

---

[26] *Legal Consequences of the Construction of a Wall in the Occupied Palestinian Territory (Advisory Opinion)* [2004] ICJ Reports 136, para. 106. See also: *Armed Activities on the Territory of the Congo (Democratic Republic of the Congo* v *Uganda)* [2005] ICJ Reports 168, para. 216.

[27] Working paper on the relationship between human rights law and international humanitarian law by Françoise Hampson and Ibrahim Salama, UN Doc. E/CN.4/Sub.2/2005/14, para. 57.

[28] General Comment No. 29, UN Doc. CCPR/C/21/Rev/1/Add.11, especially para. 3.

in favour of international humanitarian law, as the International Court of Justice had suggested in *Nuclear Weapons*.

The European Court of Human Rights has considered the problem of 'incidental' loss of civilian life in cases dealing with the civil war in the Russian territory of Chechnya. It has steered clear of any attempt to address international humanitarian law or to articulate the principles governing the relationship it may have with human rights law. The European Court seems to have found an entirely adequate legal framework within human rights law, in contrast with the approach taken by the International Court of Justice.

In one case before the European Court, a bomb dropped by a Russian plane had exploded near the minivan of the applicant and her relatives, as they were fleeing the village of Katyr-Yurt through what they had perceived as a safe exit from heavy fighting.[29] In another, bombs were dropped on a civilian convoy at the border between Chechnya and Ingushetia. Russian authorities had issued a press statement denying civilian damage, and claiming that a column of trucks with fighters and ammunition had provoked the encounter by firing upon a government aircraft.[30] According to the Court, article 2 of the European Convention on Human Rights 'covers not only intentional killing but also the situations in which it is permitted to "use force" which may result, as an unintended outcome, in the deprivation of life'. The test to be applied in considering the exceptions to the right to life in time of conflict, said the Court, was one of 'absolute necessity'; 'the force used must be strictly proportionate to the achievement of the permitted aims'.[31] Nevertheless, in a situation of armed conflict 'the obligation to protect the right to life must be interpreted in a way which does not impose an impossible or disproportionate burden on the authorities'.[32]

In the Katyr-Yurt case, the Court said:

the state's responsibility was not confined to circumstances where there was significant evidence that misdirected fire from agents of the state has killed a civilian. It may also be engaged where they fail to take all feasible precautions in the choice of means and methods of a security operation mounted against an opposing group with a view to avoiding and, in any event, minimizing, incidental loss of civilian life.[33]

---

[29] *Isayeva* v *Russia*, no. 57950/00, Judgment, 24 February 2005.

[30] *Isayeva, Yusopova and Bazayeva* v *Russia*, nos 57947/00, 57948/00 and 57949/00, Judgment, 24 February 2005, para. 32.

[31] *Isayeva* v *Russia*, no. 57950/00, Judgment, 24 February 2005, para. 161.

[32] *Akhmadov* et al. v *Russia*, no. 21586/02, Judgment, 14 November 2008, para. 97; *Albekov* et al. v *Russia*, no. 68216/01, Judgment, 9 October 2008, para. 79; *Arzu Akhmadova* et al. v *Russia*, no. 13670/03, Judgment, 8 January 2009, para. 163.

[33] *Isayeva* v *Russia*, no. 57950/00, Judgment, 24 February 2005, para. 176.

In the case of the bombing of the convoy on the Chechnya-Ingushetia border, the Court said:

> [T]he situation that existed in Chechnya at the relevant time called for exceptional measures on behalf of the state in order to regain control over the Republic and to suppress the illegal armed insurgency. These measures could presumably include employment of military aviation equipped with heavy combat weapons. The Court is also prepared to accept that if the planes were attacked by illegal armed groups, that could have justified use of lethal force, thus falling within paragraph 2 of Article 2.[34]

The Court has also held that article 2 of the European Convention on Human Rights imposes a positive duty on the state to locate and deactivate mines, to mark and seal off mined areas so as to prevent anybody from freely entering it, and to provide comprehensive warnings concerning mines laid in the vicinity of non-combatants.[35]

The European Court of Human Rights pointed out in the Katyr-Yurt case that Russia had not declared martial law or a state of emergency in Chechnya. No derogation had been formulated in accordance with article 15 of the European Convention. As a result, the situation had to be judged 'against a normal legal background'. According to the Court, 'the use of aviation bombs in a populated area, outside wartime and without prior evacuation of the civilians, is impossible to reconcile with the degree of caution expected from a law-enforcement body in a democratic society'. Thus, although the Court accepted that the military operation in Katyr-Yurt was pursuing a 'legitimate aim', it could not accept that it was planned and executed with the requisite care for the lives of the civilian population.[36] In the border convoy case, the Court did not repeat the same caveat about 'normal legal background' and the absence of a declaration of martial law. It said that 'even assuming that the military were pursuing a legitimate aim in launching 12 S-24 non-guided air-to-ground missiles on 29 October 1999, the Court does not accept that the operation near the village of Shaami-Yurt was planned and executed with the requisite care for the lives of the civilian population'.[37] In another case involving an attack on civilians fleeing Grozny by way of what they had been led to believe was a safe humanitarian corridor, the Court rapidly concluded there had been a violation of the right to life absent any attempt by Russia to justify the military action.[38]

---

[34] *Isayeva, Yusopova and Bazayeva* v *Russia*, nos 57947/00, 57948/00 and 57949/00, Judgment, 24 February 2005, para. 178.

[35] *Albekov* et al. v *Russia*, no. 68216/01, Judgment, 9 October 2008, para. 90.

[36] *Isayeva* v *Russia*, no. 57950/00, Judgment, 24 February 2005, paras 191, 200.

[37] *Isayeva, Yusopova and Bazayeva* v *Russia*, nos 57947/00, 57948/00 and 57949/00, Judgment, 24 February 2005, para. 199.

[38] *Umayeva* v *Russia*, no. 1200/03, Judgment, 4 December 2008, paras 82–3.

The methodology applied by the European Court of Human Rights in considering the permissibility of exceptions or limitations to human rights proceeds in stages. The Court determines whether the limitation has a legitimate aim or purpose. If the State passes this threshold, then the Court considers the proportionality of the measure in question. The Russian examples referred to above are focussed on the proportionality debate. The analysis is very similar to that of the law of armed conflict in determining the permissibility of collateral damage. None of the European Court cases concerning armed conflict found that the respondent state had failed to demonstrate a 'legitimate aim'. In the Chechen jurisprudence, the Court recognized that Russia was entitled to repress a secessionist movement.

Isn't the issue of the legitimate aim or purpose in human rights law fundamentally the same as determining the lawfulness of the conflict? If the European Court were to hold that the use of lethal force in an internal armed conflict had no legitimate aim or purpose, it would not even consider whether such force was also used proportionality. The argument that the killing of non-combatants in a conflict conducted in violation of international law, that is, contrary to the *jus ad bellum*, would be per se contrary to the European Convention, regardless of issues of necessity and proportionality, remains to be considered by the Court.

As a jurisdictional matter, the European Convention may not apply to the conduct of hostilities in an international armed conflict. Although the United Kingdom has been found to be in breach of the European Convention for certain of its actions in Iraq, it has not yet been challenged with respect to loss of life of non-combatants resulting directly from the illegal 2003 invasion itself. Given the current state of the law, success in an application raising this issue would seem improbable. But the conclusion that the European Court of Human Rights may not have jurisdiction over such issues does not mean that fundamental human rights are not breached.

The International Court of Justice has said that when life is taken in armed conflict, a determination of whether this is 'arbitrary' within the meaning of international human rights law must be established with regard to the *lex specialis*. The term comes from a rule of statutory interpretation: *Lex specialis derogat legi generali* (the general norm is displaced by the specialized one, by implication). It serves to resolve apparent conflicts in legislation adopted by the same legislator. If a professor tells her students that the class will be held from 9 to 12, and that there will be a twenty-minute coffee break at 10.20, only someone who is thick-headed would ask for an explanation of the apparent contradiction in these instructions. The coffee break is the *lex specialis* and the class schedule is the *lex generalis*. What is troubling about the application of the concept by the International Court of Justice is that the *lex specialis* tolerates 'incidental' loss of civilian life, as long as it meets a test of proportionality, that is, it is not 'excessive in relation to the concrete and direct military advantage anticipated'. It matters little that the conflict itself may be the result of unlawful action. If the law of armed conflict is the *lex specialis* of international human rights law, with respect to application of the prohibition of arbitrary deprivation of the right to life resulting from armed conflict, it seems to follow that international human rights law should also profess indifference to the cause of the conflict.

If the law of armed conflict is the *lex specialis* of human rights law in war-time, at least as far as arbitrary deprivation of life is concerned, then the position of the 'right to peace' within human right law becomes uncertain. But if there is indeed a right to peace located within the general frame-work of international human rights law, as the Human Rights Council resolutions suggest, then it is impossible entirely to reconcile this body of law with the law of armed conflict. To the extent that international human rights law views aggressive war as a violation of the right to peace, there is a point where efforts to fuse it to international humanitarian law can never entirely succeed.

Of course, nobody has argued that international humanitarian law is a *lex specialis* of the Charter of the United Nations or of the customary international law governing the use of force. Similarly, in the field of inter-national criminal law, the International Criminal Court has jurisdiction over both war crimes and aggression. It has not been suggested that there is an incompatibility in the institution prosecuting crimes derived from the *jus in bello* as well as those of the *jus ad bellum*. Why, then, this forced mar-riage between international human rights law and international humani-tarian law, when we do not require the same of other disciplines?

In the context of the arbitrary deprivation of the right to life, which is the situation addressed by the International Court of Justice in *Nuclear Weapons* and the one where the whole debate began, defining international humanitarian law as the *lex specialis* that governs violations of the right to life in time of armed conflict is inadequate. International humanitarian law may be helpful, for example by informing concepts of necessity and propor-tionality where non-combatants are killed as a result of the use of armed force, or in determining whether or not certain weapons are allowed. But human rights law also requires that any deprivation of life can only be accepted if it pursues a legitimate purpose. The waging of aggressive war can never meet this test. The right to peace, even if it only assists in the application and interpretation of the other norms, serves to highlight this distinction between humanitarian law and human rights law.

THE HUMAN RIGHT TO PEACE

International law seems to distinguish between 'peoples' rights' and 'human rights'. The idea of 'peoples' rights' is often associated with 'group rights'.[39] Philip Alston, who is not an enthusiast for the concept, describes peoples' rights as 'the elevation of the well-recognized, but nonetheless vague and open-ended, duty of states to cooperation to achieve the objectives of the United Nations Charter'.[40] There is, of course, a close relationship between peoples' rights and human rights. Thus, for example, the African Charter is concerned with both human and peoples' rights. Its preamble says that 'the reality and respect of peoples' rights should necessarily guarantee human rights'. The two United Nations Covenants on human rights enshrine the 'right of peoples to self-determination' in common article 1. The Human Rights Committee has held that this provision does not give rise to an individual right of petition, because only 'individuals can claim that their individual rights have been violated'. However, common article 1 may be relevant in the interpretation of other rights in the International Covenant on Civil and Political Rights, especially democratic rights (art. 25), non-discrimination (art. 26) and minority rights (art. 27).[41] It also establishes the position of peoples' rights within human rights law more generally.

There have been efforts to link peace with other normative provisions. The two Human Rights Council resolutions invoke the text of article 28 of the Universal Declaration of Human Rights. There is also some support for this in academic writing, including the relevant chapter in the commentary by Gudmunder Alfredsson and Asbjørn Eide:

> It does not take much reflection to recognize that violence and war negatively affect the enjoyment of human rights. A social and political order in which all the rights in the Universal Declaration could be enjoyed would be possible only if there were peace on both the international and the national levels.[42]

Article 20(1) of the International Covenant on Civil and Political Rights requires that '[a]ny propaganda for war shall be prohibited by law'.[43] In its first General Comment on the right to life, the Human Rights Committee

---

[39] Ian Brownlie, 'The Rights of Peoples in Modern International Law', in James Crawford (ed), *The Rights of Peoples*, Oxford: Clarendon Press, 1988, pp. 1–16.

[40] Philip Alston, 'Introduction', in Philip Alston (ed), *People's Rights*, Oxford: Oxford University Press, 2001, pp. 1–6, at p 1.

[41] Eg, *Gillot* v *France*, UN Doc. CCPR/C/75/D/932/2000, para. 13.4.

[42] Asbjørn Eide, 'Article 28', in Gudmundur Alfredsson & Asbjørn Eide (eds), *Universal Declaration of Human Rights*, Dordrecht: Kluwer Academic Publishers, 1999, p. 620.

[43] Michael Kearney, *The Prohibition of Propaganda for War in International Law*, Oxford: Oxford University Press, 2007.

invoked article 20(1) in support of a more general proposition about the right to life and armed conflict:

The Committee observes that war and other acts of mass violence continue to be a scourge of humanity and take the lives of thousands of innocent human beings every year. Under the Charter of the United Nations the threat or use of force by any state against another state, except in exercise of the inherent right of self-defence, is already prohibited. The Committee considers that states have the supreme duty to prevent wars, acts of genocide and other acts of mass violence causing arbitrary loss of life. Every effort they make to avert the danger of war, especially thermo-nuclear war, and to strengthen international peace and security would constitute the most important condition and guarantee for the safeguarding of the right to life. In this respect, the Committee notes, in particular, a connection between article 6 and article 20, which states that the law shall prohibit any propaganda for war (para. 1) or incitement to violence (para. 2) as therein described.[44]

This paragraph on the right to life is rarely referred to today, and possibly would not reappear were the Committee to revise its general comment. The context of its adoption of the general comment seems to have been associated with the 1984 General Assembly Declaration. It also resonates in the academic literature of the time.[45]

There are some signs of the controversy concerning the place of peace within human rights in the case law of international tribunals. In *Varnava* et al., which concerned persons who had disappeared during the Turkish invasion of Cyprus, the Grand Chamber of the European Court of Human Rights wrote:

It may be that both sides in this conflict prefer not to attempt to bring out to the light of day the reprisals, extra-judicial killings and massacres that took place or to identify those amongst their own forces and citizens who were implicated. It may be that they prefer a 'politically-sensitive' approach to the missing persons problem and that the CMP with its limited remit was the only solution which could be agreed under the brokerage of the UN. That can have no bearing on the application of the provisions of the Convention.[46]

The Court seemed to be saying that its job was to respond to individual petitions, and not to concern itself with broader collective interests where

[44] General Comment 6, UN Doc. CCPR/C/21/Add.1, para. 2. See also: General Comment 14, para. 2.

[45] For support for a 'right to peace', see: Ved P. Nanda, 'Nuclear Weapons and the Right to Peace Under International Law' (1983) 9 *Brooklyn Journal of International Law* 283; A.B. Sajoo, 'Human Rights Perspectives on the Arms Race' (1982) 28 *McGill Law Journal* 628; A.A. Tickhonov, 'The Inter-Relationship Between the Right to Life and the Right to Peace: Nuclear Weapons and Other Weapons of Mass-Destruction and the Right to Life', in B.G. Ramcharan (ed), *The Right to Life in International Law*, Dordrecht: Martinus Nijhoff, 1985, pp. 97–113.

[46] *Varnava and Others* v *Turkey*, nos 16064/90, 16065/90, 16066/90, 16068/90, 16069/90, 16070/90, 16071/90, 16072/90 and 16073/90 [GC], Judgment, 18 September 2009, para. 193.

peace negotiations might be involved. In a dissenting opinion in a case involving discrimination in the constitution of Bosnia and Herzegovina, which was itself part of the Dayton peace agreement of 1995, Judge Bonello warned of the consequences of rigid application of human rights norms when the sensitive compromises of a peace agreement are concerned. He chided the majority for its failure to consider 'a clear and present danger of destabilizing the national equilibrium', adding: 'The Court has not found a hazard of civil war, the avoidance of carnage or the safeguard of territorial cohesion to have sufficient social value to justify some limitation on the rights of the two applicants…I cannot endorse a Court that sows ideals and harvests massacre.'[47]

There is, to be sure, no suggestion that human rights law is in some sense opposed to peace. Yet the growth in two fields that are closely related to human rights law, namely international humanitarian law and international criminal law, may have helped push the issue of peace to the periphery. The right to peace, whether presented as a peoples' right or a human right, has a legitimate position within the overall framework, even if its role today is best described as underdeveloped or latent. The evolving discussions on the right to peace within the Human Rights Council reflect both the appropriateness of its place on the agenda and hesitations about the importance that it should be given. Possibly those who are sceptical about the usefulness of a right to peace would adjust their views if they saw its potential to influence and frame the interpretation of other fundamental rights, not to mention the course of international criminal justice.

Above all, the notion of a right to peace provides a unifying principle that assists in bringing human rights law, international criminal law, and international humanitarian law closer together. Unstated or understated in human rights law, it is nevertheless implicit. The right to peace very usefully puts other rights into perspective. Similarly, it rounds off the corners of international humanitarian law, so that a body of norms that sometimes looks like rules to govern killing and destruction takes on a more anti-war dimension. The overarching theme of a right to peace was important at the dawn of international prosecutions, at Nuremberg and Tokyo, but later it seemed to lose its way. The adoption of amendments to the Rome Statute at the Kampala Review Conference in June 2010 brings the crime of aggression back to centre stage and with it the mission of international criminal justice, as well as international human rights, as a civilizer not only of individuals but also of nations.

---

[47] *Sejdić and Finci* v *Bosnia and Herzegovina*, nos 27996/06 and 34836/06 [GC], Dissenting Opinion of Judge Bonello, 22 December 2009, at p. 56.

INDEX